WITHDRAWN

*The Russian Struggle for
Power, 1914—1917*

The Russian Struggle for Power, 1914–1917

A STUDY OF RUSSIAN FOREIGN POLICY
DURING THE FIRST WORLD WAR

by

C. Jay Smith, Jr.

*Assistant Professor of History,
University of Georgia*

PHILOSOPHICAL LIBRARY
NEW YORK

Copyright, 1956, by
Philosophical Library Inc.
15 East 40th Street
New York 16, N.Y.

All rights reserved.

Printed in the United States of America.

TABLE OF CONTENTS

I. The Grand Design	3–62
II. Extension of the Design	63–134
III. The Balkan Tangle (September, 1914–February, 1915)	135–184
IV. The Straits Agreement and the Treaty of London (March–May, 1915)	185–272
V. The Collapse of Russian Power in Eastern Europe (May–December, 1915)	273–350
VI. The Partition of Turkey and the Fall of Sazonov	351–406
VII. The Eclipse of Russia as a Great Power (July, 1916–November, 1917)	407–486
Notes	487–514
Bibliography	515–525
Index	527–553

LIST OF FREQUENTLY USED ABBREVIATIONS IN SOURCE CITATIONS

M.O.V.E.I.   *Mezhdunarodnye otnosheniya v epokhu imperializma. Dokumenty iz arkhivov Tsarskogo i Vremmenogo Pravitelstv. 1878–1917 gg.* Series III, 1914–1917. Moscow-Leningrad: 1931–1938.

T.R.V.M.V.   *Tsarskaya Rossiya v mirovoi voiny.* Moscow: 1925.

E.D.I.G.   *Evropeiskie Derzhavy i Gretsiya v epokhu mirovoi voiny.* Moscow: 1922.

K.I.P.   *Konstantinopol i prolivy.* Moscow: 1924.

R.A.T.   *Razdel Aziatskoi Turtsii.* Moscow: 1926.

S.I.M.I.D.   "Stavka i Ministerstvo Inostrannykh Del", *Krasnyi Arkhiv.* Moscow: 1928.

D.M.I.D.   "Dnevnik Ministerstva Inostrannykh Del", *Krasnyi Arkhiv.* Moscow: 1928–1929.

C.V.T.D.   "Cheko-Slovatskii Vopros i Tsarskaya Diplomatiya, 1914–1917 gg." *Krasnyi Arkhiv.* Moscow: 1928.

R.-P. O.   *Russko-Polskiye otnosheniya vo vremya mirovoi voiny.* Moscow: 1925.

INTRODUCTION

BOTH BEFORE and after the extension of Soviet Russian power over nearly all of Eastern Europe (1944–1948), there have been many attempts to find the real key to the imperialism of Stalin and his successors. There is certainly much evidence that Communist doctrine alone does not provide an adequate answer, despite its remarkable elasticity after the advent of Stalin's personal dictatorship. Accordingly, many have come to believe that the key to Soviet imperialism lies in the historic aspirations of the Russian state prior to 1917.

Whether this belief is justified or not will probably be debated endlessly, just as the question of French imperialism during the age of the great Revolution and Napoleon will be debated endlessly. Must one accept at face value the claims of a revolutionary regime that it has broken with the bad, aggressive foreign policy of the old regime? Or must one assume that geography, economic factors, national charac-

Introduction

ter, and a host of other unchangeables impose on any government of a given state, with fairly stable boundaries, a more or less fixed foreign policy, regardless of its type of government?

This study, which examines certain aspects of Russian foreign policy during the First World War, does not pretend to offer any final answer to such a sweeping problem, though it is based on the belief that the Russian revolution of 1917 did not succeed in creating a permanent chasm between the old Russia of the Tsars and the new one of Lenin and Stalin. I concede in advance that between 1917 and 1921, the Soviet leaders did try to break with the past; indeed, that they sincerely thought they had broken with the past. However, I believe also that when they did awake to find themselves masters, not of a Communist world, but of the historic Russian state, they began to behave much as earlier Russian rulers behaved, certainly in the realm of foreign policy.

To be sure, the world revolution was never completely forgotten, any more than America has forgotten the dream of a world in which all peoples everywhere will recognize that the

Introduction

"American way" is the right way. Nevertheless, in practical situations, the Soviet rulers have not been reluctant to accept limited objectives which bear a strong resemblance to limited objectives sought by the Tsars.

As a consequence, there is more than a passing resemblance between the Tsarist policies of 1914–17 and those of Stalin between 1941 and 1948. During both periods, Russia was allied to the democratic West against a Germany which had effective control of the central mass of Europe. During the earlier period, Russia and her allies planned to crush Germany and her allies, and to effect vast territorial changes, which would have effectively divided Europe into a Western sphere and a Russian sphere. These plans were foiled, both by the collapse of Russia and by the entrance of the United States into the war. Thirty years later, it was supposed in the United States that the collapse of Germany would be followed by a return to the status quo of 1920, in which the twenty-odd European nationalities had an independent existence under the benevolent aegis of an international organization. Instead, in 1944–48, something similar

Introduction

to what had been planned in 1914–17 actually took place—a division of the European states between a Russian bloc and a Western bloc. The main difference was that the United States, owing to the weakness of France and Britain, played the major role after 1945 in the Western bloc. Thus, whether Stalin actually intended to do so or not, he in effect carried out the plans of Nicholas II and his ministers.

Just what the real intentions of Stalin were during and just after the Second World War will not be known until the Soviet archives are opened. However, the Soviets have opened the archives of the Imperial Ministry of Foreign Affairs to a rather generous degree, at least for the 1914–17 period, though up to now, the bulk of the documents for the war period have been but little studied in the West. Indeed, little is generally known of any but the main lines of Allied diplomacy during the First World War, despite the acrid controversy which once raged over the "secret treaties" of 1914–17. It is hoped therefore that this study will help to bridge a gap in historical knowledge, as well as help in explaining the bases of Soviet imperialism. It

Introduction

should be added, however, that since the British and French have not yet opened their archives for the World War I period, the definitive study of Allied wartime diplomacy in 1914–17 cannot as yet be written.

❂ ❂ ❂ ❂ ❂

I am indebted to many persons without whose help and cooperation this study would never have been undertaken or completed. It had its genesis in a doctoral thesis prepared under the direction of Professor Michael M. Karpovich of Harvard University, to whom I, along with many other Americans who have undertaken Russian studies, owe an overwhelming debt of gratitude. I am also indebted to Professor Robert L. Wolff of Harvard, who gave abundantly of his time to read and criticize the original manuscript, and from whose extensive knowledge of Eastern Europe I profited much. However, neither Professor Karpovich nor Professor Wolff is responsible in any way for any errors of omission or commission which may appear in the completed version of the book. My studies in Byzantine history under the late Professor

Introduction

Robert Blake of Harvard, of twentieth-century European history under Professor Harry Rudin of Yale University, and of modern French history under Professor Donald McKay of Harvard were of the greatest help in providing the background for this work; however, none of these gentlemen has seen this book in manuscript form, and none of them is therefore in any sense responsible for it. Many fellow graduate students at Harvard University, colleagues at the University of Georgia, and co-workers in the Office of the Chief of Naval Operations contributed, wittingly or unwittingly, to the book. I should particularly like to thank Professor Basil L. Crapster of Gettysburg College, Professor Wilbur Jones of the University of Georgia, and Lieutenant Robert W. Herrick, U.S.N. I am much in debt to the staffs of Widener Library, Harvard University, the Library of Congress, the Army Library, and the University of Georgia Library for providing the necessary materials for my researches.

Finally, and most important, I owe an immense debt of gratitude to my wife and my par-

Introduction

ents, without whose patient encouragement and active assistance this study could never have been pushed through to completion.

C. JAY SMITH, JR.

Athens, Georgia

*The Russian Struggle for
Power, 1914–1917*

I

THE GRAND DESIGN

AT THREE o'clock on the afternoon of Sunday, August 2, 1914, all the top military and civil officials of the Russian Empire, numbering five to six thousand, assembled in the St. George's Gallery of the Winter Palace, which fronts the Neva quays in St. Petersburg, about to become Petrograd, before receiving its present name of Leningrad. Full-dress was worn by the court, but field dress by the officers of the garrison. The only foreigner present was M. Maurice Paléologue, ambassador of a French Republic which had gone to war following Germany's August 1 declaration of war on her ally, Russia. Sir George Buchanan, the British ambassador, was not invited, and was indeed, quite busy at the moment pacifying impatient crowds outside the British embassy demanding to know if Russia could count on the support of his country.

In the center of the St. George's Gallery was

placed an altar, on which was the miraculous ikon of the Virgin of Kazan. In 1812, Mikhail Kutuzov, before going to face the great Napoleon, had prayed before this same ikon.

At the appointed moment, in a hushed silence, Nicholas II, Emperor, Autocrat, All-Russian Tsar, entered the gallery, accompanied by his pale, glassy-eyed wife, Alexandra Fedorovna, and a numerous suite, and crossed to the altar. While the court chaplain chanted the liturgy of the Orthodox mass, Nicholas knelt before the ikon and fervently prayed. At the close of the mass, the chaplain read the Tsar's proclamation announcing the existence of a state of war with Germany.

The reading finished, Nicholas approached the altar, and raised his right hand towards the gospel held out to him by the chaplain. Gravely he swore:

Officers of my guard, here present, I greet in you my whole army and give it my blessing. I solemnly swear that I will never make peace so long as one of the enemy is on the soil of the fatherland.

It was the oath taken by Tsar Alexander I in

The Russian Struggle for Power, 1914–1917

1812. A tremendous cheer filled the gallery, and was echoed by a crowd of thousands of citizens who filled the Winter Palace Square. The French ambassador was crushed in a bearhug by Grand Duke Nikolai Nikolaevich, Supreme High Commander of the Russian armies, while the crowd shouted *"Vive la France!"* The Tsar now proceeded to the balcony at the front of the Winter Palace overlooking the square, which was black with an enormous crowd holding flags, banners, ikons, and portraits of Nicholas. On sighting the Little Father, the massed populace fell on its knees and sang *God Save The Tsar.*

On Wednesday, August 5, at 5 A.M., Sir George Buchanan received a laconic message from the British Foreign Office: "War—Germany—Act." At a Roman Catholic mass held by the French colony in Notre Dame de France that afternoon, the Union Jack was displayed along with the Tricolor and the Russian double-headed Byzantine eagle over the altar. On the next day, the Austro-Hungarian ambassador handed Foreign Minister Sazonov a declaration of war, based on the Russian attitude in the Austro-Serbian dispute, and the fact that Russia had begun hostilities against Germany.

Tsar Nicholas now determined to recall, at least for a formal sitting, the recently prorogued Fourth State Duma, since he wished to be "in perfect union with my people." Accordingly, the Duma met on Saturday, August 8, in its ornate quarters, the Tavricheskii Palace.

The session was opened by a normal sample of the sonorous oratory delivered by the President of the Duma, V. I. Rodzyanko. Thereafter, feeble Ivan L. Goremykin, an incompetent old courtier who had been made Premier in February, 1914, shuffled to the tribune. Exhausted by the strain of a task beyond his powers, this aged relic summoned enough energy to say that Russia had not wanted war, and had clung to the slightest chance of "damming the deluge of blood which threatens to engulf the world." Russia would not, however, shrink from the challenge offered by Germany, and, ending on a note of fatalism—"if we had yielded, our humiliation would not have changed the course of affairs." The Minister of Foreign Affairs, Sergei D. Sazonov (in office since 1910), followed him, and spoke more vigorously, but in a spirit no less conscious of coming trials. "When history brings the day of unbiased judgment, I am convinced it will justify us," he confidently asserted. Cheering arose when he mentioned France and Britain. He closed with a flourish: "We will not accept the yoke of Germany and her ally in Europe!" Shortly after, the Duma enthusiastically and overwhelmingly voted for war credits. The Social Democrats abstained from the vote, but advised workingmen to defend their country.

A final pageant took place in Moscow on Tuesday, August 18. The Tsar and Tsarina, with their four daughters and one haemophiliac son, and Buchanan and Paléologue, journeyed to the Kremlin. There, in the St. George's Hall of the Palace, the Tsar addressed a crowd of court officials and Moscow merchants in this fashion:

From this place, the very heart of Russia, I send my soul's greeting to my valiant troops and my noble allies. God is with us!

The imperial cortège then passed through several rooms, down the famous Red Staircase, across a covered bridge, and down more stairs to the Uspenskii Cathedral. A mob packed in the Kremlin courtyard shouted an enthusiastic welcome. While bells tolled and onion-shaped domes gleamed in the August sun, the procession passed within the cathedral. There, greeted by a host of metropolitans, bishops, archimandrites, and other clergy, the Imperial family prayed before various ikons and the tombs of former patriarchs.[1]

The war having now officially begun, it remained for the generals and diplomats to wage it, on both the military and political fronts, in order to achieve the desired victory. As the grey-clad regiments of Grand Duke Nikolai moved slowly towards the German and Austrian frontiers, Sazonov and his frock-coated diplomats found much to occupy their time.

PROCLAMATIONS TO THE POLES, UKRAINIANS, AND "PEOPLES OF AUSTRIA-HUNGARY"

The most urgent immediate problems facing the Russian Foreign Ministry were the Polish and Ukrainian Questions. Officially, these were still internal problems in the Russia of 1914,

The Russian Struggle for Power, 1914–1917

and hence less the concern of Sazonov than of the reactionary Minister of Internal Affairs, V. A. Maklakov. However, Russia had good reason to believe in August, 1914, that Austria-Hungary would seek to stir up revolts among the Russian Poles and Ukrainians, using the Austrian Poles of Galicia, and the Austro-Hungarian Ukrainians of Galicia, Bukovina, and Ruthenia for that purpose.[2]

Sazonov claims in his memoirs that all along he had thought that Russia should give her Polish subjects, who formed the majority of that submerged and oppressed nationality, autonomous status within the Russian Empire. Whether this be true or not, he certainly understood that the war with the Central Powers had shattered the century-long understanding with them regarding the suppression of Poland, and that a new settlement of the Polish Question was bound to come, especially since Russia was allied to France, the traditional champion of Polish liberties.[3]

At all events, during the first three weeks of August, 1914, Sazonov was able to persuade Nicholas II that the reunification of Poland as an autonomous state within the Russian Empire, and the annexation of Austria-Hungary's Ukrainian areas, should be proclaimed as official Russian war aims.

The appropriate proclamations were drawn up in the Ministry of Foreign Affairs, and the one regarding Poland was vigorously combatted by the reactionary Minister of Internal Affairs, as well as by Premier Goremykin. However, Sazonov triumphed over his ministerial colleagues; the only concession the latter got from the Tsar was that the proclamations should be issued in the name of the Supreme High Commander, Grand Duke Nikolai, rather than in the name of the Tsar. During the struggle for the proclamations, Sazonov was cheered on by assurances from Maurice Paléologue that they would make a most favorable impression in France.[4]

Drawn up by Prince G. N. Trubetskoi, Chief of the Second Political Division of the Foreign Ministry, and an ardent expansionist of liberal leanings, the proclamation regarding Poland was issued on August 16. It had much more to say about the reunification of Poland under the

The Russian Struggle for Power, 1914–1917

Russian Tsar than about the measure of self-government which would be granted. The Poles were promised that the dreams of their fathers and grandfathers, defined as "the resurrection of the Polish nation and its fraternal union with Russia," would at last be realized, that the frontiers which had divided the Polish people would be broken down, that Poland would be reunited under the sceptre of the Russian Tsar, and that "the morning star of a new life" was rising for Poland. In addition, the promise was made that, under the sceptre of the Russian Tsar, Poland would "come together, free in faith, in language, and in self-government." This last, as it turned out, was the really critical phrase. To be sure that it was not misconstrued, the next sentence admonished the Poles that Russia expected "an equal consideration for the rights of nations with which history has linked you."[5]

The proclamation regarding the Ukrainians came eight days later, on August 24, just as Russian troops were about to invade Galicia. In part, it was probably a concession to Rightist Russian nationalists, who feared that the reunited Poles might lay claim to the Ukrainians of Eastern Galicia. The word "Ukrainian" was not actually used, of course, since, from the official Russian viewpoint, the Austro-Hungarian Ukrainians were only a branch of the Russian nationality.

Announcing that for centuries the Russian people had languished under a foreign yoke, the proclamation asserted that "there are no forces which will halt the Russian people in its striving for unity." The Ukrainians of Austria-Hungary were reminded that they were "the patrimony of Saint Vladimir, the land of Yaroslav Osmomysl, of Princes Danilo and Roman,"[6] and were called upon to "cast off the yoke, . . . hoist the banner of great, undivided Russia," and complete "the blessed cause of the great reunion of the Russian Land, . . . the cause of the Great Prince Ivan Kalita."[7] These "liberated Russian brothers" were exhorted to "stand forth to greet the Russian warrior," to find their places "in the bosom of Mother Russia," and to lift their swords to the enemy "with a prayer for Russia, for the Russian Tsar."[8]

Meanwhile, the lumbering Russian military

The Russian Struggle for Power, 1914–1917

machine had at long last reached the western frontier, and the Supreme High Commander had established his Stavka or headquarters in Baranovichi, on the frontier between Byelorussia and Poland. Grand Duke Nikolai intended to smash the Austrians in Galicia, while overrunning German East Prussia as far as the Vistula. Both campaigns had been planned before the war; hence the Russian attack on East Prussia was not delivered solely to help the French, especially since the forces sent against Austria-Hungary were twice the size of those sent against Germany.[9]

The East Prussian campaign was ruined by the defeat of Samsonov at Tannenberg (August 26–30), but the Austrians were badly mauled in the south at the same time. By August 29, the Russians had occupied Tarnopol, in eastern Galicia; five days later, they entered Lvov (Lemberg). By mid-September, they had taken Chernovets (Czernowitz, Cernauti), capital of Bukovina, and were besieging Przemysl, whose fall would destroy the Austrians north of the Carpathians. Since the French victory on the Marne occurred at about the same time, it seemed that France was about to defeat Germany, while Russia dealt with Austria-Hungary.[10]

Flushed with a premature feeling of imminent victory, the Russian Ministry of Foreign Affairs had already come to wonder, towards the beginning of September, whether it had been unnecessarily generous towards the Poles. To anxious inquiries regarding the exact nature of the autonomy which would be given the newly reunited Poland, emanating from Paris, the Vatican, and Washington, Sazonov sent cautious answers. The Poles, he said, must wait until the war was won. In any case, the Russian Duma would probably have to be consulted about the limits of future Polish autonomy.[11]

During the second week of September, the Supreme High Commander was embarrassed by eager efforts on the part of the Russian Poles to fight for the liberation of their countrymen in Germany and Austria. Offers of an army of half a million men, supported by contributions from Polish Americans, were received. They were, after some wavering, declined, on the plausible ground that Russia had declined to grant the

The Russian Struggle for Power, 1914–1917

rights of war to Austrian Poles fighting as Poles, and could not accept help from such detachments herself. It would be a matter of another six weeks before the Grand Duke would reverse himself and urge the fulfillment of the promises of August 16.[12]

Meanwhile, largely as a result of his victories, the government in St. Petersburg had come to give serious attention to the Czech Question. Only on the very eve of the First World War had any serious consideration been given in Russia to the possibility of espousing the cause of the Czechs, and then only because of the pleas of Karel Kramář and other Czech nationalist leaders. Even so, Sazonov appears to have warned the Czechs in April, 1914 not to count on Russian help. True, the Russian consul in Prague on the eve of the war seems to have intrigued with some nationalist leaders, though he also seems to have exceeded his instructions. He apparently discussed the formation of a vague Pan-Slavic federation, with Russia as its protectress, and with the Czech lands included.[13]

The impetus towards some Russian action was given by the numerous Czech colonists in

The Russian Struggle for Power, 1914–1917

Russia, who lived chiefly in and around St. Petersburg, Moscow, and Kiev. On August 4, the Moscow Czechs laid before the Russian government a scheme for a Czecho-Slovak Legion within the Russian Army. This request was repeated two weeks later, when a Czech delegation, representing organizations in St. Petersburg, Moscow, Warsaw, and Kiev, saw Nicholas II on August 20, during the latter's ceremonial visit to Moscow. At the same time, the following additional request was made:

> The Czech people, sons of the Pan-Slavic Mother, having miraculously survived for a millennium as sentinels in the West, turn to you, Great Sovereign, with flaming hope and a request: revive the independent Czech kingdom, and cause the glory of the Crown of St. Vaçlav to shine again in the rays of the great and mighty dynasty of the Romanovs...[14]

Nicholas was glad enough to create a special Czech army detachment, composed at first only of Russian subjects, and later filled with Austro-Hungarian prisoners. It was named the *Druzhina*, and by the end of October, had left for the front. However, both he and Sazonov were still hesitant to go further.[15]

The Russian Struggle for Power, 1914–1917

Early in September, Sazonov granted an audience to eleven members of a Czech National Committee. The main item of discussion was a plan brought forward by the Czechs to re-create the Kingdom of Bohemia-Moravia, and to make some member of the Romanov family its ruler, either as king, or as the viceroy of the Russian Tsar. Sazonov expressed grave doubts as to the success of either alternative, since he regarded the idea of placing an Orthodox ruler in a Catholic country as an act of political folly. However, according to notes kept by the Czechs, he went so far at this time as to say that

Should God grant decisive victory to Russian arms, the reestablishment of an entirely independent Czech Kingdom would be in accordance with the intentions of the Russian Government; this question was considered before the beginning of the war and decided in principle in favor of the Czechs.[16]

It seems highly probable that the phrase "an entirely independent Czech Kingdom" does not convey precisely what Sazonov said at this time. In any case, he did agree to arrange a meeting of the delegation with Nicholas II.[17]

The Russian Struggle for Power, 1914–1917

Before it took place, he had decided to issue, again in the name of Grand Duke Nikolai, a proclamation to the "Peoples of Austria-Hungary." After reminding them that Vienna had declared war on Russia because the latter would not desert Serbia, and that Russia had "already shed her blood more than once for the liberation of peoples from a foreign yoke," the proclamation went on to claim that Russia sought nothing but right and justice. To that end, she was bringing to the peoples of Austria-Hungary "freedom and the realization of your national strivings." Pointing out that Austria-Hungary had used the principle of *divide et impera,* the proclamation claimed that

Russia, on the other hand, strives for only one thing, that each of you shall develop and prosper, preserving the dearest possessions of your fathers —language and faith, and that, united with blood brothers, you may live in peace and friendship with your neighbors, respecting their independence.[18]

In closing, the proclamation asked that the peoples of Austria-Hungary cooperate with invading Russian troops "as with true friends and fighters for your highest ideals."[19]

The Russian Struggle for Power, 1914–1917

The day when the proclamation was issued, September 17, coincided with the promised reception of the Czech committee by Nicholas II. The Tsar received it with his usual graciousness and examined on a map the frontiers of the proposed new state, which now included not only Bohemia and Moravia, but also the Slovak area of Hungary and that part of Austria north of the Danube. Even the city of Vienna was included! To these proposals, Nicholas made only the vague statement, "I thank you, gentlemen, for what you have told me. I trust that God will help us and that your wishes will be realized." He did, however, grant permission for the creation of a single Czecho-Slovak organization in Russia at this time. Along with the general proclamation to the peoples of Austria-Hungary, that was as far as the Russia government would go until November, 1914.[20] As a matter of fact, as will appear below, Sazonov had told Britain and France only three days before that Russia would be content if Czecho-Slovakia were made a third unit in a remodeled Hapsburg monarchy, on a plane with Austria and Hungary. Obviously, he wanted to be sure of his ground before definitely committing Russia to the Czech cause.

THE WOOING OF ITALY AND RUMANIA

The Polish, Ukrainian, and Czech questions were of primary concern to Russia during the first six weeks of the war, because they affected the operations of her own armies. However, from military considerations alone, the positions taken by Italy and Rumania were also matters of vital concern to the St. Petersburg government and its allies.

It was not safe to assume that either country would not join the Central Powers, though both were rightly regarded as either on the fence, or perhaps, more than halfway over into the camp of the Triple Entente. Russia and Italy had pledged to consult each other before consenting to further changes in the Balkans (Racconigi Agreement, 1909), though this understanding had been strained by Serbia's ambitions for Albanian territory during the First Balkan War (1912). The visit of Nicholas II and Sazonov to Rumania in June, 1914 had crowned a year of careful Russian diplomacy, which had whetted

The Russian Struggle for Power, 1914–1917

Rumania's desires for the Rumanian territories of Austria-Hungary.[21]

Nevertheless, Sazonov took no chances. Even before all the declarations of war had been made, he had made preparations to offer Italy and Rumania Austro-Hungarian and other territory as the payment for joining the Triple Entente. Hurried consultations with Gaston Doumergue, French Foreign Minister at the outbreak of war, and with Sir Edward Grey, British Foreign Secretary since 1906, led to the offer of the Trentino and Trieste, as well as of the Albanian port of Valona, to Marquis Carlotti, Italian ambassador in St. Petersburg, on August 7.[22] In return, Sazonov asked that Italy immediately declare war on Austria-Hungary "on any pretext she chooses, blockade the exit from the Adriatic of the Austro-Hungarian navy, and invade and seize the Trentino." He added that "time is flying, and . . . Italy must decide quickly, since her help . . . will become less dear to us, and the opportunity . . . to achieve the agreement of the three powers to such significant gains will be missed."[23]

Italy had obviously been waiting for an Entente offer, but felt insulted by Sazonov's highhanded tone, and aggrieved by the meagre gains offered. Complaints were made to the British and French ambassadors in Rome, and were received sympathetically in Paris and London. Doumergue complained to Sazonov that his words to Carlotti had had the character of an ultimatum. At Grey's orders, Sir Rennell Rodd, British ambassador in Rome, soothed Italian Premier Antonio Salandra on August 13, and was rewarded with the statement that Italy's joining Austria was "unthinkable," and that her joining the Triple Entente was "not excluded in the future." Substantially the same promise was made by Foreign Minister San Giuliano to the Russian ambassador on the next day. However, San Giuliano stipulated that negotiations, when they took place, must be handled in London.[24]

Sazonov now became worried over the possibility that Italy might demand some of the coast of Austrian Dalmatia, which the Russian Foreign Ministry had already planned to present to Serbia. On August 24, he warned Grey and Doumergue that this coast must not be presented to Italy. Three days later, he wanted to

The Russian Struggle for Power, 1914-1917

resume negotiations with the Italians, after rumors of an impending partition of Albania between Italy and Greece reached St. Petersburg. However, Grey and Théophile Delcassé, who had just succeeded Doumergue, thought that the moment was inopportune.[25]

Thereafter, Russia ceased to be interested in bringing Italy into the Triple Entente, so long as she seemed likely to remain neutral. The entrance of Italy was henceforth viewed solely from the standpoint of its possible effect on Russia's Balkan plans.

Meanwhile, the early negotiations of Russia with Rumania were leading to the successful conclusion of the first of the Allied secret treaties of World War I. On the outbreak of the war, the real ruler of Rumania was not aged King Carol I, who died on October 12, disconsolate over his failure to push his kingdom into the war on the German side, but rather the all-powerful Premier, Ion Bratianu. Rumania had both pro-German conservative leaders and pro-Entente liberal leaders, both of which groups favored intervention, though on different sides, of course. However, neither of them was really important, or perhaps they simply balanced each other off. In any event, Bratianu made all the decisions in the end, and proved himself more than a match for the statesmen of countries far more powerful than his.

While the crisis over the Austrian ultimatum to Serbia (July 23) was in its last stages, Sazonov offered Bratianu Transylvania if Rumania would join Russia in the oncoming war (July 29–30). Bratianu immediately asked whether France and Britain would sanction this offer. A partial answer was given on August 1, when France joined in the Russian proposal. With the offer in hand, Bratianu was able to defeat the pro-Germans in a critical Rumanian Crown Council on August 3, and to assure Rumanian neutrality, for the time being.[26]

However, he was fearful of an attack upon Rumania by Bulgaria, on account of Rumania's seizure of the southern Dobrudja from the latter in 1913. Brushing aside these fears, Sazonov proceeded to work out the text of a treaty which promised Rumania "the states of the Austro-Hungarian Monarchy which are inhabited by a Rumanian population" (August 7).[27]

The Russian Struggle for Power, 1914–1917

At this point, however, Russia's Western allies brought matters to a halt. Britain refused to join in a collective guarantee by the Triple Entente of Rumania's existing borders. Instead, on August 12, Grey proposed that Rumania be offered Transylvania as the payment for joining a pro-Entente bloc of Balkan nations whose formation had just been suggested by Greece. Doumergue thought it better that Rumania remain neutral, in order to assure the neutrality of Bulgaria and Turkey, and cautioned Sazonov against being over-hasty in his negotiations with Bucharest.[28]

Meanwhile, Bratianu had come to feel that he deserved a promise of Transylvania merely for remaining neutral (August 12). During the third week of August, he was visited by the Turkish Foreign Minister, Talaat Pasha, who offered tempting territorial gains at Russia's expense (Bessarabia), if Rumania would join in a pro-German bloc with Bulgaria and Turkey. Though Bratianu turned down this offer, he was emboldened to ask Poklevskii, the Russian ambassador, on August 30, for an Entente promise of the inviolability of Rumania's existing frontiers and "compensations in the form of Austrian territory with a Rumanian majority of the population," provided Rumania remained neutral, the Entente won the war, and there was a change in the existing Balkan balance. He made this request at a time when it seemed that Paris might fall to the Germans. When the Entente military situation had improved (September 9), he modified it somewhat, asking only that Russia promise Transylvania for neutrality.[29]

Sazonov greeted this proposal with cold silence, and Bratianu thereupon resolved to shift his dealings with the Entente westward. After having asked Italy to let him know forty-eight hours in advance of her intention to join the Allies, he sent a special delegation of Rumanian diplomats to Rome. They arrived on September 16, and it soon developed that they had come mainly to see Sir Rennell Rodd, the British ambassador. He was to be asked to intercede with Grey and persuade the British Foreign Secretary to put pressure on Russia to cede southern Bessarabia to Rumania. The territory in question had been a part of Rumania from 1856 to 1878, and the Rumanians claimed that the

The Russian Struggle for Power, 1914–1917

"sense of outrage" at its loss was still very much alive. If Russia returned it, Rumania would immediately declare war on Austria-Hungary and attack her with five army corps.[30]

Meanwhile, great excitement reigned in Bucharest after the Russian capture of Chernovets, capital of Bukovina, which was inhabited partly by Rumanians. There was great popular pressure to join the Allies, and Sazonov added to it by inviting Bratianu on September 16 to join Russia in occupying Bukovina and Transylvania. However, Bratianu resisted the pressure and repeated his demand for a promise of Transylvania and southern Bukovina, as the price of Rumanian neutrality (September 21). Sazonov replied on September 24 that Rumania might have Transylvania on such terms only if the Allied Powers had to undertake no military activities to conquer it. However, he changed his mind when it was learned that Germany was promising Rumania a special regime for the Transylvanians, the cession of southern Bukovina, Bessarabia, and Odessa, and the creation of an independent Ukraine. Between September 26 and October 2, negotiations in both Petrograd and Bucharest for a Russo-Rumanian agreement were successfully completed.[31]

In return for Rumanian "benevolent neutrality," Sazonov promised to recognize Rumania's right to annex Transylvania and a part of Bukovina, the division of the latter between Russia and Rumania to be decided on the basis of "the ethnic majority of the population." Bratianu demanded in addition that Russia guarantee Rumania's existing frontiers, and that the Prut River be the future Rumanian frontier in Bukovina. Sazonov agreed to the former demand, but insisted on an ethnic frontier in Bukovina, which would leave all its Ukrainians to Russia. He carried his point, and the agreement was duly signed in Petrograd on October 1–2. Later, on October 6, Bratianu was presented with a "note annexe" which stated that Russia's guarantee of Rumania's frontiers would be diplomatic only, and must not involve any military action. Moreover, Rumania's "benevolent neutrality" must involve a stoppage of communications between the Central Powers and Bulgaria-Turkey, and the easement of communications between Russia and Serbia. In reply, Bratianu hoped for an unconditional guarantee of Rumania's frontiers when she began military action against Austria-Hungary, and declined to shut off the Central Powers' line of communication completely.[32]

Thus, though the Russo-Rumanian agreement of October 1–2, 1914 definitely marked Rumania's adherence to a pro-Allied position, it left many loopholes which would later have to be plugged. In October 1914, Sazonov was so incensed by the passage of German oil and submarine parts to Turkey through Rumania that he was almost ready to withdraw from the agreement.[33] In November, 1914, he would be asking that Rumania return the southern Dobrudja to Bulgaria. The question of the future Russo-Rumanian frontier in Bukovina was destined to prevent, almost, Rumania's joining the Allies. And finally, the agreement did not even touch on the question of the Banat of Temesvar, though it contained some Rumanians, and though Russia already knew that it was coveted by Serbia. The French would later blame Bratianu's obstinate delays in joining the Allies on Sazonov's haste in concluding the agreement of October 1–2.[34] However, to a Russian Foreign

Minister, the safety of Bessarabia was bound to seem more important than the military help which Rumania might furnish the general Allied cause.

THE MACEDONIAN QUESTION

Sazonov could make trouble for Austria-Hungary at the beginning of the war by stirring up Italy and Rumania against her. However, the government of Vienna could retaliate and make trouble for Russia by stirring up Bulgaria to attack Serbia.

In August, 1914, Bulgaria still burned with resentment against her late enemies of the second Balkan War, and against Russia, which was unfairly blamed for the failure of Bulgaria to achieve her maximum ambitions in 1912–13. King Ferdinand had appointed a pro-German cabinet, headed by Vassili Radoslavov, in 1913, and had negotiated a large loan in Berlin. To be sure, Bulgaria classified her enemies as primary and secondary. In 1913, Serbia had taken not only the "contested zone" of Macedonia, whose ultimate fate was to have been decided by the Russian Tsar, but also the "uncontested zone," promised by the Serbs to the Bulgarians in 1912. Serbia was therefore regarded in Sofia as the primary national enemy. Only a little less hated was Greece, for her seizure of the Aegean port of Kavalla and its hinterland in 1913, at a time when Bulgaria hoped even to gain Salonika. Bulgarian resentment against Turkey, which had won back Adrianople after its seizure by the Bulgarians, and against Rumania, which had taken the southern Dobrudja, was less intense.[35]

Sazonov knew that he had to counter inevitable Austrian offers of Serbian Macedonia to Bulgaria with a counter-offer of the same territory, despite the fact that Russia had gone to war to save Serbia. Nevertheless, since he was now free to offer Serbia limitless Austrian territory, he saw no reason why Nikola Pashich, the Serbian Premier, should not agree to exchange Macedonia for Bosnia-Herzegovina and Dalmatia, in order secure Serbia's southern frontier.[36]

On July 29, in Sofia, Premier Radoslavov admitted to the Russian ambassador, Savinskii, that if Austria-Hungary offered him Serbian Macedonia, he would, of course, "take it with both hands." The initial reaction of the Russians was to bluster, and on August 3, while appealing to Slavic solidarity, Savinskii warned King Ferdinand of all the dire consequences which would probably follow an Austrian victory over Serbia, including the possibility that Bulgaria would become for Austria-Hungary only "an unimportant vassal organism, which could not hinder the achievement of the ardent striving of Austria towards Salonika, towards the Aegean Sea."[37]

However, on August 5, in Nish, the temporary Serbian capital, the Russian Chargé was telling Pashich that he must fling aside "petty considerations" and act decisively and quickly to keep Bulgaria neutral, or better still, acquire her as an ally. She should be promised that part of "uncontested" Macedonia east of the Vardar, including Ishtib and Kochana, for neutrality, and all of "uncontested" Macedonia, from Kriva Palanka to Lake Okhrida, for joining the Triple Entente. Russia would consider any hesitation "directly pernicious."[38]

Pashich was dismayed by the demand, since he had already encountered opposition in the

The Russian Struggle for Power, 1914–1917

Serbian government and army to a proposal for territorial offers to Bulgaria. Cooperation between his countrymen and the Bulgarians was, he said, impossible. He finally consented, however, to let Russia hold out hopes of undefined gains in Sofia, and even mentioned a small strip of Macedonia, between the Lakavitsa and Bregalnitsa Rivers, which might be worth Bulgaria's maintenance of neutrality. For even this, Bulgaria must promise not to send guerrillas into Serbia, to keep open her communications with Russia, and to fight Turkey, if the latter was induced by the Central Powers to attack Serbia.[39]

These terms were transmitted to Sofia by the Russians on August 9. At the same time, Sazonov promised Radoslavov "broader compensations if the Entente was victorious, and the support of the Russian Black Sea Fleet if Bulgaria was attacked by Turkey. The Bulgarians promised in reply (August 12) to maintain "stringent neutrality," and to defend themselves against Turkey if attacked. Encouraged by this attitude, Sazonov now demanded further concessions from Serbia, but Pashich asked, as the price of them, that Greece and Rumania also agree to make concessions to the Bulgarians.[40]

Already, Greece was involving herself, unasked, into Russia's Balkan negotiations, in which, after all, she had a legitimate concern. To be sure, the Greek nationalist war-horse, Premier Eleutherios Venizelos, was mainly concerned with the possibility of acquiring southern Albania and Turkey's Aegean coast-line, where many Greeks still lived. However, he was also concerned that a re-partition of Macedonia between Serbia and Bulgaria did not endanger Greek control of Kavalla and Salonika. When Turkey's policy began to take a pro-German turn on August 3, following the mobilization of the Turkish army, Venizelos decided that the time had come to align Greece with the Triple Entente, despite doubts and hesitations around the court (Queen Sophia, wife of King Constantine I, was the sister of the German Kaiser).

On August 7, Venizelos presented to the Russian ambassador in Athens, Prince Demidov, a suggested plan for new Balkan boundaries, and asked that Sazonov sponsor it in all the Balkan capitals. Rumania was to receive

The Russian Struggle for Power, 1914–1917

Transylvania; Serbia, Bosnia-Herzegovina; and Bulgaria, Serbian Macedonia as far west as Monastir. In addition, Albania would be partitioned between Serbia, Greece, and Italy. Venizelos explained that while Greece did not oppose Bulgaria's extension westward, she wanted to maintain her common frontier with Serbia, which would simply be moved farther west. Later, on August 12, Venizelos suggested that if Turkey joined the Central Powers, Bulgaria might be promised some of Turkish Thrace.[41]

Though undoubtedly motivated largely by considerations of Greek national interest, Venizelos' plan was statesmanlike. It recognized that the treaty of 1913 had been only a truce, forced on the Balkan nations by the Great Powers. It offered the best guarantee of a stable equilibrium in the Balkans, insofar as such an ideal situation was possible in 1914.

However, Sazonov was less interested in the future Balkan balance than in the immediate problem of reconciling the two Slavic states, Serbia and Bulgaria. On August 12, he told the Greek Chargé in St. Petersburg that Greece should not count on getting southern Albania unless she ceded Kavalla to Bulgaria. He added a threat that if Greece refused to cede Kavalla, he would support Italian claims to Albania. On the other hand, Sir Edward Grey expressed strong support for the Venizelos plan.[42]

Shortly after, the arrival of two German cruisers in Constantinople seemed to herald the immediate adherence of Turkey to the Central Powers. On August 13, Venizelos told Prince Demidov in Athens that Greece was ready to make common cause with the Triple Entente, and wanted guarantees against an attack by Turkey or Bulgaria, or both. On August 18, he made a still stronger offer to join the Entente, after the Turks began to try to swing Bulgaria and Rumania over into a pro-German bloc. The August 18 offer had the backing of King Constantine.[43]

Sir Edward Grey would later be much criticized for not accepting Greece as an ally, when she offered herself so freely. However, he rightly suspected that one of Venizelos' motives was to wriggle out of having to cede Kavalla to Bulgaria, and therefore that British sponsorship of him at this point would enrage Sazonov. Ac-

The Russian Struggle for Power, 1914-1917

cordingly, he adopted the position that Greece should be brought into the Triple Entente only if Turkey definitely joined the Central Powers, or if Bulgaria attacked Serbia.[44]

Sazonov was so encouraged by this attitude that he resolved to involve both Britain and France into his Balkan initiatives. However, Grey and Doumergue would commit themselves only to Venizelos' proposal that the Balkan states should themselves form a bloc and discuss a redistribution of territories, though they recognized the principle that both Serbia and Greece should compensate Bulgaria. (August 22-23)[45]

The Bulgarians were so delighted with this turn of events that they were willing to promise on August 24 benevolent neutrality towards Serbia, and an attack on Turkey or Rumania, if either joined the Central Powers, in return for "uncontested" Macedonia. Sazonov was encouraged to enlarge his previous demands on Serbia and Greece. On August 24, he wished the Triple Entente to demand that Serbia cede all of "uncontested" Macedonia and that Greece cede a long strip along her northern frontier, from

Doiran to Kastoria, allegedly inhabited by Slavs. On August 26, he suggested that the Entente immediately offer Bulgaria the Lakavitsa-Bregalnitsa triangle which Pashich had mentioned on August 3.[46]

However, Britain and France were dismayed when they came face to face with the Balkan hornets'-nest. Venizelos passionately refused to cede an inch of Greek territory, and threatened to take back his approval of Bulgaria's enlargement at Serbia's expense. Pashich was not even sure he could get the Serbian army and parliament to agree to the cession of the Lakavitsa-Bregalnitsa triangle, much less of all "uncontested" Macedonia. The reaction of the British and French was to try to arouse Bulgarian interest in Rumanian and Turkish territory.[47]

Sazonov was considerably irritated with this change of face, and sent sharp messages to Delcassé, who had just become French Foreign Minister, and Grey (August 27–29). He warned that any mention of the southern Dobrudja would only complicate relations with Rumania, and that any mention of Bulgarian gains in Turkish Thrace would only fortify Greek obsti-

The Russian Struggle for Power, 1914–1917

nacy. He added that it was impossible to expect the Balkan states to agree among themselves on territorial changes.[48]

Suitably chastened, the British and French went along with a demand in Nish on August 30 that concessions be made to Bulgaria in case the latter promised to oppose any Rumanian or Turkish attack on Serbia. The Serbian reply, delivered on September 1, raised for the first time the question of what Serbia would receive after the war. Provided Bulgaria defended her against Rumania and Turkey, and provided the Serbian parliament agreed, Pashich was willing to cede undefined territory in Macedonia. But in return, he demanded "the Serbo-Croatian territory, with the adjacent littoral." Sazonov greeted this with a haughtiness which speaks volumes regarding the Russian attitude towards the Balkan states at the time. He wired Pashich that "we exclude the possibility of haggling with Serbia. . . . We do not allow ourselves to entertain the thought that the Serbian Government could not conform to our desire . . ." He wanted Britain and France to join him in telling Pashich that the Entente Powers reserved complete liberty "to evaluate at the moment of the conclusion of peace, at their real worth, the efforts and sacrifices of Serbia, as well as the compensations which are due her on account of these."[49]

Britain and France thus glimpsed this early in the war the true face of their ally, which had been so admired a month before for taking up arms in defense of Serbia's integrity. With the German army bearing down on Paris, they could hardly afford to look too closely, but they could and did drag their feet in the Balkan negotiations. Delcassé still thought that concessions in Turkish Thrace were enough for Bulgaria, and Grey remained decidedly in favor of the Balkan states' settling their own territorial problems. On September 3, Grey insisted that it was now impossible to ask concessions of Greece; hence, they should not be asked of Serbia. On September 4, he firmly rejected a suggestion from Sazonov that the Entente guarantee King Ferdinand of Bulgaria his throne, on the ground that it involved too much interference in Bulgaria's internal affairs.[50]

Sazonov, however, had none of Grey's tender

The Russian Struggle for Power, 1914–1917

susceptibilities regarding the rights of small nations, and anyway, was irked by the Western attitude towards his Italian and Rumanian initiatives. He insisted on the policy of browbeating Serbia and Greece, warning that Russian military operations might be affected by a Bulgarian attack on Serbia, and that Britain's "indecisiveness" would be to blame. Russia, he added, while fighting the Central Powers, could not be drawn into a war with Turkey and Bulgaria, as a result of "the folly of Greece, which relies on the toleration of the English."[51]

However, the danger of a split between Russia and her allies at this point was averted. Venizelos made two threats to resign (September 5 and 9), if Kavalla were again demanded of him. Before the spectre of a new, pro-German government in Greece, even Sazonov hesitated. Then, the French won the Battle of the Marne, which caused both Turkey and Bulgaria to hesitate in their pro-German course. Sazonov therefore temporarily dropped the Bulgarian negotiations in mid-September to attend to more urgent matters.[52]

THE "ALLIED POWERS" AND SAZONOV'S TWELVE POINTS

The first six weeks of the war had been hectic ones, during which Sazonov had had to formulate war aims on the spur of the moment, to meet various threatening situations as they arose. After the victories in Galicia and on the Marne, it was possible to relax somewhat and to take a longer look at the purposes for which Russia was fighting the war, a war which she had not wanted, at least in 1914.

Willy-nilly, Sazonov had already committed himself to at least a partial partition of the Austro-Hungarian monarchy, since Galicia, Bukovina, Ruthenia, Transylvania, the Trentino, and Trieste had been either claimed or promised to someone else, while vague promises of independence had been made to the Czechs. In addition, Russia certainly intended from the start that Serbia should gain considerable Hapsburg territory. In his memoirs, Sazonov candidly admits that from the war's beginning, he was resolved to destroy Austria-Hungary.[53]

On top of that, there had been the Russian

The Russian Struggle for Power, 1914–1917

promise to liberate the Poles of Germany, the various schemes to partition Albania, and finally, the plan to enlarge Bulgaria at the expense of Serbia and Greece, and possibly, of Rumania and Turkey, too. Moreover, during the negotiations with Italy, Doumergue had said (August 6) that the return of Alsace-Lorraine to France "must, in any case, be made certain."[54]

It remained, however, to tie all the loose ends of Russian foreign policy together in a master plan, to reach definite agreement with Britain and France on the points already raised, and to decide the really crucial question—what war aims were to be pursued with respect to Germany?

As early as August 7, Sazonov was urging Doumergue to persuade the British to accede to the Franco-Russian alliance of 1891–93, and in particular, to agree not to sign a separate peace. However, Sir Edward Grey liked at first the freedom of action which the absence of formal ties with France and Russia gave him. Not until it seemed that the Germans would take Paris did he consent to discuss a formal alliance (September 1). Even then, the British cabinet refused to become a party to the Franco-Russian alliance. Instead, on September 5, a short, new treaty of alliance was signed in London. It read:

> The Russian, British and French Governments mutually agree not to conclude a separate peace in the course of the present war.
>
> The three governments agree that when the time has come to discuss peace terms, none of the Allied Powers will offer conditions of peace without previous agreement with each of the other Allies.[55]

Thus did the old Triple Entente evolve into the "Allied Powers."

Meanwhile, the French ambassador in Petrograd had been animatedly discussing with Sazonov the future of Germany. Paléologue was addicted to flights of showy rhetoric, which probably went sometimes beyond his actual instructions from Paris. In addition, he was a convinced believer in the policy of crushing Germany. Hence, what he said to Sazonov cannot always be taken as a precise statement of French policy; nor can what he wrote in his memoirs be always taken as an exact statement of Russian policy.

The Russian Struggle for Power, 1914–1917

On August 6, he emerged from an audience with the Tsar, cheered by the "implacable determination" of the latter "to put an end to German tyranny" and to "crush Germany." On August 20, he entertained Sazonov at a luncheon in the French Embassy, and both men discussed the future peace "in an academic sort of way." They agreed that Germany must be defeated definitely, that she must not be given an easy peace like those given Austria in 1860 and 1866. The war must be "a war to the death," on whose outcome both sides staked their very existence.

Sazonov thought the correct Allied formula was the destruction of German imperialism, and that great political changes were necessary if "Kaisertum" were not to "rise from its ashes to aspire to universal dominion." Among such possible changes he mentioned the return of Alsace-Lorraine to France, the restoration of Poland, the enlargement of Belgium, the reconstitution of Hanover, the return of Schleswig to Denmark, the liberation of Bohemia, and the transfer of the German colonies to Britain, France, and Japan. Paléologue concurred, adding that the Allies must realize such a program, "if we want our work to be lasting."[56]

On August 20, of course, it still seemed that the Entente Powers would be lucky to save themselves from Germany, much less to crush and partition her. However, the victories of early September suddenly gave significance to what had been the idle musings of a luncheon conversation. By September 14, Sazonov had prepared a definite list of Russian war aims, and on that day presented it to Paléologue and Sir George Buchanan at their usual morning conference (they met together at a regular time every morning after the outbreak of war).

For the 1914–17 phase of the war, Sazonov's Twelve Points are comparable to Wilson's Fourteen Points for its 1917–18 phase, though they were destined to be modified somewhat. The difference between the two sets of points measures the difference between Tsarist Russian and American goals. Because of their importance, the Russian points are here reproduced in full:

1. The principal objective of the three allies

should be to strike at German power and its pretensions to military and political domination.

2. Territorial modifications ought to be determined by the principle of nationalities.

3. Russia would annex the lower course of the Niemen and the eastern part of Galicia. She could annex to the Kingdom of Poland eastern Posen, Silesia . . . and the western part of Galicia.

4. France would regain Alsace-Lorraine, adding to it, if she wished, a part of Rhenish Prussia and the Palatinate.

5. Belgium would obtain in . . . an important increase in territory.

6. Schleswig-Holstein would be restored to Denmark.

7. The Kingdom of Hanover would be restored.

8. Austria would constitute a tri-partite monarchy, formed of the Empire of Austria, the Kingdom of Bohemia, and the Kingdom of Hungary. The Empire of Austria would include only the "hereditary provinces." The Kingdom of Bohemia would include present Bohemia and Moravia (the Slovaks). The Kingdom of Hungary would have to reach an understanding with Rumania on the subject of Transylvania.

9. Serbia would annex Bosnia, Herzegovina, Dalmatia, and northern Albania.

10. Bulgaria would receive from Serbia compensation in Macedonia.

11. Greece would annex southern Albania, with the exception of Valona, which would devolve on Italy.

12. England, France, and Japan would partition the German colonies.[57]

One point of capital importance is the first one, which makes it clear that Russia recognized Germany as the main enemy. Sazonov knew that it would not be enough merely to partition Austria-Hungary, and that the partition of Germany must be justified. Therefore, in the second point, he espoused the "principle of nationalities," in an obvious bid for the support of Western liberals, whose regrets over the destruction of the German national state might be assuaged by the disappearance of Austria-Hungary.

The Twelve Points, as will be noted, had two blanks, one relating to the future gains of Poland, the other to the future gains of Belgium. Obviously, the Russian Foreign Ministry was still uncertain whether to demand East Prussia and the mouths of the Vistula, from which the Russians had but recently been unceremoniously driven. Just as obviously, Sazonov left it

The Russian Struggle for Power, 1914–1917

up to Britain and France to decide what should be given to Belgium for her sacrifices.

There was one glaring error in the Twelve Points. The Slovaks did not live in Moravia, as Sazonov evidently thought, but farther to the east in what was then northern Hungary. However, there is no mistaking the fact that he wanted a Czecho-Slovak state created, not as an independent kingdom, but as a Slavic third of the Hapsburg monarchy. Obviously, it was his expectation that Austria-Hungary-Bohemia would be so greatly altered by the war that it would be dependent on Russia. This is the more likely, in that the Slovenes and Croatians were not to be joined to Serbia, but to remain within Austria-Hungary-Bohemia, to help the Czechs and Slovaks make it a Slavic state.

It may be wondered whether the loss of "the lower course of the Niemen," eastern Posen, Alsace-Lorraine, Rhenish Prussia and the Palatinate, Schleswig-Holstein, Hanover, the colonies, and possibly East Prussia and the mouths of the Vistula would indeed have reduced Germany to impotence. Much would have depended on whether Russia and the Western powers remained friendly after the war. In any event, it is doubtful whether such an abbreviated Germany could have successfully challenged a Russia which dominated a reunited Poland, a Slavicized Danubian Monarchy, and a trio of grateful Balkan states—Rumania, Bulgaria, and Serbia, all enlarged under Russia's benevolent aegis.

On the other hand, it should be noted that on September 14, 1914, Sazonov was anxious that the West should not leave the war empty-handed. Moreover, his benevolence extended to such Western protégés as Italy, Greece, Belgium, and Denmark. What he wanted, basically, was a Western Europe dominated by Britain and France, an Eastern Europe dominated by Russia, and a weak Germany as a buffer in between.

MILITARY OBJECTIVES OF THE ALLIED POWERS

Sazonov urged Buchanan and Paléologue on September 14 to "attribute no official importance" to his presentation of the Twelve Points, which he described as "this sketch of a tapestry whose warp has not yet been tied." However,

The Russian Struggle for Power, 1914–1917

Paléologue reported to Delcassé that certain words the Russian Foreign Minister let drop made the presentation more official and indicated a strong desire on the part of Russia for "close contact" with her allies. Moreover, just after his talk with Buchanan and Paléologue, Sazonov told Carlotti that the future peace conference would "only confirm . . . the *faits accomplis* and the positions taken by the victors." The peace terms would be dictated, "so to speak, arms in hand, and not with a view to future negotiations."[58]

At all events, Sazonov certainly expected some sort of reply from Britain and France. When no response came from either country, he began to fear that Russia's allies were about to sign a peace of reconciliation with Germany, even, perhaps, to relinquish the French claims to Alsace-Lorraine. The Stavka was hastily consulted, and it was decided to sound out Franco-British military plans. A message was sent on September 17 to General Joffre, in the name of Grand Duke Nikolai. The Supreme High Commander professed to believe that the Germans were about to withdraw behind the Rhine and shift their forces eastward for a knockout blow against Russia. Joffre was asked what he intended to do if this occurred.[59]

The British and French recognized that this was only a roundabout way of getting an answer to Sazonov's proposed peace terms. They therefore presented a joint memorandum (September 17) on the subject of the "definitive objectives" of the Allied Powers, that is, "on the results of the general policy which they are pursuing with respect to Germany and Austria-Hungary." Since the initial objective of the alliance of September 5, the repelling of the aggression of the Germanic powers, had been achieved, the time had come to settle the final aim of Allied efforts. The Allies were not seeking special advantages, but the institution of a new order, which would "ensure for many years the peace of the world." Manifestly, this "work of high civilization" implied the destruction of the German and Austro-Hungarian forces; since those of Austria-Hungary had been shattered in Galicia, the three Allied armies must now "carry the war to the very heart of the German homeland."[60]

The Russian Struggle for Power, 1914–1917

All this was somewhat vague, so on September 19, A.P. Izvolskii, former Russian Foreign Minister (1906–1910), and ambassador to France from 1910 to 1917, frankly confided to Delcassé the real reason for the transmission of the Grand Duke's message. He was rewarded with the assurance that France would not stop her counter-offensive at the Rhine, or at any other point, but would "carry on the business until the end."[61]

However, Delcassé decided to consult his colleagues. On September 20, a full-dress meeting of the Council of Ministers, presided over by Raymond Poincaré, President of the Republic, was held in Bordeaux, the temporary capital of France. It considered Paléologue's report of Sazonov's Twelve Points, the Grand Duke's message of September 17, and a later message from the Russian Supreme High Commander revealing his intention to advance on Berlin as soon as Austria-Hungary was destroyed, and independently of events in East Prussia.[62]

After some discussion of these messages and reports, the French cabinet decided that the aims pursued by Russia and France were identical, and that military activities must continue until French and Russian forces joined hands in the heart of Germany. The decision was unanimous, both the socialists present, Jules Guesde and Marcel Sembat, concurring.[63]

The British did not feel it necessary to hold a cabinet meeting, but on September 21, Grey sent to Sazonov the message that "His Majesty's Government are determined to carry on the war with the utmost vigour and to continue it till the conclusion of a lasting peace is assured." He pointed out that General Joffre, as the commander of the most troops on the Western Front, would determine activity on that front, but added that British military men thought the Grand Duke's decision to march on Berlin was wise.[64]

WAR AIMS OF BRITAIN AND FRANCE

Despite the assurances now given that Britain and France were agreed on crushing the German military power, Sazonov was still without any answers to his exposition of September 14. Ultimately, Grey had to be prodded by Count Alexander Benckendorff, the able Russian am-

The Russian Struggle for Power, 1914–1917

bassador in London, and Delcassé, by Izvolskii.

Grey resolutely refused to make any comprehensive reply, though he would, apparently, discuss some of the points raised by Sazonov, as individual matters. Finally, Benckendorff had to forward to Petrograd on September 28 only an unsatisfactory and unofficial approximate summary of British war aims, based on conversations with a number of leading British statesmen. He warned, however, that no person had envisioned every detail.

Benckendorff's views as to what the British wanted ran as follows: Britain would acquire some of the German colonies, although units of the British Empire might keep them for themselves "if they want to." The Kiel Canal would be neutralized, or the same result obtained by other means. Many Englishmen were reported favorable, in connection with the Kiel Canal question, to the annexation of Schleswig to Denmark, "if possible, without Holstein," and the British Government would give its consent to this proposal. All the essential part of the German fleet must be handed over to Britain to be scuttled. Belgium must be compensated at the expense of Holland, by the cession of the mouth of the Scheldt and Luxembourg to her, Holland to be indemnified with German Frisia. A war indemnity must be levied, to weigh as heavily as possible on the Germans. Britain did not expect to participate directly in a future reorganization of Germany, but it was expected that "the disaster of Prussia will lead to the forced abdication of Prussian supremacy in Germany, which will neutralize her power."

In general, the principal aim was regarded as "the destruction of the military power of Germany." France would receive Alsace-Lorraine and some of the German colonies. Russia would receive all the Polish provinces of Prussia and Austria, "without discussion, but with the strong hope that Russia would take into account for these provinces the Grand Duke's manifesto." Besides the Polish provinces and "the Russian [Ukrainian] regions in Galicia and Bukovina," Austria-Hungary would lose Transylvania, Bosnia-Herzegovina, the Adriatic littoral, and the Trentino, which were "to be divided between the Slavic states and Italy to the degree necessary." These latter cessions, however, would depend on whether Italy or Rumania entered the war on the Allied side.

In the event that Italy and Rumania did not intervene, Benckendorff doubted that "people in England have fixed ideas yet." However, he felt that all the English influence would weigh, in any case, "in favor of a large rectification of the European map on an ethnological basis—a result which can be obtained only at the expense of Austria especially." The British drew this last conclusion from their principal aim, which was "the necessity of guaranteeing peace in the future by suppressing the causes of conflicts"; however, they drew the conclusion "with certain regrets, Austria being so generally regarded as the instrument and victim of Germany, against whom is directed all the power of English national sentiment." In British minds, the question of Turkey remained open. If she took up arms against the Allies, it was thought that "she would have to cease to exist, which would result in a modification of the status of Egypt."

Benckendorff stated further on the subject of Turkey that he had never even indirectly brought up the question of the Straits, but did not doubt that "commercial liberty" entered into the future British program. He thought that the British expected Russia to take the initiative in picking the time and place for further negotiations on the future peace terms. He closed his report by emphasizing that "it is a division on an ethnological basis which preoccupies England above all as the only basis of a durable peace." For this reason, he found that the British hoped that France was not ambitious for the line of the Rhine, "which would open the door to new conflicts in the future."[65]

Later, on October 8, Benckendorff reported that Grey definitely believed that Belgium should be compensated with territory, but was vague about what territory and how much.[66]

After some delay, Delcassé proved to be more obliging than Grey. On October 13, nearly a month after the presentation by Sazonov, he expressed himself rather freely to Izvolskii. Remarking that it was still too early "to sell the bear's skin," and admitting that he had avoided any discussion of war aims with his colleagues, he nevertheless conceded that "it would not be unthinkable for the Allies, at an early date, to clarify among themselves their mutual opinions and desires." He was convinced that "on this subject no difference can arise between Russia, France, and England."

For herself, France did not seek in Europe any territorial gains, "with the exception, of course, of the return of Alsace and Lorraine." In Africa, also, she would not strive for any new gains, and would be satisfied with "the destruction of the last remnants of the Act of Algeciras and the rectification of several colonial frontiers."

The chief goal of France—and in this all three Powers were completely agreed—was the destruction of the German Empire and the weakening, as much as possible, of the military and political might of Prussia. It was necessary to do this so that the various German states might themselves come to have an interest in the destruction. It was still too early to speak of the details of the future structure of Germany. Britain would probably demand the reestablishment of an independent Hanover, and to this, of course, neither Russia nor France would object. Schleswig and Holstein must be returned to Denmark despite the latter's equivocal conduct over the two and a half months preceding.[67] Britain did not seek conquests in Europe, but would demand colonial gains at the expense of Germany, and to such demands, France would have no objections.

Russian territorial demands were already formulated in general terms, and it went without saying that "France is agreed to them beforehand." Russia would, of course, demand also freedom of the Turkish Straits and sufficient guarantees in this regard; she would receive in this matter the wholehearted support of France, which could exercise useful pressure on Britain.

Delcassé was somewhat less definite on the subject of the future of the Austro-Hungarian monarchy. This question interested the French much less than did the fate of the German Empire. Izvolskii warned Sazonov that "despite Delcassé's assurance to the contrary, it is necessary to keep in view several indubitable sympathies of the French for Austria-Hungary, based on the completely false proposition of the so-called inherent striving of the latter for independence from Germany, and the concessions made by her to France at Algeciras."

Delcassé asked Izvolskii, among other things, where, in the latter's opinion, the peace congress should take place. Izvolskii answered that this would probably be decided at the last moment; however, in his opinion, there was no reason why "the negotiations on peace or even the preliminary conversations between the three Allies should indispensably take place under the aegis of Sir Edward Grey." Later, he suggested to Sazonov that if the latter did not desire to take the negotiations into his own hands, then it would be best "to present the leadership in them to Delcassé, who simultaneously enjoys complete confidence both in London and in Petrograd . . ."[68]

THE DEADLOCK AND THE
RISE OF NEW PROBLEMS

By the time Grey and Delcassé had pronounced themselves, the discussion of war aims had come to take on an increasingly theoretical air, owing to the military rally of the Central Powers. The French and British did not drive the Germans to the Rhine, but to a line in northern France which could not be broken for four long years. Moreover, though the Germans did not send the bulk of their forces eastward in 1914, they did send enough to Poland to bolster the exhausted Austro-Hungarians. Instead of marching on Berlin, the Grand Duke was quite busy in October, November, and December, parrying Hindenburg's thrusts towards Warsaw. Moreover, the last Russian forces were driven from East Prussia, and the Austrians held on grimly to Przemysl, which barred the way to a Russian sweep across the Carpathians, somewhat as Plevna had barred passage of the Balkans to the Russians in 1877-78. By mid-December, the Russian striking power was so blunted that the Grand Duke had to confess his inability to wage more than defensive warfare.[69]

Meanwhile, what was for the Russians virtually a new war had begun with the entrance of Turkey on the side of the Central Powers (November 2). As a consequence, it was necessary to enlarge Russian war aims to a significant degree.

II

EXTENSION OF THE DESIGN

THE THEORY that Russia started the first World War in order to gain Constantinople and the Straits has long since been exploded,[1] and it hardly needs disproving here. On the other hand, there is no doubt that from 1908, the year of the Young Turk revolution, the Russians were very concerned over the possibility that the artery through which passed thirty-seven per cent of their overseas trade would be closed, not to speak of the possibility that their Black Sea ports would be in danger of another attack like that of 1854–55.

In 1908, A. P. Izvolskii, as Minister of Foreign Affairs, was so concerned at the possibility of a revival of Turkish military power that he was willing to hand over the Serbs of Bosnia-Herzegovina to Austria, in return for Austria's consent to Russia's having control of the Turkish Straits. However, neither the French nor the British would agree to his desire that Russian warships be given an exit through the Bosporus, the Sea of Marmora, and to the Dardanelles to the Mediterranean.

Four years later, in 1912, Turkey closed the Straits after she was attacked by the Balkan states. The economic consequences to southern Russia were serious, since transportation westward of Ukrainian grain was twenty-five per cent more expensive by land than by sea. It was estimated that Russian grain growers lost 30 billion rubles a month while the Straits were closed. The Russian balance of trade in 1912 was worsened to the extent of a hundred million rubles, and the State Bank had to raise its discount rate ½% in the spring of 1913.[2]

As a result, in 1912–13, a powerful demand arose among the Russian landlord, commercial, and banking interests for assurances that nothing like such a débâcle should happen again. Economic interests, something vastly different from sentimental, Pan-Slavist, Orthodox dreams of placing the cross atop Santa Sophia, had entered the picture. Aside from the question of exporting Ukrainian grain, many Russian merchants, bankers, and promoters hoped to reap a

The Russian Struggle for Power, 1914–1917

rich profit out of the exploitation of the economic hinterland of the Black Sea, including Transcaucasia and northern Persia, the latter having been assigned by the British as a Russian sphere of influence in 1907. A guarantee of an exit through the Straits was needed if these dreams were to be realized, especially since the British were installed in southern Persia and Mesopotamia.[3]

In 1912, Sazonov had been very jittery over the possibility that the Bulgarians might take Constantinople. In 1913, he became more jittery still over the possibility that Turkish naval strength in the Black Sea was about to become greater than that of Russia. As a consequence, a great naval building program was inaugurated at Nikolayev in 1913, but the new Russian battleships and cruisers could not be completed until 1916–17. After the reinforcement of the Turkish fleet by the Germans in 1914, the Turks actually had naval superiority in the Black Sea during most of the First World War.[4]

However, Sazonov and most Russians were even more alarmed, just before the war, by the prospect that the Germans might establish a protectorate over Turkey. All members of the Triple Entente had acquiesced in Germany's "Berlin-to-Baghdad" railroad project, but when the announcement was made in December, 1913 of the appointment of a German general as commander of the Turkish First Army Corps in Constantinople, the Russians were in a frenzy. A crisis was avoided by changing the nature of General Liman von Sanders' appointment with the Turkish forces, but Sazonov was far from pacified. In February, 1914, a top-level meeting of Russian ministers and generals decided that in case of a general war involving Turkey, Russia must obtain control of Constantinople and the Straits.[5]

However, this was planning for an eventuality which might not occur for years. The most effective way in which the Russians could counter the Liman von Sanders appointment was by adopting a threatening attitude towards Turkey on her Transcaucasian frontier. This was all the more possible in that Russia was in effective control of northern Persia. Russian interest in Turkey's oppressed Armenians was revived, and in February, 1914, the Young Turks

The Russian Struggle for Power, 1914–1917

were forced to agree to a program of reforms in their Armenian districts. Later, in April, 1914, the Young Turk leaders visited Nicholas II and Sazonov at Livadia, in the Crimea, but no meeting of minds occurred.[6]

THE TURCO-GERMAN TREATY OF ALLIANCE

There is no doubt at all that the abler of the Young Turk leaders, including especially War Minister Enver Pasha, had made up their minds prior to the Austrian ultimatum to Serbia on July 23, 1914, to join Germany and Austria-Hungary in any war between them and Russia-France. Aside from the possibility thus offered to deal a crushing blow to Russia, the Young Turks hoped to revive national spirits, depressed by the wars of 1911–13, and to recover Lemnos, Lesbos, and Chios, which guarded the sea approaches to the Dardanelles and Izmir (Smyrna), and whose seizure by Greece in 1912–13 had never been recognized. Moreover, there was some hope of improving the frontier in Thrace at the expense of Bulgaria.

However, the Young Turks made the terrific miscalculation that Britain would remain neutral in a war between the Central Powers and Russia-France. The reason is not too hard to find. While tightening the bonds of the Triple Entente, the British were helping in the build-up of the Turkish Navy, constructing Turkish dreadnoughts in British yards, and sending a British admiral to command the Turkish sea forces.

Secure in a false sense of British support, the Turks began to importune the Central Powers for an alliance the moment the war crisis opened on July 23. The Germans had not, apparently, even given consideration to the possibility of a Turkish alliance, and were at first extremely reluctant to assume the burden of defending not one, but two decadent, multi-national empires. However, Austria-Hungary strongly supported the Turkish request, and ultimately Berlin gave way, after gaining assurances that the Turks would attack Russia as soon as war broke out between her and Austria-Hungary, and that Germany might have effective control of the Turkish army. The treaty of alliance was signed in Constantinople on August 2, the day after the German declaration of war on Russia.[7]

The Russian Struggle for Power, 1914–1917

Turkish mobilization followed, on August 3. Then, to their consternation, the Turks discovered that the British took a dim view of their activities. Orders were given that the Turkish dreadnoughts in British yards were not to be delivered, and the British naval mission was recalled. On August 5, Britain declared war on Germany, and the Turks began to scuttle for shelter.

THE QUESTION OF TURKEY'S JOINING THE ENTENTE

On the day of British entry into the war, Enver Pasha turned to the Russians with an offer of an alliance. In his *L'histoire diplomatique de la France pendant la grande guerre,* M. Albert Pingaud assumes that the offer was only a blind to cover Turkish military preparations. Such an interpretation places too high an evaluation on the Turkish sense of self-confidence in August, 1914. Enver fully realized that the Ottoman Empire would be greatly endangered if it had to fight Russia and the British forces in Cyprus, Egypt, Aden, and India, not to speak of Greece and Bulgaria. On the other hand, he also realized that the Triple Entente might now be ready to pay a high price for a guarantee of Turkish neutrality.[8]

On August 5, he told the Russian military attaché in Constantinople that the Turkish army of 250,000 to 300,000 men would be placed at Russia's disposal if he were guaranteed Lemnos, Lesbos, Chios, and a small strip of Bulgarian territory on the right bank of the Maritza River. He added that, of course, the Straits Question would "fall of its own weight," if an alliance were signed. He denied that the Germans had control of his army, and pointed out that Turkey's support would make it unnecessary for the Russians to keep an army in Transcaucasia and assure the loyalty of Russia's Moslem population, while exerting a powerful, pro-Russian influence on the Balkan states.[9]

Sazonov knew that the return of any liberated Christian territory to Turkey was almost impossible, but was greatly impressed by the offer, and resolved to play for time. Meanwhile, the Germans, alarmed over Turkey's failure to honor the alliance of August 2, pulled off a brilliant coup which later made it possible for them

The Russian Struggle for Power, 1914–1917

to drag an unwilling Turkey into the war. On August 9–10, while Enver was still pushing for an answer to his offer to Russia, two German cruisers, the *Göben* and *Breslau,* which had been stranded in the Mediterranean, sneaked through the Straits of Messina, the Aegean, and the Dardanelles, and arrived in Constantinople. They were promptly offered to the Turks as replacements for the dreadnoughts Britain had failed to deliver. Turkey bought them, but left the German officers and crews aboard.[10]

The British and French were terribly upset by this development, and on August 11, Doumergue demanded of Sazonov a Russian guarantee of Turkish territorial integrity, despite the fact that some officials in the French Foreign Ministry thought it best to let Turkey join Germany, "in order, in this way, to put an end to her." Sazonov was agreeable to such an offer, so long as the agreement on Armenian reforms was preserved.[11]

Russo-Turkish talks began in both St. Petersburg and Constantinople. The Turks still wanted territorial concessions, while the Russians now demanded the suppression of the German military mission as the price of a guarantee of territorial integrity. Sazonov finally concluded that an offer of the Greek island of Lemnos, which guarded the Dardanelles, should be made, but Sir Edward Grey firmly and officially refused his consent, on the grounds that the offer would only complicate Balkan negotiations and would estrange Greece, whose help Britain wanted in case of war with Turkey (August 16–17).[12]

Neither Britain nor France was happy over another Russian suggestion—that Turkey be offered the return of German railroad concessions in Asia Minor. Russia could well afford to make such an offer, since she had no economic concessions of any sort in Turkey, but Britain and France feared an analogy would be made between the German concessions and their own. Finally, it was agreed that the ambassadors of the Triple Entente should merely offer Turkey territorial integrity for neutrality; this was done on August 18.[13]

However, the Russians made the offer with some reservations. On August 20, Prince G. N. Trubetskoi, author of the proclamation to the

The Russian Struggle for Power, 1914–1917

Poles, produced an important policy paper on the subject of Constantinople and the Straits. He began by pointing out that the acquisition of the mouth of the Niemen by Russia and of the mouths of the Vistula by Poland (the East Prussian campaign had not yet failed) was only the "inevitable payment of a historic debt," incurred when Catherine II and Alexander I had agreed to partition Poland with the Germanic powers. Whatever gains the Russians might make at the expense of Germany, "evidently, before everything, our thoughts are turned towards the Straits." No one could as yet tell what Turkey might do, or under what circumstances peace would be made. If Turkey remained neutral, her territorial integrity might be guaranteed, but she must be forced to give free passage through the Straits to the warships of Black Sea powers. If she attacked Russia, or the Balkan states, Russian control over the Straits must be established in a manner which would cause the least trouble with Britain. Perhaps Turkish fortifications along the Straits could be destroyed, and Russia could obtain a naval base on the Dardanelles. On the other hand, the seizure of

Constantinople could not be envisaged except in an "academic way," and Russia must not repeat the mistake of Germany, "which has armed all the people against her by her manifest desire to overturn the European equilibrium."[14]

Meanwhile, the Young Turks were complaining that the Entente offer of August 18 was not enough to meet German offers of Russian territory in Transcaucasia. They now wanted a territorial guarantee of 18 to 20 years' duration and the end of all western extra-territorial rights in Turkey. Sazonov supported the abolition of capitulations, but Russia's allies rejected this demand.[15]

After the Entente Powers learned that Turkey was trying to align Bulgaria and Rumania in a pro-German bloc, Delcassé made the firebrand proposal (August 27) that Bulgaria be invited to seize Turkish Thrace as far as the Enos-Midiya line. Both Britain and Russia rejected this suggestion, but by August 28, Grey had come to believe that Turkey would probably join Germany, and had stated that it was important to him only that her rupture with the Entente be manifestly her own doing. After that,

The Russian Struggle for Power, 1914-1917

Sazonov gave up his own efforts to keep Turkey neutral, though hardly with a heavy heart, in view of the Trubetskoi memorandum of August 20. By August 30, he was instructing the Viceroy of Transcaucasia to prepare an uprising of the Turkish Armenians and Kurds, since war seemed imminent.[16]

The Turks were unquestionably disappointed by the meagre Entente offer of August 18, and would probably have joined the Germans before the end of August, had Bulgaria and Rumania done so. Finally, from a sense of frustration as much as anything else, they decided on September 8 to announce the abolition of all capitulations within the Ottoman realm. This was stepping on German, as well as Franco-British toes, and aroused protests from both sides. However, it was more a sign of weakness and general irritation with the European powers rather than the prelude to further action. Owing to the Allied successes in early September, the Turks dared not honor their alliance with the Germans. On the other hand, the Allies still disdained to make Turkey the same glowing territorial promises they were making to Italy, Rumania, and the Balkan states, and the Turks would not fight for the Allies *gratis*. For a month after September 8, Turkey sank into a state of sullen and uneasy neutrality.[17]

TURKEY JOINS THE CENTRAL POWERS

The Germans looked upon Turkey's failure to honor the pledges of August 2 as an act of base treachery, especially after the sale of the *Göben* and *Breslau*. The blame was laid on certain Young Turks believed to be pro-Ally, and in September, a proposal to kidnap these offenders was seriously entertained. It was finally dropped, however. The only striking success won by German diplomats in Constantinople during the six weeks following the Battle of the Marne was to persuade the Turks to close the Straits on October 8. This step was apparently taken partly because of the Russo-Rumanian agreement of October 1–2, and partly because Allied counter-offensives were grinding to a halt. However, Turkey still refused to go further.[18]

Meanwhile, the Russian government had made it clear to its allies that it hoped to prevent any future closures of the Straits after the war. The initiative was taken, not by Sazonov, but by Minister of Agriculture A. V. Krivoshein, whose relatively liberal political views did not prevent his enjoying the special favor of the Russian Emperor and Empress.

Krivoshein approached Paléologue on September 25, just after returning from an audience with the Emperor. Apparently, his main purpose was to find out if Paléologue knew anything about Delcassé's attitude towards Sazonov's Twelve Points. He claimed to be convinced that the Central Powers were about to make peace offers, and said the Allies ought not to be caught without a program. When Paléologue pleaded ignorance of Delcassé's views, the Russian minister then turned to the subject of Constantinople and the Straits. He thought that the city itself must be internationalized, somewhat like Tangier, and that absolute freedom of passage through the Straits should be allowed. Paléologue pricked up his ears. Warning that the British might oppose such a project, he asked if Krivoshein was speaking for the Emperor. The minister hastily replied that he was voicing only his personal views.[19]

Nevertheless, Paléologue took the matter up with Sazonov the next day, in the presence of Buchanan. Sazonov showed some irritation at the invasion of his field by a colleague, and insisted that he was in favor of leaving Constantinople in the hands of the Turks. However, he thought the occasion suitable for broaching Trubetskoi's plan for Russian naval control of the Straits, with some modifications. Russia wanted, he said, the destruction of the Turkish fortifications and the establishment of a Russian naval base at Buyukdérè, on the Bosporus. However, she was willing that the Straits be officially under an international commission with warships at its disposal.

Buchanan voiced the purely personal opinion that Britain would probably oppose such a plan. However, no further reply was made by the Western powers at this point, and the Straits Question remained on ice for yet another month.[20]

Then, at the end of October, the Germans brought the Turks into the war by a second bril-

The Russian Struggle for Power, 1914–1917

liant *coup de main*. The *Göben* and *Breslau* had remained in charge of their German officers and crews, under strict orders from the Turkish Naval Ministry not to leave Constantinople. Nevertheless, their German commander, Admiral Souchon, with Enver Pasha's connivance, sneaked the two cruisers out of the Bosporus on October 28, in company with a few small Turkish naval units whose commanders were in on the plot. This German-Turkish flotilla then streaked across the Black Sea to the Russian coast.

On October 29 and 30, various units of the Souchon task force attacked Russian shipping off Sevastopol, Feodosiya, and Novorossiisk, and nearby coastal installations. They sank a total of twenty-one ships and set afire fifty oil tanks and a number of grain warehouses, while laying mines off the Crimea. Russian shore batteries at Sevastopol scored three hits on the afterdeck of the *Göben,* but with this exception, the task force had returned without a scratch to Constantinople on November 2.[21]

On the morning of October 29, Buchanan and Paléologue met a Sazonov flushed with anger and excitement. The Russian Foreign Minister said that the Near Eastern Question had been put on the order of the day, and that Turkey must be made to pay dearly. On the other hand, he promised that not a soldier would be withdrawn from the front against Germany to fight Turkey, since Germany was still the main enemy. Nevertheless, Buchanan soberly reported to Grey that the Russian masses were wildly enthusiastic over the new war, since none of them had thought that Russia would profit from a war with Germany and Austria-Hungary. It was a well-timed warning that despite Sazonov's promises, Russia was likely to be tempted by the prospect of gains at Turkey's expense to neglect the war with the principal opponent of the Western powers.[22]

However, Sazonov kept his head sufficiently to fasten upon Turkey indubitable responsibility for the war, remembering Grey's words of the preceding August. On October 30, a Russian ultimatum was delivered in Constantinople, with a twenty-four-hour time limit for acceptance. Turkey must either send home the German military mission and the officers and crews

The Russian Struggle for Power, 1914–1917

of the *Göben* and *Breslau,* and promise not to give shelter to any more German warships, or face a break in relations with Russia. The Turkish moderates could only wring their hands helplessly, and on October 31, Russia broke off relations. Britain and France followed suit on November 1.[23]

On November 2, the Tsar issued his declaration of war on Turkey. After reciting the list of recent Turkish outrages, he expressed confidence that Russia would defeat "the ancient oppressor of the Christian faith and of all the Slavic peoples." He added that Turkey's "unjustified" intervention in the war would "only hasten a course of events fatal for her, and ... open to Russia the path towards the settlement of the historic tasks bequeathed to her by forbears on the shores of the Black Sea."[24] When Paléologue asked Sazonov what this last phrase meant, the Russian Foreign Minister promptly replied:

We shall have to make Turkey pay dearly for her mistake of today. We must have tangible guarantees on the Bosporus. As regards Constantinople, personally I don't want the Turks to be cleared out. I'd gladly leave them the old Byzantine city with a good-sized kitchen-garden all around. But no more![25]

THE BOND OF BRITAIN

In retrospect, there seems to be no doubt that Russia was vastly rejuvenated by the prospect of gaining control of the Straits after November 2, 1914. Despite the successes in Galicia and the prospect of realizing Sazonov's Twelve Points in Eastern Europe, a large and influential segment of the Russian ruling class, including Count Sergei Yu. Witte, an ex-Premier, thought that the war with Germany and Austria-Hungary was an enormous mistake.[26] They hated Sazonov because of the proclamation to the Poles, and would have been glad to see him dismissed as the prelude to a settlement with the Central Powers. Grey and Delcassé looked on his continuance in office as the surest guarantee that the Russians would fight to the finish, and were willing to make concessions to him which they would have denied to another Foreign Minister.[27]

After November 2, Grey realized that some

The Russian Struggle for Power, 1914-1917

important gesture was necessary if Sazonov was to be successful in preventing a diversion of strength from the Russo-German front in Poland. The Russian reactionaries would gladly sacrifice Poland for Constantinople and the Straits, and Sazonov would need some weapon with which to fight them. Grey gave him that weapon in November, 1914—a British promise that Russia might have both Constantinople and the Straits after the war.

We now know that it is only a legend that the cardinal principle of British foreign policy in the nineteenth century was to keep Russia out of Constantinople and the Straits (it is also legend that throughout the nineteenth century Russia wanted to gain actual possession of Constantinople and the Straits). This theory of British foreign policy has been developed mainly by historians who see everything through German eyes. The Germans thought, indeed, hoped, that Britain would always fight to keep the Tsar out of the Bosporus and the Dardanelles. Actually, in 1840-41, the British were as much interested in saving Turkey from France as from Russia.

The Russian Struggle for Power, 1914-1917

The Crimean War came because British liberals hated Nicholas I, and wanted to restore the European balance. In 1877–78, again, Britain intervened in the Balkans to save the European balance, and shortly after, the British occupation of Egypt (1882) reassured those who feared that Russia might close the Empire's lifeline to India. Off and on, from 1882 to 1906, the British frequently indicated that they would not necessarily, come what might, try to keep Russia out of the Straits.[28]

True, Sir Edward Grey had blocked the Russian initiatives of 1908 and 1911. But that was mainly because the radicals in the British Liberal government disliked intensely the entente with Russia. In addition, Grey himself was greatly provoked with the Russians over their behavior in northern Persia, which, under the terms of the Anglo-Russian convention of 1907, the St. Petersburg government regarded as a sort of colony.[29]

Upon the outbreak of war with Turkey, Grey was very fearful of the probable effect on the Moslems of India and Egypt, especially if the Russians committed further violations of Persia's

The Russian Struggle for Power, 1914–1917

integrity. On November 2, he voiced these fears to Sazonov, while assuring him that he thought Turkey "neither deserves nor should receive any consideration, as she has shown herself incorrigible."[30]

Sazonov urged the Viceroy of Transcaucasia to use care in handling Moslems, but at the same time warned Grey that the defense of Transcaucasia would make it necessary for Russia to violate Persia's integrity. He suggested, therefore, that Persia be brought into the war by an offer of the Shiite Holy Places, Nedjef and Kerbela, in Mesopotamia.[31]

Grey and Benckendorff discussed this question at length in London (November 9). The British Foreign Office opposed the offer of Nedjef and Kerbela, since it would offend the Sunnite Moslems of India and Egypt. Moreover, Grey still wished that Russia would not violate Persia's neutrality, at least until Turkey did so. Then suddenly, in the midst of the conversation, he remarked casually that if Germany were destroyed, the fate of Constantinople and the Straits could be settled this time only in accordance with Russian convenience. When this remark evoked a startled expression of surprise from Benckendorff, Grey added that he had wired Buchanan of his attitude, but not in so clear a form. He promised to send the latter further instructions.[32]

Four days later, on November 13, Benckendorff was received in audience by King George V at Buckingham Palace. The king talked mostly about the fighting in progress in Flanders, and then shifted to the topic of war aims. He thought the military power of Prussia must be destroyed, but favored no intervention by the Allies in the post-war internal structure of Germany. The smaller German states, he said, would lessen the power of Prussia. Then, shifting abruptly to the Near East, he remarked casually, "As far as Constantinople is concerned, it is clear that this city must be yours." Benckendorff was well aware of the fact that the British monarch would not have spoken thus had the cabinet not already discussed and resolved the question.[33]

After the audience, he hastened to the Foreign Office. Sir Arthur Nicolson, the Permanent Undersecretary, confirmed what the king had said, and permitted Benckendorff to read the instructions which had been sent to Buchanan regarding Britain's attitude towards proposed Russian troop movements into Persia. In them, Grey insisted that the protection of second-rank powers had become the basic principle of the political harmony of the Allies. Should Russia insist on violating Persian integrity, fears might arise in Britain that German military hegemony was about to be replaced by Russian military hegemony. There might arise, as a result, opposition in Britain to Russian acquisition of Constantinople and the Straits—an acquisition which now aroused no opposition. In other words, if Russia behaved well in regard to Persia, she might have Constantinople and the Straits.[34]

On the next day, November 14, Buchanan transmitted this message, and at the same time indicated that King George V had faithfully conveyed the intentions of his ministers. In a note to Sazonov, he stated that Grey feared an analogy would be made between a Russian violation of Persia and the German violation of Belgium. Grey granted, however, that the mere presence of Russian troops in Persian Azerbaijan was not enough to cause such an analogy to be made, and admitted that if Turkey violated Persian territory, Russia and Britain would have the right to take measures against such an attack. Grey, however, agreed with the Russian military leaders that all Russian efforts should be directed against Germany, and thought that Russia should go on the defensive on the Turkish front. He pointed out that only the minimum number of British troops were being left in the East for defensive purposes.

Buchanan then reached the climax of his message:

> But whatever limitations are imposed on Russia and Great Britain in their defense with regard to Turkey—until the favourable issue of the struggle against Germany, on which depends all the rest—Sir Edward Grey thinks that the conduct of the Turkish Government will render inevitable the complete solution of the Turkish problem, including the question of the Straits and Constantinople, in agreement with Russia. The solution of this question can naturally come only after the defeat of Germany, independently of a prior breakup of the Turkish State, which is possible as a result of the march of military operations.[35]

The Russian Struggle for Power, 1914-1917

DISCUSSIONS ON THE FUTURE OF POLAND, NOVEMBER, 1914

Grey's important concession could not have been better timed, despite its off-hand and somewhat vague nature. It arrived at a moment when Sazonov was engaged in a bitter struggle with the reactionaries, who were in favor of sacrificing the war with Germany and the cause of Poland for the sake of gains at Turkey's expense. The Polish Question had come to the fore again mainly because of the bad conduct of reactionary Russian civil and religious officials in occupied Galicia. After most of it had been cleared of Austrians, Count Vladimir A. Bobrinskii, an ardent nationalist of narrowly Orthodox views, had been installed in Lvov as Military Governor-General, with Metropolitan Antony of Volhynia, a favorite of Rasputin, as his assistant for religious matters. This precious pair began an ardent campaign to stamp out Ukrainian nationalism and the Uniate faith, along with the Galician Jews, who were regarded as the natural enemies of Russia. In all fairness, it should be added that previous to the arrival of the Russians, the Austrians had tried to stamp out the "Muscophile" intelligentsia in Galicia.[36]

The Russians arrested eight thousand Galicians, including the entire Uniate priesthood, and sent them eastward to prison camps. Galician schools were closed down until January 1, 1915, and all Ukrainian newspapers and societies were discontinued. An ardent campaign for the conversion of the Uniate laity to Orthodoxy was instituted. Only the intervention of the Supreme High Commander caused this campaign to be somewhat mitigated, and plans for *pogroms* against the Jews to be halted.[37]

Grand Duke Nikolai was profoundly disgusted with the whole business, and deeply concerned over its possible effect on the Poles. The latter were beginning to ask whether Bobrinskii's regime would be extended to western Galicia, which was wholly Polish, and to insist on a clearer definition of the vague promises made by Russia on August 16. On October 2, the Supreme High Commander began to demand of Premier Goremykin that the Polish and Ukrainian policies of Russia be given "a definiteness which is more in accord with contemporary conditions." However, the incompetent Goremykin was in no hurry to act, and it took the outbreak of war with Turkey to produce a meeting of the Council of Ministers devoted to the Polish Question.[38]

Four of such meetings were eventually held in November, on the 2nd, the 12th, the 18th, and the 28th. Sazonov had now dropped his wavering attitude of the previous August, and had emerged as the strong protagonist of the Polish cause. V. A. Maklakov, Minister of the Interior, Justice Minister Shcheglovitov, and Acting Minister of Education Taube were leaders of the opposition. Only Krivoshein gave Sazonov strong support, but the other ministers, feeling that the Tsar and the Supreme High Commander leaned in the direction of the Foreign Minister, were reluctant to take an anti-Polish stand.[39]

Maklakov was intelligent enough to realize that he must make some concessions, but he insisted that the promise of August 16 must be interpreted to mean only that Russia would give her Poles some of the rights previously accorded to the Empire at large, but denied to the Governor-Generalship of Warsaw, or the "Vistula Region." For example, the zemstvo institutions established in Russia proper in 1864 might now be given to the Poles, and as an added concession, zemstvo business in Poland might be conducted in the Polish language. Moreover, Russian bureaucrats serving in Poland might be required to learn Polish, and Russian-speaking Poles admitted to the Russian bureaucracy. However, the Polish zemstvos must be limited to the discussion of purely local economic matters, and except for their establishment, everything must go on as before. Moreover, the Suwalki Province, populated mainly by Lithuanians, ought to be cut off from the Warsaw-Governor-Generalship, after western Galicia and Posen were added to it.[40]

Sazonov opposed to this viewpoint a scheme which was much nearer the desires of the Poles, one which would have come close to reinstituting the real autonomy enjoyed by Poland between 1815 and 1831. The new, reunited Poland must have a Viceroy, instead of a mere Governor-General, a *Sejm* or parliament, and a local Polish bureaucracy. The use of the Polish lan-

The Russian Struggle for Power, 1914–1917

guage must be allowed in the administration, the law courts, the legislative bodies, and the schools, with a few exceptions. Only Poland's foreign and defense affairs must remain wholly in the hands of the Russian government and Duma. In other matters, there would be a clear demarcation of authority.[41]

By November 28, an official project of the Council of Ministers had been worked out. Sazonov's plan had been accepted in its broad lines, but the reactionaries had obtained the elimination of the *Sejm,* for which were substituted zemstvo institutions. The project removed existing restrictions on the Roman Catholic Church in Poland, and permitted the use of Polish in the administration, law courts, and schools, with certain exceptions.[42]

Despite the concessions they had wrung from the Council of Ministers, Maklakov, Shcheglovitov, and Taube insisted on attaching a special minority opinion to the project. In it, they attacked bitterly the policy of fighting for the reunification of Poland, asserting that it could well lead to the failure of other, more important war aims.

The Russian Struggle for Power, 1914–1917

The reactionaries insisted that three over-all principles should guide the establishment of Russian war aims:

1. *The possible strengthening of Russia proper*, with respect to population, economy, and strategy;
2. *The possible weakening of Germanism*, as the chief enemy, at the present time, of Slavdom and Russia, and,
3. *The possible liberation of other Slavic peoples* from the rule of Germany and Austria-Hungary (as long as such would not be in opposition to the direct interests of Russia).

These general principles would be fulfilled first by the conquest of the Austro-Hungarian Ukrainians, who must be reunited to their Russian motherland. After that, the annexation of Constantinople and the Straits was most important. Thirdly, Russia should make territorial gains at the expense of Germany in East Prussia, and at the expense of Turkey along the Asiatic frontier. Fourthly, Germany must be weakened internally by her "complete territorial reconstruction." For example, some of the territory of Prussia should be given to France, Belgium, Luxembourg, Denmark, and the smaller German states, and the kingdoms of Hanover and Hesse-Nassau should be established.

Only after all these aims were accomplished did the reactionaries think it possible to consider the reconstitution of Poland, with ethnographic frontiers, and the liberation of the Austrian Slavs. Moreover, the unification of Poland might actually be contrary to Russian interests, since acquisition of western Galicia and Posen could make the western frontier harder to defend. In any case, great care must be taken to assure that Britain and France did not interfere in the settlement of the Polish Question, and that the Polish intelligentsia did not extort concessions relative to Poland's eastern frontiers.

Finally, the reactionaries suggested, it would be well to consider whether the inclusion of a Slavic element within the future Germany would not serve "sooner her internal weakening than her strengthening." Only in case Germany were completely destroyed did it seem to them unavoidable that Poland be reunited under the Russian crown. There was no chance that Britain and France would push Russia into "an unacceptable reestablishment of Poland because of the risk of losing Russian Poland," since "history knows no example of a power which emerges victorious from war being compelled to give up its territory."[43]

The ministerial project of November 28, with the attached minority viewpoint, reached the Tsar at Baranovichi, while he was visiting the Stavka. Since the Polish Question seemed to be arousing so much controversy, Nicholas ultimately lacked the courage to go ahead with the implementation of the project. He returned it to Goremykin with the weak excuse that its details needed further development, and that perhaps it ought to be presented to the Duma. To salve his conscience, however, he reaffirmed his intention to grant Poland autonomy, and ordered the appointment of a new Governor-General of Warsaw, who must be a person sympathetic to the proclamation of August 16. Thus, the reactionaries won only a partial victory at this time. Grey's promise of Constantinople and the Straits had done yeoman work for Sazonov and Poland.[44]

The Russian Struggle for Power, 1914–1917

FRANCE AND THE STRAITS QUESTION

Meanwhile, it had become necessary to acquaint France officially with the extension of Russian war aims which the war with Turkey had produced. Back in September and October, the British had been uncooperative about discussing any overall plan of war aims, though Delcassé had been willing, after some urging, to communicate his general views. Since Britain had voluntarily conceded the fulfillment of Russia's Straits ambitions, it was decided to ignore her for the time being, and to try to reach an agreement with the French, in which Russia's new ambitions were linked to those previously announced in September.

Two days after Buchanan handed Sazonov his note on the Straits, Paléologue reported to Delcassé that Premier Goremykin had recently spoken to him in a private fashion on the general aims which the three Allied Powers ought to pursue during the war (November 15). Goremykin's views in this regard were "identical to those of M. Sazonov." In addition, the Premier insisted on the necessity of making Constantinople a free city, with an international regime, and believed that Russia "would be obliged to annex a part of Armenia."

During the interview, Goremykin developed five chief points:

1. The general terms of peace ought to be secretly agreed upon between the governments of the three Allied Powers.

2. When the time has come, these conditions will be dictated to Germany and Austria. Hostilities will be continued without respite until the will of the three Allied Powers has prevailed.

3. There would be a conference only for the settlement of secondary questions.

4. It would be necessary that the governments of the three Allied Powers concert among themselves on the general conditions of peace while their union is most perfect, *i.e.*, while the three countries are fighting jointly, united still by the thought that there remains to them a great task to accomplish.

5. The Russian Government firmly hopes that on the morrow of the war, the alliance of the three Powers will be sanctioned by a definitive treaty.[45]

In reply to Goremykin's proposals, Delcassé asked Paléologue to tell the Russian Premier

The Russian Struggle for Power, 1914–1917

that he was "in complete agreement with him," and was ready to proceed to the discussion of the future peace. The French Foreign Minister further expressed himself as being especially happy over the desire of Goremykin concerning the strengthening of the Anglo-Franco-Russian alliance after the war.[46]

Delcassé's expression of willingness to discuss the future peace soon made it apparent that Goremykin was sending up a trial balloon for a far more important personage. Shortly after, Paléologue received an invitation to visit the Russian Emperor at Tsarskoe Selo. On November 21, he made the short journey to the imperial residence. It was his first audience with the Emperor in three months. Sazonov had arranged the interview, but it took place in the Imperial study without the presence of a third party.

Nicholas was in a relaxed mood. He bade the ambassador be seated, lit a cigarette, and, offering his visitor a light, began the conversation in this fashion:

Great things have happened in the three months since I saw you last. The splendid French army and my dear army have already given such proof of valor that victory can't fail us now . . . Don't think I'm still under any illusion as to the trials and sacrifices the war still has in store for us; but so far we have a right, and even a duty, to consider together what we should have to do if Austria or Germany sued for peace. You must observe that it would unquestionably be in Germany's interest to treat for peace while her military power is still formidable. But isn't Austria very exhausted already? Well, what should we do if Germany or Austria asked for peace?[47]

Paléologue replied that the first question to consider was whether peace could be negotiated or whether the Allied Powers would be forced to dictate it. On this point, however moderate the Allies might be, they must obviously insist on guarantees and reparations from the Central Powers; such demands would not be accepted until the enemy was at the mercy of the victors.

The Emperor replied:

That's my own view. We must dictate the peace and I am determined to continue the war until the Central Powers are destroyed. But I regard it as essential that the terms of peace should be discussed by us three, France, England, and Russia—

and by us three alone. No Congress or mediation for me! So when the time comes we shall *impose* our will upon Germany and Austria.[48]

Paléologue then asked what were the Emperor's ideas as to the terms of peace. Nicholas began by mentioning as the first object of Allied policy "the destruction of German militarism, the end of the nightmare from which Germany has made us suffer for more than forty years." The Allies must make it impossible for the German people even to think of revenge; he predicted that "if we let ourselves be swayed by sentiment there will be a fresh war within a very short time."

Nicholas then made the sweeping statement, "I must tell you at once that I accept here and now any conditions France and England think it their duty to put forward in their own interest." Thanking him for this statement, Paléologue expressed certainty "that the Government of the Republic in turn will meet the wishes of the Imperial Government in the most sympathetic spirit." The Emperor replied that this encouraged him to speak further on "what I think," but added, "I don't like to open questions of this kind without consulting my ministers and generals."

Drawing his chair closer to Paléologue's, Nicholas spread a map of Europe on the table between them and lit a second cigarette. Russia was entitled, he said, to expect from the war certain results, "failing which my people will not understand the sacrifices I have required of them." In East Prussia, there must be "a rectification of the frontier." The Russian General Staff would like this "rectification" extended to the mouths of the Vistula, but Nicholas thought this "excessive" and promised to look into the matter. Posen too, and possibly a portion of Silesia, would be "indispensable to the reconstitution of Poland." In addition, Nicholas would ask for Galicia, which would enable Russia to obtain her "natural frontier," the Carpathians, and also northwestern Bukovina. Thus, it now appeared, Russia's desires had grown since September to include all East Prussia.

Moreover, the Emperor confirmed what Goremykin had said about Turkey. In Asia Minor, he said, he had to consider the question of the Armenians, since "I certainly could not let them

The Russian Struggle for Power, 1914-1917

return to the Turkish yoke." But there were some doubts: "Ought I to annex Armenia? I shall only do so if the Armenians expressly ask me to. Otherwise I shall establish an autonomous regime for them."

Then he came to the question of Constantinople and the Straits. He would be compelled to secure his Empire a free passage through the Straits, but was far from having made up his mind as to the method. At the moment, his conclusions were that the Turks must be expelled from Europe, and Constantinople be made a neutralized international city. Moslems would be given all necessary guarantees that their tombs and sanctuaries would be respected. Turkey in Europe, with the exception of Constantinople and its environs, would be divided between Bulgaria and Russia along the Enos-Midiya line. The Turks would be confined to Asia, with Ankara or Konia as their capital.

At this point, Paléologue interrupted the Emperor to remind him that in Syria and Palestine, France had "a precious heritage of historical memories and moral and material interests." Could he assume that Nicholas would acquiesce in "any measures the Government of the Republic might think fit to safeguard that inheritance?" The Emperor replied, "Certainly."

Nicholas then indicated his desires in the Balkans, which duplicated exactly the plan earlier offered by Sazonov. Serbia would annex Bosnia, Herzegovina, Dalmatia, and northern Albania. Greece would have southern Albania, with the exception of Valona, which must be assigned to Italy. If Bulgaria "behaved properly," she would receive compensation in Macedonia from Serbia.

The Emperor now asked the rhetorical question, "And what will become of Austria-Hungary?" As Paléologue reported to Paris, he probably wanted, by this "interpellative" form, to indicate the personal nature of the exchange of views to which he was inviting the ambassador.

Paléologue replied, "Austria-Hungary will survive with difficulty the territorial losses to which the unhappy Emperor Francis Joseph will be obliged to consent. The Austro-Hungarian union having been weakened, I believe that the units could no longer continue to get along together."

The Russian Struggle for Power, 1914–1917

Nicholas responded, "I believe this too. Hungary, deprived of Transylvania, will have trouble in keeping the Slavs dependent on her. Bohemia will, at the least, reclaim her independence. Austria will then be limited to the ancient territorial states, to the German Tyrol, and to the district of Salzburg." In other words, Russia now envisaged complete independence for the Czechs, and the separation from Hungary of her Slovaks, Ukrainians, Serbians, and Croatians. Sazonov's plan of September for a Triple Monarchy of Austria-Hungary-Bohemia had thus been dropped.

After disposing of Austria-Hungary, the Emperor again lapsed into silence, "with his brows contracted and his eyes half closed as if he were repeating to himself what he was about to tell me," as Paléologue describes the scene. Then, after casting a glance at the portrait of his father, Tsar Alexander III, on the wall, he took up the question of Germany's future.

It was primarily in Germany that great changes would take place, said the Emperor. Russia would annex the territories of "ancient Poland" and part of East Prussia. France would certainly recover Alsace-Lorraine and perhaps "enlarge herself" in the Rhenish provinces. Belgium ought to receive in the direction of Aix-la-Chapelle an important increase in territory. France and Britain might divide the German colonies as they saw fit. Moreover, Nicholas remarked, he would desire that "Schleswig and the zone of the Emperor William [Kiel] Canal be restored to Denmark." Finally, he thought it would be wise to revive Hanover, adding that

> By setting up a small independent state between Prussia and Holland we should do much toward putting the future peace on a solid basis. After all, it is *that* which must guide our deliberations and actions. Our work cannot be justified before God and History unless it is inspired by a great moral idea and the determination to secure the peace of the world for a very long time to come.[49]

At this point, while Nicholas paused, seemingly under the influence of solemn religious emotion, the French ambassador asked a rhetorical question of his own: "Doesn't it mean the end of the German Empire?" The Emperor recovered, however, to indicate that Russia was not prepared to go quite that far. He firmly answered:

> Germany can adopt any organization she likes, but the imperial dignity cannot be allowed to remain in the House of Hohenzollern. Prussia must return to the status of a kingdom only . . . . Isn't that your opinion also, Ambassador?

Paléologue replied:

> The German Empire, as conceived, founded and governed by the Hohenzollerns, is so obviously directed against the French nation that I shall certainly not attempt its defense. France would have a great guarantee if all the powers of the German world ceased to be in the hands of Prussia. . . .[50]

At this point in the conference, Nicholas ended it with a statement of the hope that France and Russia would remain united after the war to ensure the permanence of its results and to preserve the peace of the world. In the course of his remarks, he had made it clear that Russian war aims had been extended since September in three directions. First, Russia would require additional territory at the expense of Germany for herself and Poland. Second, the complete disintegration of the Hapsburg monarchy was now planned. Third, Russia expected to divide European Turkey between herself and Bulgaria, while making Constantinople an international city, and to liberate the Turkish Armenians.

Delcassé was not especially happy to learn that Britain and Russia had negotiated concerning the future of the Ottoman Empire without consulting France. His anger was particularly aroused when Britain announced on November 20 the annexation of Egypt, to which Sazonov had given his consent on November 18, at the request of Grey.[51] The British Foreign Secretary therefore sent an apologetic telegram to Bordeaux, assuring Delcassé that Britain was not seeking special advantages as a result of the war. He explained his messages to Petrograd in this fashion:

> I have also said more to Mr. Sazonov about Constantinople, the Straits, etc., without inquiring the French Government, which must, of course, be consulted in definite settlement of matters of such importance; but, I thought it important to remove from mind of Russian Government any suspicion that at end of war in which Russian arms have

contributed so large a part of success, we should hesitate in recognizing Russian interests in this question of vital importance to her.[52]

On the next day, acting upon a promise he had made when Sazonov agreed to Britain's annexation of Egypt, Grey took further steps to reassure Petrograd. The diary of the Russian Ministry of Foreign Affairs has the following entry:

On November 10/23, the English Ambassador read to the Minister Sir E. Grey's telegram, in which it is stated that if the statement which Buchanan was ordered to make about England's consent to the settlement of the questions of the Straits and Constantinople in accord with Russia's desires is less definite than what Grey said on the subject to Count Benckendorff, then Grey is ready to emphasize that his words, spoken to the Russian ambassador in London, fully correspond to his attitude towards the question. Buchanan read also Grey's telegram to the English ambassador in Paris, in which he also mentions that England considers right the satisfaction of Russia in the Straits Question.[53]

Grey was not yet prepared, however, to publicize his important decision. Speculation ran high in Russia during the last week in November over the possibility of an agreement with Great Britain on the Straits Question. On November 26, one newspaper published a report that Constantinople and both sides of the Bosporus would be Russian possessions after the war, by the terms of a Russo-British agreement, which would not be submitted to a European conference. On November 27, at the request of Buchanan, the Ministry of Foreign Affairs publicly and categorically denied this report.[54]

DEFINITION OF RUSSIAN AIMS AT THE STRAITS

Meanwhile, in the light of the promises of the British, Sazonov had felt it necessary to appoint a special committee to determine just what were the Russian desiderata at the Straits. Ignoring the citadels of reaction, he chose as members of the committee only an official of the Foreign Ministry (N. A. Bazili, then Vice-Director of his Chancellery), a representative of the Stavka (the Quartermaster-General G. N. Danilov), and two officers from the Naval Ministry (Captain First Rank A. V. Nemits, Chief of the Division of Black Sea Operations of the Naval General Staff, and Captain Second Rank A. D. Bubnov). There is much evidence that Captain Nemits had the most to do with defining Russian aims at the Straits, which were conceived largely from the naval viewpoint.[55]

The memorandum produced by the committee was a long one, since it reviewed all important aspects of the Straits Question from the beginning of the twentieth century, as well as the existing naval balance in the Black Sea. It then proceeded to differentiate between a "passive" solution of the Straits problem, which would involve ironclad guarantees that Russia could not again be attacked on her Black Sea coast, as she had been in 1854–55 and 1914, and an "active" solution, which would guarantee at all times the unimpeded egress of Russian ships, both merchant and naval, into the Mediterranean.

The "passive" solution was not rejected out of hand. It would make it possible to reduce naval forces in the Black Sea. An effort by Russia to become a Mediterranean naval power would involve a "vast and aggressive naval policy," and might make it necessary to secure "the entire maritime route from the Black Sea to the Mediterranean," involving complications with Greece.

However, Sazonov's committee was far more impressed by the advantages of the "active" solution. True, its expenses would be much greater, but even the "passive" solution, involving occupation of the Bosporus alone, would require two army corps and 150 to 200 million rubles a year. Moreover, the "passive" solution would still make it necessary to guard the Odessa Military District against Rumania and the Transcaucasian frontier against Turkey, though this latter problem would be eased if Turkey lost Armenia and southern Anatolia.

Certain specific solutions were definitely rejected. Neutralization of the Straits would never work, as the German violation of Belgian neutrality had shown; furthermore, the fleet of even an inferior power, such as Bulgaria or Greece, could conceivably establish itself in a neutralized Straits zone. Nor would an international patrol be effective, since each patrolling power would use its ships for its own purposes. Russia could take the Bosporus and share control of the Dardanelles with Britain and France, but this solution assumed that the existing combination of powers would be permanent, and would be, essentially, only a "passive" solution. Russia could return to the policy of Unkiar Skelessi and leave Turkey in control of the Straits, under a Russian protectorate, but Russian experience with Bulgaria and Korea proved that it would be impossible to hold Turkey permanently in line. Finally, it would not do simply to establish a Russian naval patrol in a neutralized Straits zone, since the range of modern artillery and the narrowness of the Straits would greatly endanger the patrol.

Even for a "passive" solution, there must be territorial gains, and these must include a zone twenty to twenty-five miles deep on both sides of the Bosporus, excluding the city of Constantinople, plus the islands of the Sea of Marmora. For the "active" solution, possession of the Gallipoli Peninsula and possession or neutralization of the Troiad, in addition, would be absolutely essential. Moreover, possession of Tenedos, Imbros, Lemnos, and possibly, Samothrace was very desirable. However, Greece might be allowed to keep Lemnos if it were neutralized, especially since Samothrace would replace it in importance if a canal were dug through the Gallipoli Peninsula. As an optimum solution, a "defense in depth," involving Russian possession of the plain of Thrace, with Adrianople, or perhaps, of the line Enos-Maritza River-Ergene-Lule Burgas-Midiya, was recommended. Bulgaria might be given what was left of Turkish Thrace, but must never be allowed on the Sea of Marmora.

Thus, the committee defined Russia's aims solely in terms of the strategic problem, which in turn involved the economic problems mentioned at the beginning of this chapter. Nevertheless, sentimental considerations were not wholly absent, and after the committee had rendered its report, Sazonov and the Tsar began to wonder if it might not be just as well to go ahead and take Constantinople, instead of making it an international city.

When Sazonov submitted the committee's report to Nicholas II, the Tsar received it with the deepest satisfaction and told his Foreign Minister, "I owe you the happiest day in my life." Sazonov then dwelt at some length on his reasons for opposing the annexation of Constantinople, despite the fact that the idea had been so long cherished by many Russians. He wanted to prevent the Tsar from taking "the sentimental attitude which patriotic Russians generally adopted towards the subject." He feared that "the glamor of Tsargrad's name and the age-long dream of Russia's placing an Orthodox cross on the cupola of Santa Sophia might prejudice the Emperor's opinion on the fate of Constantinople."[56]

The Emperor did not succumb at the time of this first report, but Sazonov could tell from some of his remarks that "he did not think it possible for us to preserve the position we had taken at the early stage of the negotiations." Sazonov himself was eventually won over to the idea of annexing Constantinople because of "the pressure of public opinion and strategic necessity which always overrules all other considerations." He adds that

> I was aware of the endless complications in which the proposed co-dominion over Constantinople would involve us. Friction and jealousy would in-

evitably arise, however justly the spheres of influence and the interests of the Powers concerned were apportioned, and, as in all cases of joint occupation, this might lead to dangerous conflicts, the consequences of which it would be difficult to foresee.[57]

PROCLAMATIONS TO THE CZECHS AND ARMENIANS—OR A SEPARATE PEACE WITH AUSTRIA-HUNGARY

At the beginning of December, 1914, the Germans began to learn some of the disadvantages of being saddled with the defense of two such decrepit empires as Austria-Hungary and Turkey. The Austrians had begun an all-out offensive against Serbia just after the Turks entered the war, only to see it end in miserable failure a month later. The Serbs even recaptured Belgrade. Just before, a weak Russian force in Transcaucasia shattered Enver Pasha's November offensive. The reaction of the Russians was to consider proclaiming the imminent liberation of the Czechs and the Turkish Armenians. That of the war-weary British and French was to consider the possibility of detaching Austria-Hungary from the side of Germany.

The Russian Struggle for Power, 1914–1917

The idea of a specific proclamation to the Czechs, singling them out as the proclamation of September 17 to the peoples of Austria-Hungary had not originated with the military, just as had the demand for a final decision on the Polish Question. The originator of the proposal was General Mikhail Alekseev, whose excellent performance as Chief of Staff on the Southwestern Front (Galicia) in 1914–15 would lead to his appointment as Chief of Staff to the Supreme High Commander, and real head of the Russian armies, in 1915–16, not to speak of a brief term as Supreme High Commander in 1917 and leadership of a White army in 1917–18.

At the beginning of November, 1914, Alekseev evidently expected that Przemysl would soon fall, and that then an invasion of Bohemia-Moravia would be possible. He contacted the Russian Czechs about political conditions in these provinces, and was assured that the Russian Army would be welcomed with open arms. He was also told that if some sort of "state act" were published, guaranteeing "the complete sovereignty and independence of Czechia, based on the rights of a historic state, and the deposition of the ruling dynasty of the Hapsburgs," a revolt would follow. His informants added that a Czech army could be quickly formed, using the Russian Czech *Druzhina* as a nucleus.[58]

Alekseev was so impressed that on November 29, he recommended to the Supreme High Commander the issuance of a new proclamation, pointing out that military advantages would accrue from a revolt behind the Austrian lines. He also suggested the formation of the nucleus of a Czech government in Russia. At first, the Supreme High Commander threw cold water on the suggestion, on the ground that it was premature. However, the Czechs now turned to Prince Kudashev, who headed the Diplomatic Chancellery at the Stavka, and who took up the matter with the Foreign Ministry in Petrograd. A proclamation was finally drawn up there, and forwarded to the Stavka. It dwelt on the duty of the Russians and Czechs "to lift the German yoke and establish a powerful Slavic state," and promised that

. . . now to the Czech people, help will come

The Russian Struggle for Power, 1914–1917

from the Slavic East, from Holy Rus, which has frequently helped the Balkan Slavs in their difficult struggle against the oppressor.[59]

However, when the text of the proclamation was revealed to the Russian Czechs at the Stavka in January, 1915, it was made plain that it would be issued only when all was ready for the invasion of Bohemia-Moravia. Since such an invasion never took place, it was never issued. Nevertheless, its preparation confirms the change in Russian policy towards the Czechs which took place between September and November, 1914.

This is made even plainer by Sazonov's reaction to a Franco-British proposal for a separate peace with Austria-Hungary in December, 1914. Hopes along these lines were undoubtedly aroused largely by the defeats inflicted on the Dual Monarchy by the Serbs.

On December 3, Benckendorff discussed the general military and diplomatic situation with Grey. The peaceable Foreign Secretary was visibly exasperated over the attitude of Germany which had provoked the war, but towards Austria-Hungary, his unwonted anger was less intense. To a question regarding the proposed losses by Austria-Hungary, Benckendorff answered that he thought the minimum must be Galicia, Bukovina, Bosnia-Herzegovina, Transylvania, and the Italian provinces. Grey then asked how Sazonov would look upon the idea of a separate peace with Austria, "if, by agreeing to the necessary sacrifices, she decided to separate herself from Germany."[60]

Benckendorff said he could not answer the question, since it presupposed a case he personally believed very improbable, at least during the lifetime of Emperor Franz Josef. It would be above all a question of the conditions to which Austria would resign herself, and even then, Hungary might offer great difficulties. Grey did not pursue the matter, and Benckendorff assured Sazonov that the conversation had not been the result of any advance on the part of Austria. The ambassador thought Grey probably had in view the concentration of the struggle against Germany, "which he always looks on as the key to the whole situation."[61]

However, two weeks later, on December 16, Izvolskii was wiring Sazonov for instructions on

The Russian Struggle for Power, 1914-1917

how to proceed in case Austria asked for a separate peace. Sazonov replied that the rumors of a separate peace were completely indefinite, and that the basis for them seemed hypothetical. In any case, the initiation of such negotiations was a matter for Austria, and the Allies must hear her proposals before establishing their terms.[62]

Towards the end of the year, on December 29, Grey wired Buchanan that the question of a separate peace with Austria-Hungary affected Russia most of all. France and Britain would not oppose the conclusion of peace with Austria-Hungary, but only if she proposed conditions satisfactory to Russia.[63] Evidently the Quai d'Orsay failed to send such explicit instructions to Paléologue, however. On January 1, 1915, Paléologue, Buchanan, and Sazonov met to discuss the problems to be faced by the Allies during the coming year. All agreed that illusions about a speedy victory could no longer be entertained, but also that the tremendous effort necessary for victory must be made, since "nothing less than the independence of our national life" was at stake.

Paléologue then remarked that the military experience of the preceding months embodied a valuable lesson, which it would be wrong not to turn to account. He went on, addressing Sazonov:

> As the German bloc is such a hard nut to crack, we should endeavor to detach Austria-Hungary from the Teutonic coalition by any and every method of force or persuasion. I believe we should succeed in a very short time. The Emperor Francis Joseph is very old; we know he bitterly regrets this war and only asks to be allowed to die in peace. You have beaten his armies in Galicia again and again; the Serbs have just won a brilliant victory at Valievo; Rumania threatens and Italy is doubtful. The Hapsburg Monarchy was in no greater peril in 1859 and 1866, yet the same Francis Joseph then accepted serious territorial sacrifices to save his crown. Quite between ourselves, my dear Minister, if the Vienna Cabinet agreed to cede Galicia to you and Bosnia-Herzegovina to Serbia, would not that seem to you an adequate return for making a separate peace with Austria-Hungary?[64]

Sazonov's response was immediate: "What about Bohemia and Croatia? Would you leave them under the present system? . . . It's impossible." Paléologue then begged forgiveness for pointing out that in "this terrible hour of trial for France," the Czech and Yugoslav problems seemed to him secondary. Sazonov was unmoved, and replied, "No. Austria-Hungary must be dismembered."

Paléologue tried persuasion. The defection of Austria-Hungary from Germany would have important consequences, both strategic and moral. Russia would be the first to profit from an Austrian defection. The whole effort of the Allied Powers must be directed against Germany. The granting of a generous measure of self-government to the Czechs and Croatians would be "a resounding victory for Slavism." However, the most that Sazonov would say was that the matter needed thinking over.[65]

Ultimately, the French Government, like the British, backed away from the idea of a separate peace with Austria-Hungary. Though Paléologue reminded Delcassé of "the unquestionable advantage to France of the preservation of a great political system in the Danube basin," he was ordered on January 9 not to say another word "which might lead the Russian Government to think we do not hand over Austria-Hungary *in toto*."[66]

Meanwhile, since the beginning of the fighting in Transcaucasia, Russia had been occupied in defining her Armenian policy, which had still been very vague when the Tsar talked with Paléologue on November 21. Early in December, the Armenian Catholicos, religious leader of his people, asked the Russian Viceroy of Transcaucasia in Tiflis to issue a proclamation to the Armenians modeled on that to the Poles. The Viceroy turned the matter over to Stolitsa, a representative of the Foreign Ministry on his staff.[67]

Stolitsa forwarded the request to the Ministry on December 7 with a recommendation that it not be granted. He believed that the proclamation to the Poles had been "influenced exclusively by the desire to forestall the going over of the Poles to the side of our enemies." As for the Armenians, he noted that those serving in Armenian military organizations, those serving in the Russian Army, and those living in the Ottoman districts now occupied by Russia "exhibit, if not a hostile attitude towards us, then one that is

The Russian Struggle for Power, 1914-1917

far from the benevolent one on which we should have been able to count, it would seem, in view of the complete solidarity of our interests." Thus, it was wrong to consider the Armenian case as analogous to the Polish.

Stolitsa further asked particularly that no proclamation to the Armenians be issued in the name of the Tsar, and that none be issued until Russian troops had penetrated deeply into Turkish Armenia. He pointed out the touchy problems of Cilicia and Kurdistan. The Armenians considered Cilicia as theirs, but since the district was on the Mediterranean, difficulties with Britain and France might arise. As for Kurdistan, its boundaries overlapped those of Armenia, and its wild Moslem inhabitants hated Moslem Turks and Christian Armenians about equally; their possible reaction to an Armenian proclamation should be considered.[68]

A reply to Stolitsa was drafted on December 15 by Gulkevich, Counsellor of the Second Political Division of the Foreign Ministry. Stolitsa's basic recommendation was accepted, since the Ministry feared that a premature proclamation, issued before Russian troops penetrated deeply into Turkish Armenia, would set off a new wave of Armenian massacres by the Turks. However, Gulkevich thought Stolitsa's attitude towards the proclamation "negative," and enlightened him on the ministry's general policy towards the Armenians:

Of course, the hour has still not come for the decision of the question as to whether an autonomous Armenia will remain under the suzerainty of Turkey, or be placed under a protectorate of Russia. But in either case, Armenia must be in the sphere of our direct influence and this completely independently of the desires of our Allies. Also, the territorial limits of the future autonomous district definitely must be defined by us exclusively from the viewpoint of Russian state interests.[69]

Gulkevich conceded that during the working out of the project of Armenian reforms just before the war, Russia had been compelled by the force of circumstances to reckon with Germany's pretensions to a position of predominance in Cilicia. This consideration no longer applied, and Russia must strive towards "the secure future of Armenia, and, as a consequence, an exit to the Mediterranean Sea for us." The separation of Great Armenia, or the part near the Caucasus, and Little Armenia, the Cilician portion on the Gulf of Alexandretta, was "not permissible;" nor should any other European power be permitted to establish itself in Cilicia.

Denying Stolitsa's contention with respect to the Polish proclamation, Gulkevich alleged that it was designed "to lay the foundations for a lasting rapprochement of the two great Slavic peoples." In any case, Russia must eventually "proclaim far and wide to the Armenians the intention of the Russian Sovereign to liberate them from the age-old yoke and to grant them autonomy." Germany was trying to attract the Armenians to her side by persuading the Porte to grant them autonomy, and

> The appearance of a Turkish manifesto, in place of the expected Russian one, in connection with the creation of a district parliament in Erzerum or Van, could cause disputes in the ranks of the Armenians, could deliver a blow to the fascination which the Russian name has in the eyes of the whole population, and could perhaps even make difficult to a significant degree the task of our troops in Armenia.[70]

Later, added Gulkevich, a proclamation to the Kurds could be issued, after their attitude towards Russia was clarified. As for the Kurds living in Armenian districts, an unfavorable impression could be avoided by the method used in the Polish proclamation, *i.e.*, telling the Armenians that Russia expected "some respect for the rights of those nationalities with which their history is linked." In fact, it could be specifically promised that in an autonomous Armenia, the rights of Kurds and Turks would be secured in all respects.[71]

THE FUTURE ATTACK ON THE STRAITS

Towards the end of 1914, the Russian Naval Ministry began to become very excited over the prospect of a future amphibious operation for the capture of Constantinople and the Straits. It recognized that such an operation would not be possible before the completion of the new construction in progress at Nikolayev, not to speak of the necessity of further success on the main front against Germany. However, to ensure that the Stavka was planning a Straits operation, the

The Russian Struggle for Power, 1914–1917

Navy sought the support of the Ministry of Foreign Affairs.

On December 14, Captain First Rank A. V. Nemits, who had sat on Sazonov's Straits committee, and who would presumably be in charge of planning any amphibious operations at the Straits, submitted to Sazonov something called "Preliminary Considerations on the Constantinople Operation." It was a long paper, full of rather extravagant political reasons why Russia should seize the Straits. The captain evidently thought it would impress Sazonov greatly.

Nemits rambled blithely over a long series of complex questions, claiming that the Germans, who thought the Slavs fit only for a labor force, feared a renaissance of the southern and western Slavs, and that Russia's fundamental policies tended towards "making the Slavic rivers flow into the Russian sea." In order that Russia might fulfill her "Pan-Slavic role," that of the "political center" and arbiter and protector" of the Slavic peoples, she must not ignore the fact that the "hand of destiny" was removing Austria-Hungary and Turkey from the world scene. This involved future Russian control of Constantinople and the Straits, for, according to Nemits,

> Russia has always seen clearly the importance, in fact vital for her, of her political position in the Balkans and over the Straits which lead by "Tsargrad" towards the East and West. The best of her statesmen have never doubted that the Turks, sooner or later, would be chased from that "world position" and that their place would be taken by the government of a powerful new Eastern Empire, the government of our Fatherland. It is only by installing herself with a firm foot on the Bosporus and Dardanelles that Russia, in fact, could accomplish her historic mission of forming into a single state the peoples of all Eastern Europe and a part of Asia, of making peace reign between them, and of giving them "European" culture.[72]

The captain admitted, however, that in addition to solving the "Germano-Slav" and Eastern Questions, Russia must destroy first German and Austro-Hungarian efforts to end Russia's position as a great power and thus put an end to the "excessive militarism" of 1904–1914. Therefore, the proper moment to take Constantinople and the Straits by force would be when the French had reached the Rhine, and the Russians, the

The Russian Struggle for Power, 1914–1917

Oder. On the other hand, there must be no illusions about the necessity of fighting to take this vital area from the Turks.

In his memorandum, Nemits seems to have assumed that Russia would take Constantinople as well as the Straits. However, he thought it must be given a special regime, not just that of another Russian provincial city. Moreover, he seems to have decided, at this point, that perhaps the Bulgarians might be allowed on the Sea of Marmora, with a port at Rodosto.[73]

Sazonov may have considered Nemits' political maunderings somewhat innocent, but he seems to have been impressed by the idea of planning for a future attack on the Straits. On December 21, he wrote General Yanushkevich, the Grand Duke's Chief of Staff, asking what operations were planned to reach and occupy the Straits.[74]

Yanushkevich replied on December 25 that no such operations were being planned, owing to the necessity of directing all Russian efforts against Germany and Austria-Hungary. Only after victory had been won against them could such operations be begun, and it was difficult to give any details prior to that time.[75]

The Ministry of Foreign Affairs was considerably perturbed by this message. Since an overland march through Asia Minor seemed out of the question, and also an immediate amphibious operations against the Bosporus or the Bulgarian coast, consideration was given to making new offers to Rumania to persuade her to permit the transit of a Russian army, as in 1877–78. There was talk of giving her control of the lower Danube, by abolishing the international commission set up by the Paris Convention of 1856; the question of modifying the frontier in Bessarabia was even raised.[76]

General Danilov, the Quartermaster-General thought the overland march through Rumania, Bulgaria, and Turkish Thrace the only practicable way of taking the Straits. There was not enough shipping to transport troops even to the relatively undefended Asiatic side of the Bosporus, and a landing on the European side was out of the question. The Black Sea Fleet had just enough forces to assist the overland campaign with a landing in Bulgaria and bombard-

The Russian Struggle for Power, 1914–1917

ment of the Chataldja lines. Eight to ten army corps would be required for the entire campaign; therefore the Straits campaign was impossible until the victory over Germany.[77]

Sazonov preferred not to request passage of Russian troops through Rumania and Bulgaria, and on December 29, asked the Grand Duke himself whether or not the Black Sea Fleet could effect a landing in Turkey. In reply, the latter said he thought that all would depend on the political situation at the time operations became possible. If Bulgaria and Greece attacked Turkey, and Italy and Rumania attacked Austria-Hungary, Russia could finish off Turkey without British and French help. If a separate peace with Austria-Hungary were signed, and the Balkan states remained neutral, then all forces could be turned against Germany, though in this event, enough troops could probably be transferred southward to gain the Straits. However, the Grand Duke was skeptical of the whole idea of a Straits campaign. He recommended that "in political talks with our Allies, we ought not to go further than we have gone, and . . . we ought to limit ourselves to what we have already obtained from France and England, that is, to the declaration that these two powers have made that our interests will be taken into consideration at the time of settlement of the question of the Straits and Constantinople."[78]

France had never made any such declaration, and Sazonov was thus put on notice that diplomacy, rather than arms, must gain the Straits for Russia in this war. It was up to him to see that the Russian Army captured "Tsargrad" by fighting the Germans in Poland.

III

THE BALKAN TANGLE
(SEPTEMBER, 1914–FEBRUARY, 1915)

AFTER THE Battle of the Marne, Russia had ceased temporarily to dabble in the Balkan hornets'-nest, primarily because a Bulgarian attack on Serbia was unlikely while the Allies were winning. In addition, the August–September negotiations had revealed profound differences of view between Russia and her allies over how the Balkans should be handled. However, the policy of abstention could not last. In September and October, it became obvious that a real struggle between South Slavic and Italian interests was inevitable. Then came Turkey's entrance, and the Balkan lid was off again. By this time, Sir Edward Grey had long since overcome his Liberal queasiness over dealing with the Balkan states as if they were spoiled children, who needed to be told where their real interests lay. As a consequence, the Balkan states were inundated with Allied *démarches,* which had accomplished exactly nothing when the British began their attack on the Straits on February 19, 1915. Perhaps the most significant Balkan development during these six months was the threat that Rumania would join Italy in a bloc to thwart Russian hegemony over southeastern Europe.

SERB AND ITALIAN AMBITIONS

The struggle between South Slavic and Italian ambitions arose in September primarily because law and order broke down completely in the new state of Albania, following the flight of Prince William of Wied, ruler of the turbulent country for six months in 1914. The Serbs, Montenegrins, and Italians promptly began to intrigue with rival Albanian political groups in order to advance their own interests. Sazonov had to warn Serbia and Montenegro not to let themselves be distracted from the struggle with Austria, and to urge the British and French not to let Italy take Valona without Allied permission.[1]

The turmoil in Albania persuaded the Italians that they must now inform the Allies of their asking price for intervention in the war. On September 24, the staff of the Italian Embassy in Constantinople revealed to A.A. Giers, then Russian ambassador in Turkey, that Italy wanted, in addition to the Trentino, Trieste, and Valona, the following territory: all of Istria, coastal Croatia, and Dalmatia, including the cities of Šibenik (Sebenico), Split (Spalato), and Dubrovnik (Ragusa).[2] On the next day, the efficient Russian secret service intercepted and decoded a telegram from San Giuliano to Carlotti, the Italian ambassador in Petrograd, which made it clear that Italy wanted even more. San Giuliano said that Italy still wanted to remain neutral, but if Austria-Hungary was unable "to maintain the balance in the Adriatic," Italy must protect her vital interests by joining the Allies. Her price would be the Trentino and all of Istria, an unspecified part of Dalmatia, and Valona. Montenegro, Serbia, and Greece might partition the remainder of Albania, but the coastline of that country must be neutralized. In case of a partition of the Ottoman Empire, Italy must be given full sovereignty over the Dodecanese Islands, and an Anatolian zone around Adalia. If Germany were forced to give up her interests in Anatolia, the sphere of Italian influence should be extended to Mersina. Italy would also demand a share in any war indemnity and in the German African colonies, if the latter were partitioned between Britain and France. Finally, the Allies must give Italy diplomatic support in case of difficulties with Ethiopia.[8]

Serbia, too, decided at this point to make her desires clear. On September 21, Pashich circularized Serbian diplomats abroad with a statement of their country's claims, so that they might be introduced into conversations "concerning the claims of other states." Serbia, it appeared, would demand all the South Slav territories of Austria-Hungary, including those inhabited by Croatians and Slovenes. What Pashich wanted was approximately the present frontier of Yugoslavia, plus additional territory. The new Serbia must include a broad belt across what was then southern Hungary. It comprised all of the rectangular Banat of Temesvar, enclosed by the Marosh, Theiss, and Danube Rivers (with the city of Temesvar or Timiso-

The Russian Struggle for Power, 1914-1917

ara), the Serbian Voivodina or Slavonia of the eighteenth century, including the territory north from the Save River as far as the latitude of Baia on the middle Danube, and all of Croatia. In addition, Pashich desired Bosnia-Herzegovina, Dalmatia, and most of the Slovene territories of Austria, including Carinthia, Carniola, southern Styria, and Istria. However, he was willing that Italy have Istria if she joined the Allies immediately. Admitting that the Banat of Temesvar had a large Rumanian population, he insisted that nevertheless this province was needed to protect Belgrade.[4]

On October 3, Pashich complained to Sazonov that Italian diplomats and the Italian press were asserting that Serbia must receive only part of Dalmatia and Albania, and that a portion of Dalmatia must be joined to the Croatian-Slovene lands to form an autonomous area. Pashich asked that the question of the Catholic South Slavs be taken up in London and Paris, since he feared Britain and France were abstaining from an attack on Dalmatia, out of fear of the possible reaction in Rome. He added that the Dalmatians preferred Austrian to Italian rule, and that most of all, they wanted to join Serbia. Indeed, annexation to Serbia was "the everlasting desire of all the Serbo-Croatian people." Italy should be satisfied with the Trentino and Istria, and not think of "seizing Slavic lands for which Slavic blood is being shed—without any sacrifice on her part."[5]

Pashich had some reason to be concerned. Italy, fearful of Greek intervention in Albania, was on the point of occupying Valona, and had approached the British for their views on the subject, requesting that Grey sound out the French and Russians. Grey complied, since he had been promised that the occupation would be provisional and would not prejudice future negotiations. He feared that Allied opposition might cause Italy to turn to the Central Powers, which would certainly give their consent.[6]

Sazonov bowed to the request, but complained of Italy's increasing appetites, and expressed the fear that her desires ran counter to Serbian interests.[7] On October 13, Izvolskii presented to Delcassé the Croatian leader, Frano Supilo, former deputy in the Hungarian Diet and newspaper editor in Rijeka (Fiume). Supilo impressed Delcassé with his presentation of "the Yugo-Slav idea," which Izvolskii defined as "the idea of a united, strong Serbo-Croatian state, including Istria and Dalmatia, as a necessary counterweight to Italy, Hungary, and Rumania."[8]

On October 14, the Italians tried to sound out Serbia's ambitions in Nish, but were told that the question was still under study. They then frankly stated their desires for Valona, Trieste, Pola, and the Dalmatian islands, and for the creation of an autonomous Catholic province including Dalmatia and parts of Bosnia and Slovenia. Serbia, they said, should be satisfied with the port of Dubrovnik (Ragusa). Shortly afterwards, a delegation of Serbo-Croatian leaders went to Rome to lay their case before the Allied ambassadors there.[9]

In late October, Italy was negotiating in Athens over a possible partition of Albania, and raising in Petrograd the question of Constantinople and the Straits. When the Souchon task force attacked Russia, an Italian naval force occupied the Albanian island fortress of Saseno, just off Valona, though there was no movement to the mainland.[10] However, for the moment, no further steps were taken, owing partly to the sudden death of San Giuliano, who was finally succeeded during the second week of November by Sidney Sonnino.

THE BALKAN REACTION TO THE TURKISH ATTACK ON RUSSIA

Everyone realized, after Admiral Souchon's batteries blasted Sevastopol, Feodosiya, and Novorossiisk on October 29 that the Balkans would surely erupt. In London, Prime Minister Asquith, who rarely intervened in Grey's bailiwick, was moved to ask the Russian ambassador whether Russia could not now agree to cede Bessarabia to Rumania in order to assure the latter's position. He claimed that the British believed that only a re-division of Europe along lines of nationality would assure a lasting peace.

Benckendorff understood the British too well to take this inquiry too seriously, and actually, it apparently represented nothing more than the personal views of Asquith and the radicals in the cabinet. The Russian ambassador deftly parried the inquiry, and since Grey never brought the matter up, Bessarabia was not further discussed.[11]

Bulgaria had maintained a sullen neutrality since the Battle of the Marne, punctuated by threats of attacking Rumania if the latter attacked Austria-Hungary (September 29), and the prohibition of the passage of war material to Serbia through her territory (October 1).[12] Britain had refused, however, to permit the reopening of negotiations, despite these provocations (October 4).[13]

On October 29, Sazonov warned the Bulgarian ambassador in Petrograd against an attack on Serbia, but also, for the first time, offered Russian consent to Bulgarian seizure of Turkish Thrace to the Enos-Midiya line. France supported this offer, and also promised to support a demand for territorial concessions from Serbia and Greece. In Athens, Russian diplomacy worked for the formation of an anti-Turkish Graeco-Bulgarian alliance.[14]

On November 1, there was much enthusiasm in Sofia for an attack on Turkey, and even King Ferdinand and Radoslavov seemed to be wavering. Pro-Russian Bulgarians indicated that an attack on Turkey was possible if Russia offered parts of Turkish Thrace and Serbian Macedonia, a guarantee against attack by Rumania or the Turkish navy, and freedom of command over Bulgarian troops.[15]

There was also good news from Bucharest and Athens. Bratianu promised to join the Allies if Bulgaria attacked Serbia, and Greece came to the latter's aid. He wanted to help bring Bulgaria over to the Allied side, though not with a promise of the southern Dobrudja. Meanwhile, Venizelos had refused a German request for a promise of neutrality vis-à-vis Turkey, though he had no intention of attacking Turkey until Bulgaria's position became clear.[16]

Finally, Radoslavov made it clear on November 2 that Serbian Macedonia still interested him more than did Turkish Thrace. He revealed to Savinskii, the Russian ambassador, that Austria-Hungary was now offering not only all of Serbian Macedonia, but also part of pre-1912 Serbia, and intimated that the Allies must meet these new offers. Sazonov's response was to offer part of Turkish Thrace if Bulgaria attacked Tur-

The Russian Struggle for Power, 1914–1917

key, and part of Serbian Macedonia, if she also attacked Austria-Hungary. He was willing to offer a guarantee against a Rumanian attack, and also to guarantee Bulgaria's coast if Burgas were turned over as a Russian naval base. He was agreeable that questions regarding joint military action be settled by the Russian and Bulgarian general staffs.[17]

Meanwhile, both Britain and France were displaying great concern over the Balkan situation. Recognizing that Greece and Rumania would not join the Allies unless Bulgaria at least remained neutral, Grey, without any prodding from Petrograd, suggested that the cession of part of Turkish Thrace be mentioned in Sofia. Delcassé was trying to persuade Bratianu to intervene. On November 5, a joint Anglo-French proposal for an offer of part of Turkish Thrace to Bulgaria reached Sazonov. He consented, but expressed the view that only part of Serbian Macedonia would be enough to gain Bulgaria's help. He suggested that Serbia be offered part of Dalmatia for part of Macedonia, and that Albania be partitioned between Serbia and

Greece. Delcassé approved this proposal, but suggested that Greece be asked only to cede the inland towns of Drama and Seres to Bulgaria, and not Kavalla.[18]

THE AUSTRIAN ATTACK ON SERBIA

Before Allied plans for a joint *démarche* in Sofia could mature, Austria-Hungary undertook a major attack on Serbia, in order to back up her offers in Sofia. Even before the nature of the attack became fully apparent, Pashich had claimed that concessions to Bulgaria were impossible, owing to existing Serbian hatred of the Bulgarians.[19] On November 9, after a visit to the front, Pashich told the Russian Chargé that the Serbian High Command was very bitter over the failure of the Allies to send munitions. The generals had said that it was better to lay down arms than to submit to concessions in Macedonia. Pashich himself continued to believe that Greece would attack Bulgaria, if the latter attacked Serbia.[20]

Prince-Regent Alexander of Serbia sent a dramatic appeal to the Russian Tsar on Novem-

The Russian Struggle for Power, 1914–1917

ber 10 for more munitions and a Russian offensive against Hungary. He added that the Serbs could neither explain nor justify, "either from the moral viewpoint or the political viewpoint," the demands of Russia that " at the very moment when we suffer in the struggle for the defense of our independence and that of Slavism, that we recompense Bulgaria, traitor to Slavic solidarity, by ceding to her territory watered so many times by our blood." Alexander added that, to spare the army certain destruction, the Serbian General Staff had proposed that the Government either sue for peace or declare the cessation of the defense of the country. However, the cabinet had threatened to resign before taking such a step.[21]

Sazonov took Pashich sharply to task the next day for the talk of a separate peace. Promising that munitions would be sent through Rumania, he was at the same time strongly critical of the General Staff for its negative attitude towards concessions to Bulgaria. Russia, he said, would be able to deal with Austria-Hungary, but the Serbians must accept full responsibility if their stubborn attitude led to trouble with Bulgaria.[22]

DIPLOMATIC CONFUSION IN THE BALKANS

The new attack on Serbia produced a cacophony of Balkan negotiations rarely equalled at any time when the "Eastern Question" was a live one. Each of the three major Allied Powers had its own plans and suggestions, subject to change at a moment's notice. Small wonder that no results were achieved!

On November 9–10, the British minister in Sofia, Bax-Ironside, to the great chagrin of his Russian and French colleagues, was negotiating independently with Radoslavov on the basis of Bulgarian entrance for Thrace to the Enos-Midiya line and Macedonia east of the Vardar. Savinskii thought this insufficient inducement, and complained to Sazonov that Bax-Ironside wanted to play a "big role", and was unfit for his position. He added that "the preeminent position which Ironside is trying to take in the eyes of the king and government . . . is little in accord with the traditional position of Russia, which, in Balkan questions, is accustomed to seeing the co-operation of her friends shown her only in the form of the cooperation of assistants." Belatedly, Sazonov informed Savinskii that he had transferred to Grey the initiative in the Bulgarian negotiations.[23]

Meanwhile, Britain and France were becoming convinced that only fear of Russia was preventing Rumania from joining the Allies. The Rumanians complained of Russia's "protective attitude" and Straits ambitions. Not as yet knowing of Grey's promises to Sazonov, Delcassé asked the latter on November 9 to let Rumania know that Russia would not oppose internationalization of the Straits and freedom of transit through them. Sazonov haughtily replied that Russia did not have to make Rumania any explanations whatever regarding the Straits.[24]

Nevertheless, Sazonov sent to Bucharest on November 10 an urgent request for immediate intervention, based on the danger to Serbia. Bratianu was not wholly unco-operative. Though he could not intervene until the Allies sent more munitions, and until there was security from Bulgaria, he agreed to send Serbia artillery shells. He also promised that if both Serbia and Greece made territorial concessions to Bulgaria, he would be willing to return Dobrich and Balchik in the southern Dobrudja.[25]

Sazonov next proposed a new Allied *démarche* in Sofia (November 13), demanding a promise not to attack Rumania, in return for a promise to safeguard Bulgaria's "special interests." Delcassé agreed, but wanted to go further and make specific promises to Bulgaria. He was now disgusted with all the Balkan states, and thought the Allies must settle their territorial problems. In addition to Turkish Thrace, he wanted to offer Bulgaria that part of Serbian Macedonia mentioned by Pashich on August 19, while offering Serbia compensations "which correspond to her national desires." Sazonov agreed, and suggested that Serbia be offered Bosnia-Herzegovina and southern Dalmatia from Split to the Montenegrin frontier. The French, however, feared that such an offer would alarm Italy, and it was decided not to mention specific territory in talks with the Serbs.[26]

Sazonov now produced a proposed text for the *démarche* in Sofia, but both Grey and Delcassé feared that it had too much the character

The Russian Struggle for Power, 1914–1917

of an ultimatum. On November 14 and 15, there was much haggling over its wording.[27]

Before agreement could be reached, the irrepressible Bax-Ironside acted. Without consulting his Allied colleagues, he made to Radoslavov a definite offer of Turkish Thrace to the Enos-Midiya line and Serbian Macedonia to the Vardar, if Bulgaria would join the Allies (November 15). Radoslavov was grateful, and promised not to attack Rumania if she joined the Allies. However, he revealed that Bulgaria was determined to remain neutral during the coming winter.[28]

Grey was greatly impressed by these results, and on November 17, proposed an all-out effort to win Bulgaria. He now wanted to offer Radoslavov all of Serbian Macedonia, and Serbia, Bosnia-Herzegovina and an exit to the Adriatic. Then, to everyone's amazement, Sazonov proved unco-operative. He wanted instead to send Radoslavov the following vague and noncommittal message:

The governments of the three Allied Powers receive with a feeling of satisfaction the news of the statement made by the president of the Council of Ministers of Bulgaria to the minister of His Majesty the King of Great Britain in Sofia.

If, in accordance with this statement, Bulgaria takes on herself the obligation to preserve towards Rumania, Greece, and Serbia stringent neutrality, the Powers of the Entente will guarantee her that at the time of the definite regulation of all questions after the war, they will take into consideration the line of her conduct and present her with significant territorial compensations.

These compensations will be increased in case Bulgaria should decide to advance against Turkey or Austria-Hungary.[29]

Just why Sazonov should have taken such a position when the British were willing to risk relations with Italy in order to promise Serbia territory on the Adriatic, is hard to understand. Perhaps he was greatly impressed by the impassioned messages sent from Nish to Petrograd. More likely, he disliked intensely the idea that Serbo-Bulgarian reconciliation should take place at the urging of Britain, rather than of Russia.

Grey protested strongly against the Russian attitude, as did Bulgaria, which, it now seems, was only waiting for an offer of all "uncontested" Macedonia to join the Allies. The Bulgarian ambassador in Petrograd tried in vain to see Sazonov at this point, and had to complain to a lesser official that Bulgaria was filled with Macedonian refugees persecuted by the Serbs, that much new territory was being promised other Balkan countries, and that his own country was being asked to fight the Turks without any assistance.[30]

Meanwhile, though the Bulgarians had said nothing about Kavalla since the beginning of the November negotiations, Sazonov, acting on a suggestion of Pashich, had turned to Venizelos with a demand for concessions to Bulgaria. However, the Greek Premier was even more unyielding than he had been in August, and now thought that if Bulgaria gained part of Serbian Macedonia, she must give up her claims to Turkish Thrace.[31]

On November 24, *faute de mieux*, the Allies gave way to Sazonov, and presented the Bulgarians with the vague *démarche* proposed by the Russian Foreign Minister. Radoslavov was about to make a reply on November 29, when

Sazonov asked that it be delayed, since the Allies would soon have a new proposal to make. Radoslavov consented.[32]

What had happened was that Sazonov had come to the conclusion that an immediate partition of Albania between Serbia and Greece was the way out of the Balkan impasse. On November 27, he proposed that the two countries divide Albania between themselves along a line proceeding from Pograditsa along the watershed between the Skumbi and Devol Rivers to the Adriatic. This would give to Serbia the Albanian provinces of Shiak, Durazzo, Kavaia, and Tirana, as the reward for ceding part of Macedonia to Bulgaria, but annexation of these provinces would in no way lessen her right to Austro-Hungarian territory. Sazonov seems to have thought that Greece would be most grateful, not only for southern Albania, but also a common frontier with Serbia, and would gladly cede Kavalla.[33]

Though Delcassé consented to this plan, Grey decided that it was his turn to be unco-operative. He expressed fear that Italy would oppose the partition of Albania and the belief that

The Russian Struggle for Power, 1914–1917

neither Bulgaria nor Rumania would intervene during the winter. Therefore, he wanted to wait for an answer to the November *démarche* in Sofia.[34]

At this point, the Serbian front began to disintegrate under Austrian pounding, and the Albanian partition proposal had to be laid aside for more urgent business. Sazonov sent an urgent appeal for intervention to Bucharest, and the Tsar wanted to take back the promise of Transylvania unless Rumania helped Serbia (December 3). An appeal was sent to Greece on December 1, but Venizelos refused to move unless guaranteed against a Bulgarian attack. Bratianu also declined to do more than he was already doing.[35]

Sazonov appealed to Grey and Delcassé on December 1, asking them to join in an offer to Greece of southern Albania and security against Bulgaria for immediate help to Serbia. Also, he was now willing to offer the Bulgarians Turkish Thrace to the Enos-Midiya line and an undefined part of Serbian Macedonia. Later, he wanted the Allies to extract from Bratianu a promise to guarantee Greece against a Bulgarian attack.[36]

Grey, meanwhile, had come to the definite conclusion that Greece would not help Serbia if the Allies forced the latter to cede Macedonia to Bulgaria, and that it would be too dangerous to partition Albania, in view of the Italian attitude. He wanted to press Radoslavov for an answer to the *démarche* of November 24. However, when Venizelos announced on December 3 that he would enter the war after Rumania had done so, Grey changed his mind, and agreed to Sazonov's proposals of December 1. Delcassé followed suit.[37]

Accordingly, on December 5, the Allies offered Greece southern Albania, with the exception of Valona, and protection against Bulgaria, if she would immediately come to the aid of Serbia. Venizelos at first seemed content, but on December 6, said he still wanted a Rumanian guarantee against Bulgaria, and complained that he was being offered "only crumbs." He now wanted to discuss the Dodecanese Islands, which were held by Italy.[38]

In the meantime, the Allies had turned to

The Russian Struggle for Power, 1914-1917

Bratianu, asking for a guarantee of Greece against Bulgaria, in case the Greeks helped Serbia. Bratianu replied on December 6 that he would not remain "an onlooker" if Bulgaria attacked Serbia, but said Rumania's entrance depended on the Allies' reconciling Nish, Sofia, and Athens.[39]

Sazonov now asked that Bratianu ease the Allies' task by ceding some of the southern Dobrudja to Bulgaria. However, the Rumanian Premier repeated his earlier statement that he could cede part of the Dobrudja only if a general Balkan agreement were reached, leading to Bulgarian adherence to the Allied cause.[40]

Meanwhile, Radoslavov was still waiting impatiently for the promised new Allied *démarche*. Finally, he asked the Russians on December 5 on what he could count if he joined the Allies. Sazonov, playing for time, asked that he formulate his own desires. In reply, Radoslavov asked for the "Big Bulgaria" which Russia had tried to create through the abortive Treaty of San Stefano in 1878. Then having heard nothing more from the Allies, he announced on December 9 his reply to the Allied *démarche* of November 24:

> In view of the fact that nothing has happened to change the line of conduct of Bulgaria, which has maintained neutrality up to this time, the Royal Government intends not to depart from this path, preserving in this way the interests of the country, which, among all other considerations, must have primary significance.[41]

THE SERBIAN VICTORY AND THE TRUBETSKOI MISSION

A reaffirmation of neutrality was now the safest course for Radoslavov, since the Serbians had just decisively defeated the Austrians. On December 2, the Hapsburg forces had taken Belgrade for the second time during the war, but on the next day, the Serbians struck back with a formidable force on the Morava River. After the great Serbian victory at Kolubara (December 3–6), the Austrians began to retreat, and on December 15, the Serbians re-entered Belgrade.

While the battle was still in doubt, Sazonov had decided to send Prince G.N. Trubetskoi to

The Russian Struggle for Power, 1914–1917

fill the vacant post of Russian ambassador to Serbia and to bring about the long-desired reconciliation with Bulgaria. As one of the most prominent officials of the Foreign Ministry, Trubetskoi had already achieved a certain notoriety for his 1913 book, *Russia As a Great Power*, and had written both the proclamation to the Poles and the first wartime policy paper on Constantinople and the Straits.[42]

He left Petrograd on December 4 with instructions which were later approved by the British and French. He was to point out to Pashich that the Allies were trying to prevent a Balkan war, "whose events would have no influence on the course of the general European war," and this was why they were asking Serbia "to hand over to their review and responsibility the question of territorial concessions on the part of Serbia, unavoidable for the salvation of Serbia herself." Serbia was to be asked to cede "uncontested" Macedonia east of the Vardar for Bulgarian neutrality; other concessions would depend upon any military help the Bulgarians might be asked to give the Allies. In return, Serbia might have "significant districts" of Austria

The Russian Struggle for Power, 1914–1917

and an exit to the Adriatic. Serbia should be grateful, since without Allied intervention in Balkan affairs, she could not strike through to the sea, and none of the Balkan territorial disputes would be settled. A week after Trubetskoi's departure (December 11–12) Sazonov revealed that he did not want Bulgaria to join the Allies until the new ambassador to Nish had had a chance to bring Serbia, Rumania, and Greece into a Balkan Bloc to discuss compensations to Bulgaria. Grey gave hearty endorsement to this policy, which he had himself proposed, after it was suggested by Venizelos, back in August.[43]

After stopping off in Bucharest for talks with Bratianu, which will be discussed later, Trubetskoi arrived in Nish on December 16, just after the re-capture of Belgrade. He was so impressed with the Serbs' "exalted sense of national honor" that he asked to be allowed to offer them more than was planned, including the Banat of Temesvar, in addition to Bosnia-Herzegovina and southern Dalmatia.[44]

However, Sazonov did not consent, and in his first conversation with Pashich (December 22), Trubetskoi had no luck. Pashich insisted that no Serbian political leader could agree to the line of the 1912 Serbo-Bulgarian treaty. Trubetskoi countered with the argument that a lesser price would buy Bulgarian neutrality and Rumania's intervention, and then raised the spectre of the war ending in such a way that Serbia might lose Macedonia without gaining anything at the expense of Austria-Hungary. Presumably he was referring to the possibility that the Allies might make a separate peace with Austria-Hungary and let Serbia and Bulgaria fight it out over Macedonia.[45]

On the next day, Trubetskoi joined Pashich in a railway journey from Nish to Serbian headquarters at Kraguevats, in order to see Prince-Regent Alexander. During the trip, he tried to impress the Premier with the sincerity of Russian friendship for Serbia, and then went over all the arguments in favor of Macedonian concessions. Pashich insisted again that acceptance of the 1912 line would mean justifying Bulgaria's "criminal" attack on Serbia in 1913 and recognizing as "unimportant" the sacrifices then being borne by the Serbs. He said that Serbia might reconcile herself to a violent seizure of

Macedonia, since then it might be later recaptured, but she could never give voluntary consent to its cession.[46]

Four days and two conferences later (December 27), Trubetskoi had made no further progress, but was not entirely discouraged. He thought Bulgaria's intervention after substantial concessions by Rumania might still cause Pashich to change his mind. True, Bulgaria would no longer be important if Italy and Rumania intervened, but it was impossible to be reconciled with a permanent impasse in Serbo-Bulgarian relations, which meant a continuation of "that atmosphere of contrariness and dissatisfaction in the Balkans of which Russia's enemies always try to take advantage."[47]

Meanwhile, on December 20, Delcassé had expressed the view that Bulgaria would try to take Turkish Thrace in the spring, if Rumania attacked Austria-Hungary. Pending that development, the Allies ought to abstain from new Balkan *démarches,* while preserving their position that Serbia must make concessions to Bulgaria in return for Austro-Hungarian or Albanian territory. In the meantime, the Bulgarians could be told unofficially that Rumania was willing to make concessions in the southern Dobrudja. Sazonov concurred in this position (December 23).[48]

THE ITALO-RUMANIAN BLOC

Meanwhile, there had been disturbing indications that Italy and Rumania were acting together against Russian interests in the Balkans. Trubetskoi had stopped off in Bucharest for a two-day visit (December 6–8) on his way to Serbia, and had found Bratianu much impressed by an Italian refusal to intervene during the winter. Though distrustful of Bulgaria, Bratianu was still willing to cede some of the Dobrudja.

Trubetskoi asked Bratianu why Rumania did not take the initiative in forming a Balkan bloc, a step which would emphasize the Balkan nations' independence of Russia. Bratianu answered that while he valued such a self-sacrificing attitude on Russia's part, he feared that bad relations with Bulgaria prevented any Rumanian approach to her.

In conversations with other Rumanians, Trubetskoi learned that Rumania was beginning to link her policy with that of Italy, and to claim that Italo-Rumanian intervention against Austria-Hungary would have much greater effect if the two nations attacked simultaneously. The Italian minister in Bucharest admitted to Trubetskoi that one reason Italy and Rumania were delaying was the likelihood of the progressive weakening of both sets of major belligerents. "As a result," said the minister, "the voice of Italy and Rumania gains more significance the later they put their forces on the balance of the scales."

Trubetskoi warned that, on the other hand, "they might be completely shunted aside," if Austria-Hungary proposed a peace acceptable to both Russia and Serbia. Later, he warned the Rumanian Foreign Minister that "any subjection of Rumanian policy to orders from Rome was not understandable." He pointed out that Italy would not mind "taking Austria's place in the Balkans," and claimed that Russia wanted only "the independence and equality of states," and was not seeking "any hegemony." Later, he

The Russian Struggle for Power, 1914-1917

suggested that Germany was about to sacrifice Austria-Hungary to Italy.[49]

A week later, on December 15, Marquis Carlotti expressed to Sazonov concern over the talk of a partition of Albania between Serbia and Greece; he warned that this could involve "a certain danger" to the two small states, since Italy had important interests in Albania. Sazonov haughtily replied that "no one will force Serbia and Greece not to take these territories," and moreover, that "the presentation to Serbia of part of Albania will not lessen her right to annex lands in Dalmatia."

Somewhat chastened, Carlotti asked meekly what would happen to the Moslem part of Albania between the Skumbi valley and Epirus, adding that "this locality gravitates towards Valona." Sazonov replied that it was his duty "to state positively" that if the Allies had left Valona for Italy, it was not necessary to expect them "to cut off a significant hinterland for Valona." In any case, Russia would never recognize Italian possession of a large part of Albania, even under the form of an Italian protectorate.[50]

Two days later, on December 17, Sazonov expressed to Buchanan uneasiness over the possibility that Italy was trying to form a Balkan bloc of Rumania, Bulgaria, and Greece, under her leadership. He thought something must be said in the Balkan capitals about the exclusion of Serbia from such a bloc. Buchanan doubted that Greece would exchange Serbia for Bulgaria, and Sazonov seemed reassured, adding that Serbia's joining the bloc would remove all his objections. This must have been said with a touch of grim humor, for Italy was unlikely to welcome Serbia into her bloc. Nevertheless, Grey was rather upset by the conversation, until he was assured by Sonnino the report of such an Italian bloc was groundless.[51]

Despite this assurance, Rumania became more difficult, from the Russian viewpoint, in mid-December. Sazonov wired Bratianu on December 16 that he no longer desired immediate Rumanian intervention, but did expect him to cooperate with Trubetskoi's efforts in Nish by making concessions to Bulgaria. In reply, Bratianu still insisted that Serbia must make concessions first, and in addition, withdrew part of his own previous concession. He had now

The Russian Struggle for Power, 1914–1917

decided that he could not part with Balchik, on the Danube, though he was still willing to let Bulgaria have back Dobrich. On the other hand he was now willing for Trubetskoi to hold out the hope of Rumanian intervention to Pashich.[52]

On top of this, Bratianu came to the defense of Italy's interests on December 21. When the Russian ambassador spoke of the possibility of Serbia's gaining part of Dalmatia, Bratianu spoke of "the desirability of taking special care," since Italy had pretensions to part of Dalmatia, and "the active cooperation of Italy has greater value for us than even the military help of Bulgaria." Though he had no official data, Bratianu thought Italy wanted the Dalmatian coast as far south as Šibenik.[53]

This was bad enough, but on December 24, rumors from Athens indicated that Bratianu was approaching Greece regarding joint opposition to Bulgaria's moving into Turkish Thrace, too near to Constantinople. At the same time, he seemed to be trying to form a Balkan bloc to oppose future Russian influence in southeastern Europe, since his views were summed up as follows:

He thinks that at the end of the war, whatever may be the result, the political situation of the little states will not be as favorable as in the past, because up to now an almost perfect equilibrium of European forces has assured them protection. Consequently, he thinks that a sincere union of Balkan peoples on the basis of the equilibrium and parity of forces is most desirable of all.[54]

A few days later, though Bratianu did not know it, the groundwork was being laid for other disputes between Russia and Rumania. On December 26, the Russian Stavka asked the Ministry of Foreign Affairs to indicate "the desirable limits by which the sphere of our administration in Bukovina ought to be bound, without prejudicing the question of the final settlement with Rumania." The Stavka was unwilling to inform the Rumanians of these plans, and Sazonov concurred in this view. He hoped that as much of Bukovina as possible would be conquered, in order to help along future negotiations. Though reluctant to be pinned down on the future frontier, he finally suggested that the line of the Suchav (Suceava) River, with some alterations, would be about right as a frontier.

The Russian Struggle for Power, 1914-1917

Though this line would have followed the approximate line of the Ukrainian and Rumanian parts of Bukovina, it was far from being the Prut boundary for which Bratianu had once asked, and for which he would ask again.[55]

On the same day that this matter arose, Italy landed troops in Valona, allegedly to protect her citizens from an Albanian uprising. Sazonov could hardly object when officially informed of the landing by Carlotti, since he had already consented to a temporary Italian occupation in October. He warned Carlotti, however, that a permanent occupation would result in the partition of the rest of Albania between Serbia and Greece.[56]

AFTERMATH OF THE VALONA INCIDENT

Sazonov soon found it impossible to maintain his original calm and detached attitude towards the Valona incident, since it threatened to blow the lid off the Balkan boiling-pot again. Pashich demanded of Russia on January 6, 1915 permission to send Serbian troops into Albania, and Sazonov felt he had to agree, reluctantly. Greece also sent in troops, and Sonnino began to bristle, only to be mollified by assurances from Venizelos that the Allies intended that Italy should share in a future partition of Albania.[57]

Trubetskoi warned from Nish on January 11 that Italy seemed to be trying to take the place of Austria-Hungary in the Balkans, with the help of Rumania, and that the Serbs were freely predicting that their next war would be with the Italians. Nevertheless, Sazonov counselled calmness in Nish and Athens, and warned Pashich not to weaken the front against Austria for the sake of Albanian adventures.[58]

The Russian Foreign Minister had been encouraged by a report from Sofia that Bulgaria, like every other Balkan state, was very much disturbed over Italy's evident intention to succeed Austria-Hungary in the role of meddler in Balkan affairs, and was happy to see Serbia moving to stop her. On January 12, he informed London and Paris that he thought the time ripe for a third round of Balkan negotiations. Serbia could now be offered part of Albania and Dalmatia from Split southward, in addition to Bosnia-Herzegovina.[59]

However, this proposal died a-borning. Tru-

The Russian Struggle for Power, 1914–1917

betskoi predicted on January 14 that a new demand for Serbian Macedonia would surely be refused, owing to the excellent situation of the Serbian military position. He counselled an attempt to ascertain the likelihood of Bulgaria's intervention first, and more precise definition of future Serbian gains. A week later, on January 21, he did take up with Pashich the possibility of future concessions in Macedonia, but was told that the Army would never permit them while the war was in progress. He then advised a soft tone in Serbia, where resentment over Russia's support of Bulgarian ambitions was growing. For the moment, Sazonov was willing to desist.[60]

Italy, meanwhile, was making it clear that the occupation of Valona was only a preliminary to intervention on the Allied side. On January 15, the Rumanians were certain that Italy intended to enter the war in March. She was increasing her preparations for war, and had told Rumania she would never fight on the side of Austria-Hungary. The Italian minister in Bucharest told his Russian colleague that Italy did not want "to be left with empty hands at the coming redrawing of the map of Europe." He added that his country would want Dalmatia as far south as Šibenik, but might be willing to exchange the Dodecanese, except Rhodes, for the Vilayet of Adalia in Anatolia.[61]

From Paris, there came other rumors. These indicated that Italy might want Dalmatia as far south as the Narenta, as well as the creation of a Croatian state. On the other hand, she was willing that Serbia gain an exit to the Adriatic, and would enter into negotiations with "the great protector of the Slavic peoples who have vital interests in the basin of the Adriatic Sea." Other Italian demands would include a large part in any partition of Turkey, and "parity" with Britain and France in the Mediterranean.[62]

Rumors of the same sort evidently reached Nish, for on January 26, Trubetskoi was forwarding to Petrograd details of the plans being drawn up by Serbian scholars, who had been called on to find justifications for Serbia's right "to become a huge state, which unites Southwest Slavdom." The scholars were prepared for wide concessions to the Croatians, including a change in the name of the country to the "United Serbo-Croatian Kingdom." However, there was little knowledge in Nish of the true state of Croatian, Slovene, and Dalmatian opinion, and there was some fear that they might want to form their own state.

Despite a tendency among some Serbian leaders "to assert the prime position of the present Serbia in the future aggrandized state," Pashich was willing to make great concessions to the Croatians. He had sent the first Serbian ambassador to the Vatican, so as to regulate relations with the Roman Catholic Church in the regions to be acquired. Trubetskoi was warning him "what a responsible task will fall on the shoulders of the Orthodox Church in Serbia, when it must struggle with a militant and well-armed Catholicism."

The Serbs were willing to recognize a distinction between the Orthodox-Moslem and the Catholic regions which they wanted to acquire. It was planned to give the latter autonomy and also the right of participation in the Serbian parliament for the management of "general state matters," somewhat after the fashion of the relationship planned for Orthodox Russia and Catholic Poland.

Trubetskoi warned that it was impossible to predict "into what the present Serbia will be changed," since the Croatians and Slovenes would bring "new habits and new ideas." He feared, moreover, that the annexation of vast Catholic areas might cause Serbia to hold Orthodox Macedonia more dear, a very shrewd observation.[63]

Meanwhile, the Croatians had formed a Yugo-Slav Committee in Zagreb. On the very day of Trubetskoi's report Frano Supilo, a wandering worker for the Yugoslav cause, arrived in Nish, as representative of this committee. He was to try to reach an agreement with the Serbs, and if he failed, he was to take up with Russia the possibility of a Catholic Yugoslavia, embracing Croatia, Slovenia, and Dalmatia.[64]

While in Nish, Supilo did yeoman work for Russia in trying to persuade Prince-Regent Alexander and Pashich to turn their eyes away from Macedonia and the exit on the Aegean, and instead serve as a Piedmont for a future Yugoslav state, oriented towards the Adriatic. Before he had left on February 15, he had made a strong impression on Prince Trubetskoi, who became a

The Russian Struggle for Power, 1914-1917

fervent partisan of the future Yugoslavia, despite earlier Russian intentions to limit Serbia's gains mainly to those areas inhabited by Serbs. Trubetskoi wired Sazonov that

> It seems to me that the interest of Russia in the fate of Southwestern Slavdom can be defined not only as a natural sympathy for the liberation of our brothers. The heartfelt concern shown by our people in the fate of the Slavs is at the same time an expression of true statesmanlike instinct. True, it sometimes involves for us heavy sacrifices, connected with wars past and present, but this attitude of ours towards Slavdom creates at the same time that position of Russia in Europe which grew so clearly out of our history and policy, that it is impossible not to consider it as something unavoidable, from which we could not withdraw without the sacrifice of our Great Power position.[65]

Sazonov would remember all this when negotiations for Italy's entrance began.

MACEDONIA—FOURTH ROUND

In the interim, Sazonov had returned to the attack in the matter of Macedonia, for the fourth time. On January 27, he asked the British and French to agree to work out a Balkan settlement which might be used in later negotiations. They consented, and on the next day, there was forwarded a draft agreement to which Buchanan and Paléologue had agreed. It provided that Serbia should cede "uncontested" Macedonia to Bulgaria as soon as she had obtained Bosnia-Herzegovina, "a large outlet to the Adriatic Sea," and enough of Albania to guarantee her common frontier with Greece. In return, Bulgaria must promise to attack Turkey as soon as the Allies asked her to, and to maintain a friendly attitude towards Serbia, Greece, and Rumania.[66]

Delcassé thought that in the light of increased Serbian pretensions, this proposal did not go far enough. On February 3, he produced a different plan. The Allies must first promise Bulgaria "uncontested" Macedonia to the Vardar for a friendly attitude towards Serbia, Greece, and Rumania, and Monastir in addition, if she joined the Allies. Then Serbia must be offered Bosnia-Herzegovina, Dalmatia as far north as Cape Planca, a part of the Banat of Temesvar and of Syrmia for the strategic defense of Belgrade, a guarantee of free access by rail to Salonika, and a common frontier with Greece in

The Russian Struggle for Power, 1914–1917

Albania. It seems likely that Delcassé hoped by this method to prevent Serbia and Italy coming to blows, since his proposed offer to Serbia would have put a limit to what she might expect.[67]

Probably because he realized that this was Delcassé's purpose, Sazonov began to make objections. At this point, Grey intervened (February 4), and claimed to believe that no territory could be asked of Serbia at this moment, because the British minister in Nish predicted the fall of the Serbian government, anarchy, and an attempt to make an arrangement with the Austrians if another request were made for Macedonian concessions.[68]

Grey's attitude almost ended the fourth round of Macedonian negotiations, but there was another flurry on February 9. The French House of Orléans, which was related to Ferdinand of Bulgaria, had sent the Duc de Guise to Sofia in an effort to win over the reluctant king to the Allies. Ferdinand was not impressed, and said that Bulgaria would never make war on Turkey.[69]

Sazonov, when he heard this, wanted to send

an ultimatum to Sofia. The Bulgarians should be offered "uncontested" Macedonia in return for immediate intervention, provided Serbia received territorial gains, and provided the cession of Macedonia took place after the war. If they refused, they should be threatened.[70]

However, Delcassé wanted to suspend all Balkan *démarches,* since Britain and France were already discussing an Anglo-French expedition to Salonika, in order to swing the Balkans into line (February 11). Grey was in favor of waiting for Bulgaria to offer herself to the Allies, which he obviously expected to happen after the British attacked Turkey at the Straits (the Dardanelles campaign had been approved on January 13). Sazonov therefore agreed to wait until "some military event opens the eyes of the Bulgars."[71]

Nevertheless, he made one more effort, on February 14. Pashich had just told Frano Supilo in Nish that he would be willing to make concessions, provided the Allies made definite promises regarding Serbia's post-war gains. Sazonov thought this development important enough to justify re-opening Balkan negotiations, but neither Delcassé nor Grey agreed. Delcassé now thought that only the presence of Allied troops would move Bulgaria, while Grey thought she had not yet been sufficiently cooperative to justify demands on Serbia. Indeed, Grey thought at this time (February 23) that Bulgaria must attack Turkey before the British could undertake to guarantee her any territorial gains.[72]

RUSSO-RUMANIAN COOLNESS—THE STRAITS AND BUKOVINA

The Russo-Rumanian coolness, which had developed when Bratianu began to draw close to Italy in December, continued on into January and February. On January 6, the Russians learned in Athens that in negotiations with the Greeks, the Rumanians had evinced much interest in the Straits Question. Three days later, the British let Sazonov know that Bratianu had told the Greek ambassador in Bucharest that it was in the interests of Greece and Rumania to struggle against "too vast an expansion of the Slavs." Bratianu especially wanted the two states to work together to obtain a satisfactory solution of the Straits Question. He had even talked of a bloc of Rumania, Greece, and Bulgaria, the last of these being described as "the least Slavic of the Slavic countries."[73]

Sazonov took the Rumanian ambassador in Petrograd sharply to task on January 10. He pointed out that although all Rumania's hopes of gaining Transylvania rested on a Russian victory over Austria-Hungary, it appeared that Rumania was about to enter a league of neutrals designed to stop the advance of Slavdom in the Balkans. He demanded an explanation.[74]

Bratianu denied having done more than talk with another government on the subject of the Straits, and said that he had refused to answer its queries about his position, since he thought the question was "not yet mature." At the same time, he pointed to the friendly attitude towards Russia since the beginning of the war, and hinted that Rumania would join Italy in intervening in March.[75]

Nevertheless, another rumor came to Petrograd on January 22, this time to the effect that Rumania was seeking an alliance with Bulgaria

The Russian Struggle for Power, 1914–1917

to oppose the "Slavic danger," in case Russia took possession of Constantinople and the Straits. This one was, however, also denied by the Rumanians (January 24).[76]

By January 29, Sazonov had decided that blustering might help in dealing with Bratianu. He told the Rumanian ambassador that he was deeply disillusioned by his country's "lack of spirit." Evidently the Rumanian Army of half a million men feared the puny Austro-Hungarian force of 40,000 which guarded the western frontiers of Rumania. In general, he thought that Bratianu's conduct was "insincere and not corresponding to the good relations which I have tried to establish between Russia and Rumania." Bratianu was reported "distressed and offended" by these remarks; he warned that Sazonov's change of attitude would make most difficult "the greater strengthening of the ties which bind Russia and Rumania."[77]

However, two weeks later, Sazonov had cooled off, and was assuring the Rumanian ambassador that Russia recognized Rumania's economic interests at the Straits, and would never destroy them (February 15). This statement had an immediate effect, since a few days later, Bratianu told the Italians that though he was opposed to the Straits being put under one power, he had no intention of raising the Straits Question.[78]

It seems likely that all along, he had been talking of the Straits at Italy's urging. In any event, on February 17 the Italians in London were raising with Benckendorff the question of the future of Constantinople. They professed to believe that the partition of Turkey was inevitable, but thought that Russia should expand in the direction of Armenia and Asia Minor, leaving Constantinople to the Greeks and establishing free passage of the Straits. Benckendorff replied that Russia was indeed interested in the fate of the Armenians, but that she "would never allow Constantinople to fall into the hands of another power, great or small." He added that Russian public opinion had "already spoken on this subject" and that consequently "the solution is now well defined."[79]

The Rumanians returned once more to the question of the Straits, in a conversation between Baron Schilling, Chief of Sazonov's Chan-

The Russian Struggle for Power, 1914–1917

cellery, and Diamandy, the Rumanian ambassador in Petrograd, on February 26. Diamandy was upset by some recent speeches of Duma members which seemed to indicate that Russia might not respect Rumanian rights at the Straits. Schilling blamed Rumanian dilatoriness in intervening for Rumania's unpopularity with the Duma members, but repeated Sazonov's promises of Russia's willingness to respect Rumania's economic interests at the Straits.[80]

Just prior to this conversation, in mid-February, new complications had arisen. The Stavka had now decided that Russia must have all of Bukovina, and even a corner of Transylvania, if she were to hold the Ruthenian area of Hungary after the war. As additional reasons for its attitude, it claimed that the Bukovinians had shown no desire to be annexed to Rumania. Moreover, most of the property of the Orthodox Church in Bukovina was located in the southern part; cut off from its source of revenue, the clergy in the northern part might become a charge on the Russian treasury. The Foreign Ministry was disturbed, for it did not want to bring more Rumanians into the Empire, in addition to those in Bes-

The Russian Struggle for Power, 1914–1917

sarabia, and feared that ultimately Rumania would not intervene in the war unless she were given all of Bukovina. However, the Stavka persisted in its attitude throughout the spring of 1915, though fortunately for Russia, without the knowledge of the Rumanians.[81]

In the meantime, the launching of the British attack on the Dardanelles had created an entirely new situation, and brought on new problems. These must be considered before further attention is given to the Balkan tangle.

IV

THE STRAITS AGREEMENT AND THE TREATY OF LONDON
(MARCH–MAY, 1915)

THE EARLY SPRING of 1915 witnessed the signing of the two best-known Allied "secret treaties" of the First World War —the Straits Agreement and the Treaty of London. Sir Edward Grey, looking backward in 1928, thought the first of these the most important of all the "secret treaties," not troubling to tell the readers of his memoirs that he had promised Constantinople and the Straits to Russia as early as November, 1914.[1] Of course, the later formal agreement was important, not only because France adhered to Russian possession of the vital area in March–April, 1915, but also because it marked the beginning of negotiations for a general partition of Turkey by the Allied Powers. Just as important was the fact that it made possible the entrance of Italy, since Russia would never have consented to sign the Treaty of London and to sacrifice Serbia's Adriatic interests, had it not been for her own desire for Constantinople and the Straits. In a way, it was a return to 1908, when Izvolskii had sacrificed Bosnia-Herzegovina to Russian Straits ambitions.

To avoid confusion, negotiations for the Straits Agreement will be treated separately from negotiations for the Treaty of London, but the reader should be always mindful that they went on simultaneously.

THE PRELUDE TO GALLIPOLI

After the First World War had ended, Winston Churchill, David Lloyd George, and others, sought to confound the critics of the ill-fated Gallipoli Campaign by pointing out that Russia might have been saved from collapse, had enough troops been sent to Gallipoli to make it a success. Russia's collapse was blamed on the shortage of munitions which became apparent as early as mid-December, 1914. Had the stubborn generals on the Western Front spared enough troops to open a sea route to her, she

The Russian Struggle for Power, 1914–1917

might have been kept in the fight to the end, and then Bolshevism would never have triumphed.[2]

This theory has led many to believe that the Russian munitions shortage produced the Gallipoli campaign. Actually, there seems to be no particle of truth in such an assumption. Certainly, there is no shred of evidence from the Russian side that the munitions crisis had anything to do with the British attack on the Straits.

What seems to have happened is that Churchill, as First Lord of the Admiralty, became very concerned as early as August, 1914 by the comparative ease with which the Germans, through the use of naval power, had drawn Turkey over into their camp. This was a serious blow to the prestige of the Royal Navy, whose main task was now to guard the exits from the North Sea. Accordingly, Churchill began in the first month of the war to advocate a naval demonstration in Turkish waters, similar to those made in the nineteenth century. Though he may have mentioned the necessity of maintaining communications with Russia, this was not his primary goal; rather, it was the maintenance of British supremacy on the high seas.[3]

However, the British Foreign Office, as well as the Russian and French Foreign Ministries were trying to keep Turkey neutral, and there was no chance of a naval demonstration until Turkey entered the war. After November 2, an entirely different strategic concept was advanced by Churchill. This was the idea of striking at the "soft underbelly" of Germany, an idea he later advocated in the Second World War. As in the Second, so in the First World War, there were those who opposed Mediterranean ventures because they would only subtract from the effort on the main front, where a decision must be reached. As in the Second, so in the First World War, the advocates of the theory of the "soft underbelly" were nevertheless able to win out, and were given a chance to try out their theories.

The Russians were not consulted in advance about the British attack on the Straits until a decision had already been reached. When they were told that it was planned, they were anything but happy, despite the prospect that munitions could afterwards be shipped through the Straits. They feared that the British were about

The Russian Struggle for Power, 1914–1917

to take over the Straits and Constantinople for themselves.

These suspicions were wholly unjustified, but they existed. Had the British really been very concerned about establishing a supply route to Russia, then surely this would have been a most effective argument to remove Russian suspicions. Yet the argument was never made, and one is led to conclude that the British were not really very worried in January and February, 1915 about Russia's seeing the war through. This conclusion is all the more plausible, in that the Russians were at that time winning over the Germans and Austrians.

It is true that the British Dardanelles expedition was justified by a request made by the Grand Duke for British help in relieving the Transcaucasian front. Early in December, 1914, Enver Pasha had thrown back Russian forces moving on Erzurum in Turkish Armenia, and had begun a movement of his own directed towards the capture of the Russian fortress of Sarakamysh. On December 20, there was grave danger of the town falling, but ultimately, owing to the severe weather and the hopeless Turkish supply system, the Turks were repulsed by General Yudenich with great slaughter (January 5, 1915). Simultaneously, a Turkish effort to capture Ardahan failed.[4]

While the crisis at Sarakamysh was at its height (December 31), Grand Duke Nikolai pleaded for a British diversion, probably expecting it to take place in Palestine or Mesopotamia. Over a month before, Churchill had tried, but failed, to persuade the British cabinet to agree to a naval attack on the Straits (November 25). Now, in the light of the Grand Duke's request, he was more successful, and on January 13, 1915, the cabinet approved the attack. Sazonov was informed of the decision on January 20, and at the same time, the Russians were asked if they could attack the Bosporus while the British attacked the Dardanelles.[5]

To Sazonov, the news gave sinister significance to certain moves initiated by the British in Greece since the beginning of the year. On January 10, Venizelos had told the British minister in Athens, Sir Francis Elliott, that his country would not fight against Austria-Hungary; such a war would be too unpopular. On the other

The Russian Struggle for Power, 1914–1917

hand, a war against Turkey to gain territory in Asia Minor would be popular. On the same day, Noel Buxton, president of the London Balkan Committee, arrived in Paris and revealed to Izvolskii a plan he intended to push in Britain, *i.e.,* persuading Greece to cede Kavalla to Bulgaria in return for Smyrna.[6]

Delcassé had given his consent to the Buxton plan, and had brought up with Izvolskii the entire question of the partition of Turkey. He claimed not to favor French gains in Turkey, but thought he must bow to public opinion and uphold French interests in Syria and Palestine.[7]

Prince Demidov, Russian ambassador in Athens, meanwhile, was taking up with Venizelos the question of Constantinople and the Straits. Venizelos denied any intention of opposing Russian ambitions, declared that only Russia could "bear such a burden," and said it was necessary "to have a sick imagination in order to suppose for a single instant that Greece may pursue any sort of political goals on the shores of the Bosporus, and take on with a light heart the one hundred and seventy million Russians, who would drive her into the sea." On the other hand, he said, Greece would definitely be interested if there were talk of Asia Minor.[8]

Meanwhile, at the request of Grey, Sazonov had given his consent in principle to an offer of Smyrna to Greece (January 13). On January 19, the British wanted Russian consent to a concrete proposal, involving an offer of compensations in Asia Minor in accordance with the military effort made by the Greeks. Greece must agree to let the Allies set the time of her entrance and the type of military and naval aid she would offer, and agree that any occupation of enemy territory by her forces would be considered temporary until general discussion and a general settlement after the war. What the British had in mind seems to have been that while their navy attacked the Straits from the sea, the Greeks should march overland against Constantinople. They were not trying, however, to conceal this from the Russians, since Buchanan offered to submit to Sazonov a plan of the Greek military and naval aid desired.[9]

Nevertheless, when the British told the Russians on the next day, January 20, that they planned to attack the Straits, Sazonov leaped to the conclusion that they were about to restore Greek rule over Constantinople and the Straits. He writes in his memoirs that he "intensely disliked the thought that the Straits and Constantinople might be taken by our Allies and not by the Russian forces" and that he would have preferred an Allied expedition to Salonika, to bring Bulgaria into line. He adds that he had difficulty in concealing from the British "how painfully the news affected me," and that he could not refrain from remarking "Remember it was not I who asked you to undertake this expedition."[10]

For a time, Sazonov tried to get the Russian military to raise military objections to the projected attack on the Straits, in case no Russian troops were available to take part in it. However, the Grand Duke was unco-operative. He thought that any operation directed against Turkey "ought to have important repercussions for the common cause," and believed that the attack would immobilize the Ottoman Empire and have a decisive effect on the Balkan states. At the same time, because of his desire not to weaken the effort against Germany and Austria-Hungary, and because of the weakness of the

Black Sea Fleet, he definitely could not take part in the projected attack.[11]

Sazonov then decided to make difficulties over the negotiations with Greece. On January 21, he demanded that she be required to cede Kavalla to Bulgaria before being promised Smyrna. Delcassé supported him to a degree, since the French thought that the whole question of the partition of Turkey must be discussed before Smyrna was offered. However, Grey overrode these objections, and on January 24, Sir Francis Elliott offered Venizelos territorial gains in Asia Minor in return for help in the forthcoming Straits operations.[12]

Reports from Athens over the next week confirmed Sazonov's worst fears. Prince Demidov wailed that

> The offer of the littoral of Asia Minor, which would very recently have still appeared a sort of chimerical plan, dreamed up by some bearer of political balloons in passing, such as Mr. Buxton, seems very natural today. This proposal, which impinges on the gravest problems of history, presupposes, in any case, a previous agreement on the subject of the liquidation of the unfortunate Otto-

The Russian Struggle for Power, 1914–1917

man Empire; it assures Greece . . . that complete and definitive establishment of Hellenism which, according to the words of Mr. Venizelos himself, is the objective of every Greek patriot. To precipitate the work of emancipation, to cause the national unification to triumph, to convert the Aegean into a Hellenic lake—such are the possibilities which will open before the shining eyes of the Greeks; they are willing to take some risks to achieve them.[13]

Venizelos was reported to be "electrified," and even willing to discuss Kavalla. He intended to ask for the whole of the Aydin Vilayet and half of the Broussa Vilayet. Noting that the northern boundary of the latter came very close to the Sea of Marmora and the Black Sea, Demidov cautioned him against making excessive demands.[14]

On February 4, Demidov warned that the Dardanelles, Russia's future exit to the Mediterranean, was going to be surrounded by Greek territory. Although he trusted in the wisdom of Venizelos, there were many Greeks in whom Russian victories in the war had inspired fear of "the imminent perils of Slavism" and "interest in the imperial attractions of Byzantium," a tendency being encouraged by the Germans. Demidov feared also that the British were hoping "to correct in the Aegean" the concessions they had had to make to Russia at the Straits.[15]

On top of all this, there were rumors from Russian spies in Constantinople that the Young Turks were trying to enter into conversations with the British and French. Sazonov felt it necessary to take up this matter with Buchanan on January 27, and was assured that though Turkey had not entered the war until two months after the signing of the Allied agreement of September 5, 1914, Grey considered that this agreement, with its guarantees against a separate peace, covered Turkey as well as the Central Powers.[16]

Ultimately, on February 10, the Commandant of the First Turkish Army Corps at Constantinople did try to get in touch with the British and French through Venizelos. He promised to take Turkey out of the war in return for a promise of territorial integrity. Sazonov consented to negotiations on February 14, after Grey promised not to go back on the guarantees he had made in November, 1914. However, nothing came of the intrigue with the Turkish general, and the attack

The Russian Struggle for Power, 1914–1917

on the Dardanelles took place on schedule on February 19.[17]

When it did occur, Sazonov was still making difficulties over the participation of Greece. During the last ten days of February, Venizelos began to push for internationalization of the Straits and Constantinople, after the manner of Crete in 1897. Thereupon, Sazonov announced that while he was willing that Greece have concessions in Asia Minor, he was unwilling that any Greek troops participate in the entrance into Constantinople of the Allied armies. Both the British and French pleaded against this attitude, but to no avail. Winston Churchill and David Lloyd George began to urge that the promise of Constantinople and the Straits be withdrawn. They were especially angry because the first attack on the Dardanelles, which was entirely naval in character, failed.[18]

However, during the first five days of March, the danger of a great rift between Russia and her allies evaporated. At a Greek Crown Council which was in session between March 3 and 5, King Constantine and his generals refused to back up an offer of three Greek divisions which

Venizelos had made to the British on March 1. Thereupon, the fiery Premier resigned, after telling the Allies that "without having any political views on Constantinople and the Straits, we have such interests of a moral and commercial order there that we could not be uninterested in their fate." His successor, Gounaris, was pro-Ally, but against intervention for the time being.[19]

THE DUMA AND RUSSIAN WAR AIMS

Two weeks before the Dardanelles campaign got underway, Sazonov had decided to try the effect of Russian "public opinion" on the West, in order to convince Russia's allies of the seriousness of her intentions with respect to war aims. For this purpose, a discussion of war aims was deliberately stirred up in the Russian Duma, when it was reconvened on February 9, following a long recess after the beginning of the war.

To be sure, since the revolution of 1905, both Izvolskii and Sazonov had frequently taken the Duma into their confidence, and had been rewarded with loyal support from some conservatives and liberals, who could be useful allies in

The Russian Struggle for Power, 1914–1917

the struggle with the reactionaries around the court. The Duma was, of course, highly unrepresentative of the Russian masses, but in a country with sixty per cent illiteracy, it probably did represent all Russians capable of having any views on foreign policy at all.

Mikhail V. Rodzyanko, president of the Duma, led off the discussion of war aims on February 9 by predicting in his opening speech that the Russian Army, "with the cross at its breast and in its heart," would "wisely carry out the Tsarist heritage and open for Russia the way to the decision of the historic tasks willed to it by its predecessors on the shores of the Black Sea, and remove the age-old threat of the German powers to the general peace and quiet."

Premier Goremykin then mounted the tribune, and boasted of the capture of Ukrainian East Galicia ("In the living crown of the Sovereign of all the Rus, a leaf absent up to now is now intertwined"), the "brotherly rapprochement" of the Russian and Polish peoples, and the strengthening of "mutual, family ties" with the majority of the Slavic peoples. He also claimed that Turkey's military forces had been shattered by "the glorious Caucasian troops," and added that "always more clearly before us appears a glorious historical future for Russia there, on the shores of the Black Sea, at the walls of Tsargrad." Despite Goremykin's general unpopularity, he had the unusual experience of being applauded for these statements.

However, real interest was centered on the remarks of the Minister of Foreign Affairs. In order to make certain that he gave the proper cues, Sazonov elected to say little about the European situation, and confined himself to a catalogue of the past sins of the Central Powers. His real climax came when he said that the recent events on the Transcaucasian front had brought near "the moment of the decision of the economic and political tasks, connected with the exit of Russia to the open sea." After a pause, followed by "enthusiastic and continuous" applause, he went on. Carrying on "the disinterested traditions of Russian policy, and our state interests," he had sought ceaselessly before the war reforms in Turkish Armenia. The agreement of February 8, 1914 had guaranteed Russia's "exclusive position" in the Armenian question, and at the end of the war, this position would be used "in a direction benevolent for the Armenian population." Finally, he said, Russia could not fail to sympathize with "the strivings of the Hellenic people to put an end to the sufferings of their fellow-nationals, who are still under the yoke of Turkey." In other words, while trying to arouse the deputies' interest in the war with Turkey, he was also preparing them for Greek acquisition of Smyrna.

The decent Russian conservatives, men formed like Sazonov himself in the mold of Stolypin, gave the most enthusiastic reception to these speeches. Nikolai E. Gepetskii, a Centrist from Bessarabia, claimed that he already saw "with quivering joy, that the pre-destination of God is fulfilled, that there are fulfilled the great legacies of our ancestors, to liberate the Slavic world from the German yoke, to snatch away from the claws of Austria Galician Rus." After discussing the need for strengthening Serbia, "the bulwark of southern slavdom," and Montenegro with new territory and exits to the sea, and the satisfaction of Italy's national strivings, Evgraf P. Kovalevskii, an Octobrist from the

Ukraine, requested that the Duma be asked its opinion before the terms of peace were worked out. In the interim, he thought that the body should establish its views on war aims, and that

> In the first place we must put the settlement of our age-old quarrel with Turkey relative to the Bosporus and Dardanelles, and also guarantee our rights in the Holy Land. The whole Black Sea half of Russia—the most populated, the most industrialized, and the richest, cannot live and develop without our control over the Black Sea, and a free exit from it . . . . The Straits are the very lock and key of our house; they must be in Russian hands with the necessary territory around these Straits . . .

After that, he thought that the important war aims were "the complete liberation of Armenia from the Turkish yoke," the annexation of the Austro-Hungarian Ukrainians to Russia (which would complete "the historic business of the great reunion of the Russian Land"), the reunification of Poland under the sceptre of the Russian Tsar, and finally, "freedom of navigation in the Baltic Sea," which might involve "the possibility of territorial gains for Russia to the injury of Germany," *i.e.*, East Prussia.

The Russian Struggle for Power, 1914–1917

At this point, Paul N. Milyukov, leader and foreign affairs expert of the liberal Kadets, arose to congratulate Sazonov on the fact that "the realization of our national tasks stands on a true path," and to suggest that Constantinople and the Straits be "simultaneously secured both by diplomatic and military means." Milyukov then began to talk about the "profound moral idea" the war was gaining, "thanks to the participation in it of the two most advanced democracies of contemporary humanity," Britain and France. The union and liberation of Poland, he added, would be "the symbol of our moral supremacy over the enemy and of our spiritual ties with our comrades." So, for that matter, would be the liberation of the Armenian people, "which has also learned to seek under the wing of Russia salvation from an age-old conqueror, on whom now sits the court of history for the sins of the past."

This ideological theme was now taken up by the conservatives, and Sergei I. Shidlovskii, another Octobrist from the Ukraine, claimed that the war had become "a war between two irreconcilable world-outlooks: that against which we fight is the world-outlook which divides humanity into two categories—the rulers and the enslaved." Shidlovskii then said that Turkey had become "no more than a geographic expression," and that no military operations against Germany could be considered settled until "the question of an exit to the warm sea, the question of the Straits, the question of Constantinople" had been settled.

V. N. Lvov, a Centrist from the Volga region, insisted that Russia was only following her historic destiny in liberating Orthodox and Slavic peoples from "cultured and non-cultured barbarians," *i.e.*, the Germans and Turks. After describing the liberation of the Balkans in the nineteenth century, he added that the Russians had found "a new threatening danger . . . the threat to our existence from the danger of Germanism." He warned that Austria-Hungary was being swallowed up by Germany, and that Russia would face a future threat from "Germany-Hungary" unless she prevented any "strengthening of Germany with parts of Austria-Hungary" by the partition of the latter. Finally, he wanted the settlement of the "age-old historic tasks in the Black Sea."

An Armenian Kadet from Russian Transcaucasia, Mikhail I. Papadzhanov, sought to disprove before his colleagues the rumors that the Turkish Armenians had been hostile to advancing Russian troops. Instead, he claimed,

> The Turkish Armenians, with hope and trust, await their liberation, and with a feeling of deep satisfaction, they will read the words of M. the Minister of Foreign Affairs concerning the disinterested legacies of Russian policy, and of the resurrection of Armenia in a direction favorable for the Armenian population.

Despite their hatred of Sazonov, the Rightists felt they must say something on this occasion. Therefore, Anatolii I. Savenko, a Nationalist from the Ukraine, rose to announce that his faith had been strengthened, and his hope "given wings," because Nicholas II would be able to realize a "great traditional dream of the Russian people: . . . the striving towards which has guided us through all our history of over a thousand years. I speak of the Straits, of Tsargrad, towards which the Russian people have striven, beginning with Oleg and Igor. . . . The Straits and Tsargrad must be ours, and only ours."

Only one sour note was sounded. The Menshevik socialist, Nikolai S. Chkeidze, a Georgian, rose to demand that the belligerent powers "immediately proceed to working out as soon as possible an end of the war, and the conclusion of a European peace," which must be "the simultaneous expression of the will of the people," rather than the expression of the will of "irresponsible diplomats." Only such a peace, he claimed would create conditions for stopping the conquest of foreign territories, and for the free self-determination of nationalities, the limitation of armaments, the introduction of "a people's militia," and the creation of arbitration courts to settle international conflicts.

Chkeidze's last words were drowned out by shouts demanding to know how much he had been paid by Germany. Nevertheless, he was supported to a degree by a young lawyer from Saratov, and member of the tiny Labor Party, Alexander F. Kerenskii. However, Kerenskii insisted that the time was not yet ripe for the steps Chkeidze proposed, and in a long, bombastic, and vague oration, developed the theme that, as in France in 1792, Russian liberty would somehow be born on the battlefield.[20]

THE WEST REACTS TO THE DUMA SPEECHES

The oratory on the floor of the Russian Duma was heard in London and Paris, and promptly produced a reaction in the press and legislative halls. Speculation ran rife when the actual attack on the Straits took place on February 19, only ten days after the Russian speeches.

Izvolskii was very distressed on February 23 to note that the French government permitted press speculation about an international regime in Constantinople, and demanded of Sazonov a precise statement of Russian desires. Thereupon, for the first time, Sazonov revealed to him, and also to Benckendorff, that Russia wanted Turkey in Europe to the Enos-Midiya line and the Asiatic shore of the Bosporus as far as the Sakkaria River, but would take into consideration the economic interests of Rumania, Bulgaria, and Turkey.[21]

Meanwhile, on February 25, Sir Edward Grey had revealed to Benckendorff that he would have to answer in the House of Commons a question as to whether Sazonov's speech of the 9th before the Duma had had the consent of the British Government. Though Benckendorff thought that the British and Russian public should know of the promises Grey had already made, he finally gave his approval to the statement in the House of Commons, which went as follows:

> I have not seen and I cannot find in the reports which have come to me of the speech of M. Sazonov the declaration which has been attributed to him by the Honorable Member.
>
> The declaration which I have seen states that events on the Russo-Turkish frontier will permit Russia to draw closer to the realization of her political and economic tasks in connection with the question of Russia's access to the open sea (Hear, Hear). This is a tendency in which we are entirely in sympathy. The precise form in which it will be realized will no doubt be determined by the conditions of peace.[22]

When news of the statement reached Petrograd, on top of the current indications that the Greeks had designs on the Straits and Constantinople, it was more than Sazonov could bear.

The Russian Struggle for Power, 1914–1917

On March 1, he demanded that Grey profit by the first possible occasion to make a new declaration which would be nearer the assurances already given to Russia.[23]

Grey was much put out by this message, especially since he had shown Benckendorff his statement before it was made. He ordered Buchanan to tell Sazonov that "I can't be more Russian than the Russian Government itself in my public utterances," and demanded of Benckendorff that he explain the true circumstances of his statement to Sazonov and the Emperor.[24]

Benckendorff complied, and pointed out to Sazonov that Grey had not provoked the question in the House of Commons and was eager to reveal the secret agreement of November, 1914. He added that there was nothing in Grey's statement to prevent a later settlement of the question in the manner desired by Russia.[25]

By March 3, there were better feelings all around, and Grey was telling Benckendorff that he had been struck from the beginning of the war by the abnormal situation that a great country like Russia could be reached only through Archangel or Vladivostok. However, he still thought that a solution of the Straits Question could be found only when peace was concluded.[26]

Benckendorff then called Grey's attention to the new requirements of "Russian public opinion." He had already indicated, in a very discreet manner, and in general terms, the boundaries of the zone Russia would consider essential for control of the Straits. On this occasion, he showed Grey on a map the Enos-Midiya line and the Sakkaria River, and added that it was necessary to receive guarantees south of the Sea of Marmora. Warning against any illusions, he indicated that Russian establishment at the Straits meant annexation. He added that, in his opinion, British public opinion was already prepared for the news.

Grey replied that he could not give an answer to such a proposal immediately. However, he conceded that there were not many Englishmen left who considered it a principle that Russia should not have Constantinople. He could not formulate any precise objections to Benckendorff's argument, but before being able to pronounce himself, he must ask the opinion of the

French. If the question arose in the Commons, it would be necessary to pose economic conditions. In fact, the territorial aggrandizement of Russia would raise the question of the complete partition of Turkey, since it would arouse the appetites of many powers.

Britain, he said, had pretensions only to some points on the Persian Gulf, not to any part of Asia Minor or Syria. He himself was against raising the idea of partition, since Turkey was not yet beaten. For this reason, he could not present the Commons with a new declaration, since it would be premature. However, whatever the theater of war in which the diverse Powers operated at the moment of peace, they would take into consideration the totality of rights of each of them, and without a doubt, the interests of Russia would have their place.

Benckendorff replied that he knew the difficulties of a new interpellation, which would require divulging more information than had the preceding one. However, a more complete affirmation had become more and more desirable. Grey then mentioned again the necessity of consulting the French, and Benckendorff replied that, owing to the military situation, it was necessary not to lose time. Afterwards, the ambassador reported to Sazonov that he thought Grey would ask only for economic guarantees at the Straits, and that difficulties were more likely to come from Paris than from London.[27]

Later, in response to orders from Sazonov on March 2 to prepare British public opinion with respect to Russia's rights at the Straits, Benckendorff assured his chief that he and the Russian press had not taken account of a progressive evolution in favor of Russia in British public opinion. He had found that "the press of all shades of opinion, the speeches of meetings, etc., all ask for a revision of prejudices and ask freely to know the national aspirations and declarations." It seemed, indeed, that Russia was almost becoming more popular in Britain than was France. Lloyd George had called Russia a pacific nation, and not militaristic like Germany; this was the explanation given for Russian defeats. At the same time, Britons had been impressed by the speed of the Russian mobilization, as well as by the publication of the Orange Books, which gave the Russian version of the outbreak of the war. Such events as the proclamation to the Poles and the measures taken against alcoholism had also boosted Russia's popularity. As for Grey's statement in the House of Commons,

> Only a little while ago, no Foreign Secretary would have been able to give such an explanation without meeting opposition in the House, in the press, and in the greater part of the population. Today, the contrary is true, and old traditions have ended. I consider this fact as one of the most significant symptoms of the progressive popularity in England of the solid Anglo-Russian Entente.[28]

DELCASSÉ AND THE TANGIER PRECEDENT

Meanwhile, Benckendorff's prediction that the French were likely to make more trouble than the British was proving to be well-founded. On March 2, Izvolskii told Delcassé that Russian "public opinion" now required more solid guarantees of Russia's access to the open sea and the security of the Black Sea coast than had been given by Grey's February 25 statement. Delcassé replied that he had always understood that Russia admitted the advisability of internationalizing Constantinople, while asking only for a part of Turkish Thrace, freedom of trade through the Straits, and international guarantees against their being closed to Russian commerce. He admitted, however, that certain recent words of Sazonov indicated a desire for Constantinople, and said he thought such a desire normal. However, he thought that Russia's demand for the Asiatic shore of the Straits would be vigorously repulsed by the British, and by all European public opinion. Existing ideas on freedom of the seas excluded the concession to one Power of the Straits, with their international interests. For example, there was the case of Gibraltar, where France had never permitted Britain to gain Tangier.

In closing, Delcassé expressed regret that he could not go to Petrograd to see Sazonov, owing to the session of the French parliament. Izvolskii therefore suggested to Sazonov that he and Grey come to Paris, in order to avoid misunderstandings in the solution of the grave questions which were beginning to arise.[29]

On March 4, Sazonov sent off a sharp message to Paris, stating that the "purely theoretical

The Russian Struggle for Power, 1914-1917

opinion" of Delcassé concerning the impossibility of Russian establishment on both sides of the Straits was refuted by the impossibility of otherwise guaranteeing a free passage through them. Since the coast of Asia Minor dominated that of Europe, the latter would be constantly menaced if the former were left in the hands of Turkey.[30]

In reply, Izvolskii tried to soothe his chief by pointing out that his conversations with Delcassé had been personal and general, and that he had made no concrete demands. However, he feared that Delcassé was about to bring the whole matter up before the French cabinet and to seek to establish a common position with the British. For that reason, he recommended again a meeting of Sazonov, Grey, and Delcassé to iron out the whole question of the partition of Turkey.[31]

In another conversation with Delcassé, on March 4, Izvolskii learned that Paléologue had just wired Paris that the Russian viewpoint had "considerably changed." Delcassé now insisted that the Straits themselves must be completely neutralized and brought under the control of an international commission, no matter who owned them. He was now willing that Russia own not only the European shore, but also the Asiatic shore, provided the problem of the partition of Turkey in Asia was settled. He added that if Russia possessed either both shores, or the European shore alone, she would, as a practical matter, be able to close the Straits any time she saw fit, but that he would not wince at this fact. He again regretted his inability to go to Petrograd, and renewed his invitation that Sazonov come to Paris.[32]

Sazonov now decided that the time had come to play one of his strongest trump cards—the conviction in the West that he had become indispensable to Russia's continued loyalty to the Allies. On March 5, he told Paléologue point-blank that if France continued making difficulties over the Straits, he would resign, which might lead to his replacement by a Minister of Foreign Affairs "from among those persons whom we still have in Russia who are adherents of the old system of the *Dreikaiserbund*." Paléologue was visibly affected by the threat.[33]

The Russian Struggle for Power, 1914-1917

THE FORMAL RUSSIAN DEMAND

Meanwhile, after conversations with Buchanan and Paléologue, and with the explicit approval of Nicholas II, Sazonov had decided to formulate Russian desires precisely in an official note to Britain and France. The note was delivered at the embassies in Petrograd on March 4, and read as follows:

> The course of recent events leads His Majesty the Emperor Nicholas to think that the question of Constantinople and the Straits ought to be definitely resolved in conformance with the secular ambitions of Russia.
>
> Insufficient and precarious would be every solution which could not permit the inclusion within the territory of the Empire of Russia of the city of Constantinople, the western shore of the Bosporus, of the Sea of Marmora, and of the Dardanelles, as well as southern Thrace up to the Enos-Midiya line.
>
> In the same way, as a result of strategic necessity, the part of the Asiatic shore between the Bosporus, the Sakkaria River, and a point to be determined on the shore of the Bay of Izmid, the islands of the Sea of Marmora, and the islands of Imbros

and Tenedos ought to be included within the limits of the Empire.

The special interests of France and Great Britain in the above regions will be scrupulously respected.

The Imperial Government is pleased to hope that the considerations indicated above will be favorably received by the two Allied Governments.

The aforesaid Allied Governments may be assured that they will meet, on the part of the Imperial Government, the same benevolence with regard to the realization of projects that they may have, as far as other regions of the Ottoman Empire and elsewhere are concerned.[34]

In the immediate wake of the demand, there were reassuring signs from Britain, but a continued lack of cooperativeness on the part of France. Buchanan told Sazonov on March 5 that operations at the Dardanelles had been undertaken solely for the common cause, and that Britain would derive no direct gain from them, since she did not intend to establish a permanent footing in the Straits area. They had been undertaken to render Turkey useless as an ally to Germany, to destroy her power to attack Russia or Great Britain, and to induce the Balkan neutrals to cooperate with the Allies. Grey had endorsed Sazonov's statements to the Duma, and had no objections to anything said by him to Buchanan. However, a precise and formal agreement must be discussed with France, and could probably not be concluded except in the final peace terms. In any event, Britain had never remotely considered installing the Greeks at the Straits.[35]

On the same day, Benckendorff reported from London that he thought Grey foresaw a British demand for compensations, though he did not yet know their nature and was unwilling to commit himself "before the whole business becomes very clear." At the same time, Grey was becoming somewhat disturbed over the negative attitude of France, and had come to desire a meeting of the three foreign ministers.[36]

Delcassé, meanwhile, was telling Izvolskii that Sazonov was still avoiding the key to the whole situation, the freedom of the Straits. A guarantee along these lines would "enormously facilitate" the cession of Constantinople and both sides of the Straits. At the same time, he still wanted a meeting of the three foreign ministers to thrash out the whole problem of the partition of Turkey.[37]

On March 7, Sazonov declared that he could not leave Petrograd, but that the question of Constantinople and the Straits, "put on the order of the day by recent events," must be settled at once by the Allies. Russian opinion would never resign itself to less than complete possession, which alone could assure the freedom and independence of Russian commerce. Neutralization of the Straits would never work, but Russia was willing to give Britain and France "all assurances as far as the free navigation of the Straits is concerned, and the economic interests of these Powers."[38]

On the same day, Benckendorff expressed fear that the British might want to neutralize Gallipoli. At the same time, he warned that in the light of discussion of a general partition of Turkey, Russia had better express herself on the subject of Armenia. The French were insisting on their interests in Asia Minor and Syria, and the British feared that not only France, but also

Italy, was going to make excessive territorial demands at the expense of Turkey. As for the British, they had as yet mentioned only their desire to keep the Moslem Holy Places in Moslem hands and to maintain existing arrangements regarding the Suez Canal.[39]

Later on March 7, Benckendorff learned that Sazonov's note was about to be submitted to the British cabinet, and that a formal request for the views of France had been sent from London.[40]

By March 8, Sazonov had resolved to return to a proposal he had made back in September, 1914, that the Allies should reach an agreement on their general war aims. He wired Grey and Delcassé that he regretted he could not leave Petrograd to talk with them, but that he considered it desirable "to raise without delay the principal conditions of the future peace." He asked that Buchanan and Paléologue be invested with authority to discuss them and to "let me know in all frankness the aspirations of their governments." He added that in his opinion, the principal conditions of the peace might be divided into three categories:

1 Conditions absolutely indispensable to this or that Ally as touching its vital interests;

2 Conditions in which reciprocal concessions are possible in view of the coordination of the interests of the three Allies; and

3 Conditions which do not touch directly the interests of the Allies, but which are important for the preservation of peace in the future, and for the continuation of good relations between the Allies.[41]

THE FIRST FRENCH RESPONSE

Meanwhile, in the four days since the presentation of Sazonov's note, the French had decided to agree to Russian desires, subject to certain qualifications. Delcassé admitted to Izvolskii later that he had decided to adopt such a policy because he understood that, in the words of Izvolskii, "if we came to doubt, however little this might be, the good will which would cause France to help us along this path, that could have a most serious repercussion on our relations as allies." For that reason, Delcassé was willing to put up a terrific fight in the French cabinet for acceptance of the Russian demands, against the socialist ministers Jules Guesde and Marcel Sembat.[42]

The Russian Struggle for Power, 1914–1917

On March 8, Paléologue delivered to Sazonov the official French answer to the Russian note of March 4:

By order of his government, and with reference to the requests formulated by the Imperial Government in its memorandum on March 4, 1915, the Ambassador of France has the honor to inform His Excellency Monsieur Sazonov that the Imperial Government can count on the good will of the Government of the Republic in order that the question of Constantinople and the Straits be settled in accordance with the aspirations of Russia. This question, as well as questions which interest France and England in the East and elsewhere, and which the Imperial Government accepts seeing settled according to the aspirations of France and England, will find their solution in the peace treaty, which, in accordance with the declaration of September 5, 1914, must be discussed in common and signed simultaneously by the three Allied Powers.[48]

Sazonov announced on the next day that he accepted this answer to his note "with satisfaction." On March 10, he was asking the Russian censors not to permit articles on Constantinople and the Straits, in order to give the French Government a chance to prepare French public opinion so that it would recognize Russia's "legitimate rights." At the same time, he asked for a project of French "economic conditions," promising that if they did not "diminish our rights in our future possessions," they would be welcomed.[44]

Meanwhile, between March 9 and 14, Izvolskii and Delcassé were having further conversations which were making it apparent that France did not feel she had waived all her claims with respect to Constantinople and the Straits. Delcassé was unwilling to empower Paléologue to represent France in general talks on war aims in Petrograd, because of his distrust of the ambassador. He was, however, still hoping that Sazonov would come to Paris to talk with him. At the same time, he talked a great deal of the necessity for guarantees of international commerce in the Straits, and Izvolskii feared that the French Foreign Ministry, which was studying the problem, might come up with something like the Danube Commission. In addition, it seemed likely that the agreement on the Straits would later be linked with other aspects of a general settlement.[45] As things turned out, Izvolskii proved to be a good prophet.

The Russian Struggle for Power, 1914-1917

THE BRITISH RESPONSE

In their discussions of Sazonov's March 4 note, the British apparently never considered demanding neutralization of the Straits, though there was apparently some desire for a guarantee of freedom of commerce. In the cabinet, the only difficulties were over making a statement on the Straits Question by anticipation, and "independently of questions having to do with the future fate of other provinces of the Ottoman Empire." In the end, however, the Liberal cabinet decided to accede to Russia's desires, and so did the Tory leaders, Landsdowne, Bonar Law, and Balfour, who were consulted.[46]

The fact that a favorable response would probably be made was indicated by Grey to Benckendorff on March 10. At the same time, Grey mentioned French interests in Asiatic Turkey. He said that while Russia already possessed a completely elaborated project defining her interests, the question of British interests had not been studied in Britain. However, he thought that a reply could be made to Sazonov's note before the end of the week. Later, Sir

Arthur Nicolson indicated to Benckendorff that Britain would require only freedom of commercial navigation in the Straits, and a free port at Constantinople for merchandise in transit.[47]

The British response arrived in Petrograd on March 12, and was promptly delivered at the Foreign Ministry. However, probably to impress the Emperor, Sazonov arranged that the note should be personally delivered to Nicholas II by Buchanan in his presence, that evening.

The Emperor received his Foreign Minister and the British ambassador in his study at Tsarskoe Selo. After a few words of friendly greeting, he said to Buchanan, "You have a communication to make?" The ambassador replied that he was charged with a message which he trusted would give the Emperor as much pleasure to receive as it gave him to deliver. He then proceeded to read Grey's note:

In case of the happy conclusion of the war, and on the condition that satisfaction is given to the requirements formulated by France and England, and applying at the same time to the territories of the Ottoman Empire and other territories, in the sense in which the question is raised in the Russian communication mentioned below, His Majesty's Government subscribe to the memorandum of the Imperial Government on the subject of Constantinople and the Straits, whose text was handed to His Majesty's Ambassador by His Excellency Mr. Sazonov on March 4th of this year.[48]

Buchanan then proceeded to read a supplementary note. It pointed out that the March 4 note had gone considerably beyond the desires foreseen by Sazonov some weeks before, and that before Britain could foresee what her desires would be at the end of the war, Russia was asking a formal promise of "the most valuable acquisition of the whole war." Grey hoped that the Russians would recognize that Britain could not give a more effectual proof of her friendship than by acceding to their desires, and that a change of British policy had taken place which was "in complete contradiction to the viewpoints and sentiments which have always ruled in England." He hoped also that "solid friendship between Russia and Great Britain" would follow the agreement.[49]

British requirements, Buchanan went on, contained no clause which could violate Russian sovereignty over Constantinople and the Straits. However, since the city would always be an entrepôt for southeastern Europe and Asia Minor, the Russian Government was asked to establish a free port for merchandise exchanged between non-Russian territories. Free passage of ships through the Straits was also asked. Moreover, now that an agreement had been reached, Russia was asked to cease her opposition to Greek support of the Dardanelles operation, and to do all in her power to reassure Bulgaria and Rumania.

Britain thought that the future interests of France and herself in the Asiatic territories of Turkey must be taken into consideration, and was ready to reach an agreement on the subject with France and Russia. In the meantime, she insisted that the Moslem Holy Places and Arabia must remain under an independent Moslem sovereignty. Grey had no other definite proposals regarding British desires, but thought one of them would be "the revision of the Anglo-Russian agreement of 1907, relative to Persia," involving the recognition by Russia of the neutral sphere, between the Russian and British spheres, as a part of the British sphere. Finally, until the Allies were able to give the Balkan states, especially Bulgaria and Rumania, sufficient assurances regarding the territory they wanted, and until there was a definite agreement on British and French desiderata, Grey wanted the Straits Agreement kept secret.[50]

After Buchanan had finished, Nicholas II asked that he convey his warmest thanks to the British Government, and asked what was the existing arrangement with regard to the neutral zone of Persia. Buchanan explained, and added that the incorporation of this zone into the British sphere would "put an end to a constant cause of friction between our two Governments and would mark a great step in advance towards a final and friendly settlement of the Persian Question."[51]

The Emperor seemed still to hesitate, and Buchanan remarked tartly that if Britain had offered Constantinople and the Straits for the neutral zone of Persia a year before, he had no doubt as to what Nicholas' answer would have been. Sazonov then interjected that if Russia acceded to the British request, she must be allowed complete freedom of action in her own sphere of Persia. Buchanan then spoke at length on the necessity of maintaining Persian independence. In the end, he told the Emperor that "after the war, Russia and Great Britain would be the two most powerful empires in the world. With the settlement of the Persian Question, the last cause of friction between them would disappear, and the world's peace would then be assured." Nicholas agreed cordially to this statement, and authorized Buchanan to report that he accepted British conditions in principle.[52]

On March 20, Sazonov ordered Benckendorff to express "the profound gratitude of the Imperial Government for the complete and definite adhesion of Great Britain" to his note of March 4. He was convinced that "the sincere recognition of their respective interests will guarantee in perpetuity the solid friendship of Russia and Great Britain." He agreed to the establishment of a free port in Constantinople and to free passage of merchant ships through the Straits.

Sazonov was also now agreeable "to obtaining on reasonable conditions the intervention of states whose concurrence is thought useful by

The Russian Struggle for Power, 1914–1917

Great Britain and France," *i.e.*, Greece. He also accepted British stipulations regarding the Moslem Holy Places, but wanted to know whether they would remain under the Turkish Sultan, who would retain the title of Khalif, or whether new, independent Moslem states would be created. He himself wanted the Turkish Sultan to lose the title of Khalif, and for "freedom of pilgrimage" to be assured.

Sazonov confirmed the Tsar's agreement to the inclusion of the neutral zone of Persia in the British sphere of influence in principle. However, he did want certain districts of the neutral zone, including Ispahan, Yezd, and an area which thrust itself in a point between the Russian and Afghan frontiers, and which touched the Russian frontier at Zulfagor, to be reserved for Russia, since they formed an "inseparable whole" with her existing zone. The construction of railroads within the neutral zone was a matter of "capital importance" to Russia, and ought to be discussed "in a friendly manner." Russia counted on Britain's recognizing her complete freedom of action within her zone, particularly with respect to economic and financial policy.

Finally, Sazonov renewed certain demands which he had made with respect to Afghanistan in the spring of 1914. These included the recognition of the 1907 Anglo-Russian agreement by the Afghan Emir, who must also agree not to tolerate any enterprise or foreign concession in northern Afghanistan, to cooperate in the completion of irrigation works indispensable to Russia in the border regions of Afghanistan, not to grant a monopoly of commerce and industry to British companies, and not to authorize the construction of railroads in northern Afghanistan without previous agreement with Russia. In return for backing these demands, Britain would receive Russian recognition of special rights for herself in Tibet.[53]

THE BARANOVICHI CONVERSATIONS AND THE SECOND FRENCH NOTE

As had been expected, the French eventually produced a set of demands regarding gains in Asiatic Turkey. On March 14, Paléologue appeared at the Foreign Ministry to present a note and ask for an appointment with the Emperor, who was then at the Stavka in Baranovichi.

The Russian Struggle for Power, 1914-1917

Since Sazonov was with the Emperor, he saw Deputy Minister A.A. Neratov, who transmitted the note to his chief on March 15. Its contents were as follows:

> I would be grateful to Your Excellency if You would be so good as to inform His Imperial Majesty that the Government of the Republic, having considered the conditions of peace which Turkey must sign, desires to annex Syria, including the province of the Gulf of Alexandretta, and Cilicia to the Taurus Range. I would be happy immediately to assure my Government of the consent of His Imperial Majesty to this desire.[54]

In passing on the note to Sazonov, Neratov pointed out that French aspirations ran counter to Armenian nationalist desires and thought that "we must tell the French that the Armenians, according to our reports, dream of Mersina, with the province inhabited by Armenians, and that including these places in the zone of French pretensions can provoke among the Armenians disillusionment towards France." The French must never be able to reproach the Russians with not having informed them of Armenian desires. However, if France considered the annexation of Mersina important and necessary, "then we, of course, will not oppose this." Paléologue had told Neratov that he thought Palestine was included in the expression "Syria," and the Deputy Minister had replied that there must be an independent governor in Jerusalem.[55]

Paléologue arrived at Baranovichi on the next day, March 16. He saw the Emperor, the Supreme High Commander, and Sazonov, and relates that he talked freely with them, and that "there was no lack of animation, no feeling of restraint." He described in detail "the full program of civilizing work which France intends to undertake in Syria, Cilicia, and Palestine." The Emperor had him "carefully point out on the map the regions which would thus come under French influence," and, according to Paléologue, then declared, "I agree to all you ask."[56]

Although the Emperor was willing to sacrifice Armenian interests in Cilicia, Sazonov made some objections with regard to Palestine. Two formulas regarding the future of the Christian Holy Places were offered by Paléologue. One would have involved maintaining the existing regime, established by the Treaty of Berlin; the other would have involved a new Franco-Russian agreement, based on the existing regime. However, Sazonov did not entirely trust his generous interpretation of the term "Syria," and asked that Izvolskii confirm it, while at the same time, assuring Delcassé that Russia was ready "widely to satisfy the desires of France relative to Syria and Cilicia."[57]

Though neither the Emperor nor Sazonov had said anything to Paléologue about Armenian desires for Cilicia, the matter was discussed with the ambassador by Baron Schilling, Sazonov's faithful Chief of Chancellery, just as Paléologue's train was about to return to Petrograd on March 17. However, Schilling made only an oblique reference to Cilicia, remarking only of "the desirability, at the time of the future partition of Asia Minor, of not depriving Turkey of some sort of suitable port on the Mediterranean Sea, in order not to create out of her a have-not state, cut off from the open sea by the Straits, which must come into our possession." He was mainly concerned with the "unfortunate impression" produced on Russia by "the difference between the statements made to us by England and France relative to the Straits and Constantinople." Though Russia had expected to encounter stiff opposition in London, Britain had given "the most positive assurances," while France had limited herself to "expressions of sympathy." On the next day (March 18), Sazonov ordered Izvolskii to tell Delcassé that "the Imperial Government desires that the French Government, following the example of the British Government, make more precise declarations on the subject of its assent to the complete realization of our desires."[58]

In Paris, Delcassé told Izvolskii on March 17 that he was very satisfied with Sazonov's reply to the French request for Syria and Cilicia. As for Palestine, he modified Paléologue's blanket demand by remarking that he would probably insist only on the possession of "some localities or other which form a part of it." He fully agreed with Sazonov that the question of the Holy Places required special and more attentive consideration. Three days later (March 20), he said that as far as he knew, Paléologue's declaration on the subject of Constantinople and the Straits

The Russian Struggle for Power, 1914–1917

had been identical to Buchanan's. However, he had no objections to a more definite statement but would have to discuss the matter with the French cabinet.[59]

Despite these promises, it took Delcassé nearly three weeks to pry out of his colleagues consent to another promise to Russia, and even so, Izvolskii had to prod him again. Despite the strict French censorship, which forbade newspaper polemics on Constantinople and the Straits, the opponents of the agreement were powerful and well-entrenched. They included all those who had financial interests in Turkey, as well as Poincaré, President of the Republic, and Bompard, former ambassador in Constantinople, who, in the words of Izvolskii, were "impregnated with the secular traditions of French policy in the Orient." A great deal was made of the fact that Russia was not taking part in the campaign to capture Constantinople and the Straits. However, Delcassé finally triumphed, and on April 10, Paléologue presented the following *note verbale* to Sazonov:

The Government of the Republic acquiesces in the memorandum presented by His Excellency, the

The Russian Struggle for Power, 1914–1917

Russian Ambassador in Paris, to M. Delcassé on March 6/19 of this year, on the subject of Constantinople and the Straits, with the reservation that the war end in final victory, and with the reservation of the realization by France and England of their projects in the East and elsewhere, in conformance with the Russian memorandum.[60]

AFTERMATH OF THE STRAITS AGREEMENT

The famous Straits Agreement was now a reality, after some thirty-seven days of bargaining, counting from Sazonov's note of March 4 to the second French note on April 10. Out of it, Britain and France had not come empty handed. Russia had promised Britain to maintain freedom of commerce in the Straits and a free port in Constantinople, while France had left the door open for a future demand for neutralization of the entire area. Britain had exacted promises which were likely to save Persia from future absorption by Russia and which were likely also to ease the future expansion of Greece in Asia Minor. Despite her desire to establish an Armenian client state, reaching the Mediterranean at Mersina and Alexandretta, Russia had conceded French possession of Cilicia, and had ob-

The Russian Struggle for Power, 1914-1917

jected only mildly to French plans of expansion in Syria and Palestine. It is certainly arguable that perhaps the Western Powers, after all, got the better of the bargain, insofar as the Straits Agreement was concerned.

That some Russians thought so, at any rate, is perhaps demonstrated by the desperate Russian efforts in the spring and summer of 1915 to make certain that they played a leading role in the occupation of Constantinople, in anticipation of its imminent capture by the British. Frantic demands upon the Stavka by Sazonov finally led the Grand Duke to concentrate a small Russian force in Batum to take part in the expected occupation of the city. However, Sazonov was so embarrassed by its small size that he almost decided it should not be used, and ultimately it had to be sent to the Polish Front.[61]

The Russians were somewhat more successful in inter-Allied planning for the future civil authority in the Turkish capital, which went on from March to September, 1915, and which became so complicated that a special conference in Paris almost became necessary. Sazonov at first wanted Russia to take over completely the heart of Constantinople, leaving the Pera and Galata quarters north of the Golden Horn to the French, and the Asiatic suburbs to the British. At Delcassé's insistence, however, he finally agreed that Constantinople should be ruled by three civilian High Commissioners, one each from the three major Allies, until the signing of the peace treaty, and that the Turkish bureaucracy and economic institutions (in which France had a large vested interest) should be left intact until that time. Later, Sazonov wanted the High Commissioners subjected to a Military Commandant, who would be the senior commander of the Allied Occupation Corps who had been longest in grade. Delcassé also repulsed this suggestion, successfully.[62]

Prince G.N. Trubetskoi, the ambassador to Serbia, was selected on April 12 to be the future Russian High Commissioner in Constantinople. However, he was reluctant to accept, and during a visit to Petrograd in May and June, explained that he feared he would be perpetually outvoted on the proposed Allied High Commission. He changed his mind only after the British and French agreed that if there was a

The Russian Struggle for Power, 1914–1917

division of votes on the High Commission, the matter in dispute would be turned over to the Allied governments for settlement.[63]

Ironic all this may seem now, but in the spring of 1915, it appeared that Turkey would surely collapse in a short time. The British had landed in Mesopotamia on November 22, 1914, taking Basra; after repulsing a Turkish counter-attack in mid-April, 1915, they began a general offensive towards Baghdad. To the north, in April, the Turks began the deportation and massacre of the Armenians, accused of helping the Russian enemy. An Armenian revolt broke out in Van (April 20), which held out against a Turkish siege until it was relieved by the advancing Russians on May 19. A Turkish attack on the Suez Canal was easily repulsed in early February, and on April 25, the British landed in force on Gallipoli.

In late March, the British were giving attention to the problem of establishing some independent Moslem power in Asia, and were considering sponsorship of an Arab Khalifate, with headquarters in Mecca. For this reason, Grey was disgruntled over the French demands for

Syria, Palestine, and Cilicia, and considered premature any discussion of the future of Arab territories.[64] However, he still hoped to secure the cooperation of Greece, and on April 13, repeated the offer of Smyrna and adjacent regions to Premier Gounaris. The latter, preferring to wait for a sure sign of Allied victory, declined the offer.[65]

The evidence of Franco-British differences over the future of Asiatic Turkey caused Sazonov to make discreet efforts to change the minds of the French about Cilicia. On April 17, he sent a Russian Armenian, Dr. Zavirev, to Paris and London to plead the cause of Armenian nationalism. Zavirev brought with him a plan for an autonomous Armenia, nominally under Turkish suzerainty, but actually under the joint protection of Russia, Britain, and France. It would include six existing Turkish vilayets and extend from Transcaucasia to the Mediterranean, embracing Mersina and Alexandretta. Later, after an anxious telegram from Izvolskii, Sazonov gave strict orders that no official Russian support be given to the plan, which was to be represented entirely as an Armenian idea.[66]

The Russian Struggle for Power, 1914–1917

Delcassé took a dim view of the whole idea, though some French officials seemed inclined towards leaving Mersina and Adana to the Armenians, while keeping Alexandretta for France. The Armenians appear to have then tried to interest the French in Kurdistan, instead of Cilicia. As later events seem to indicate, they only whetted French appetites, without achieving their objective. Consequently, the Russians withdrew increasingly into the background, insofar as the whole business was concerned, and began to think in terms of another solution to the Armenian problem.[67]

PRELUDE TO ITALIAN INTERVENTION

Meanwhile, the Russians were paying for the Straits Agreement in Europe, and paying a far more grievous price than they had had to pay in Asia. Not only did they have to sacrifice South Slavic interests to Italy; by admitting Italy to the ranks of the Allied Powers, they had to face the prospect of satisfying another ally with a greedy appetite for Turkish territory, and a frankly stated attitude of opposition to Russian claims at the Straits.

It took the Italians just ten days after the first British salvoes sounded in the Dardanelles to make up their minds to join the Allies. Germany might be able to compel Austria to return *Italia Irredenta*, but the Italians were far too sophisticated to imagine that Germany could possibly guarantee them any gains at Turkey's expense. On March 1, the Italian ambassador in Bucharest was talking excitedly to his Russian colleague about the necessity of an immediate Allied invitation to Italy that she intervene in return for "possible gains . . . on the shore of the Adriatic Sea, and . . . her participation in the eventual partition of the Turkish inheritance." He also babbled about gaining Tunisian territory from France, and of how an Italian army of 1,300,000 men was ready to advance on Dalmatia and Vienna.[68]

Sazonov's reaction was prompt. On March 2, he told Buchanan and Paléologue that Italian help had lost the better part of its value. However, he was most concerned about the possibility that Italian collaboration would make the peace negotiations more difficult:

The Russian Struggle for Power, 1914–1917

The intimate confidence which reigns among the three Allied Powers is the very principle of their strength. If a fourth Power mixed itself in their concert, would it not be necessary to fear that the latter would seek to disunite them for its personal benefit?[69]

He therefore wanted to decline Italian help, in a friendly fashion, if it were offered. A Foreign Ministry memorandum drawn up on the same day shows that he also feared Italian demands for "very significant territorial gains," and was determined that if Italy wanted to enter the war, she must herself initiate negotiations.[70]

Most likely, Sazonov was at first more fearful of the Italians' ambitions with respect to Turkey than of their claims to South Slavic lands. In reporting the reigning excitement in Rome on March 3, the Russian ambassador indicated that

. . . they fear more and more that Italy, whose interests in Asia Minor are considerable and of the first importance will be forgotten at the time of the liquidation of the Ottoman Empire . . . . The fear that Italy will remain outside the settlement of the fate of the Ottoman Empire is winning many partisans to armed intervention.[71]

On the same day, Delcassé was defending the idea of Italian intervention to Izvolskii by pointing out how much it might help the Dardanelles campaign. At the same time, he talked about locking Germany and Austria in a "vise of steel" and crushing them before August.[72]

Grey took the same position, stating on March 3 that he could not see how Italian collaboration could be "a danger for the mutual confidence and harmony which exist between the three Allies," and expressing the fear that Germany might propose "interesting conditions" to Italy, if her help were declined. At the same time, he sought to remove Sazonov's fears by stating that

If Italy or some other Power should submit her cooperation to requirements capable from the Russian viewpoint of preventing the resolution of the question of the Straits and Constantinople in favor of Russia, England and France could associate themselves with Russia in declining these conditions; granted the obligations in force, there could not be established any condition for the participation of any Power whatever, except after deliberation, and according to an agreement between France, England, and Russia.[73]

The Russian Struggle for Power, 1914–1917

This caused Sazonov to yield. On March 5 (the day after his demand for the Straits), he withdrew his opposition to Italian collaboration, so long as it did not take place in the Straits or in southern Dalmatia. However, on March 7, he was insisting that it was not necessary to offer Italy all that had been offered seven months before, that Italy must initiate negotiations, and that she must be required to fight Austria-Hungary as well as Turkey.[74]

ITALIAN OFFER AND RUSSIAN COUNTER-OFFER

Three days later, on March 10, Marquis Imperiali, the Italian ambassador in London, offered his country's collaboration to Sir Edward Grey. Paris and Petrograd were informed promptly.[75]

Imperiali stated his terms with the greatest candor. Italy was ready to go to war with Austria-Hungary and Turkey in April, and with Germany too, if the Allies wished. There must be an agreement promising no separate peace, and the Allies must agree to keep a certain number of military and naval forces engaged against Austria-Hungary. They must also promise that no representative of the Pope would be admitted to future peace negotiations, in order to prevent any discussion of the status of the city of Rome.

The heart of the proposal, however, was the list of territorial demands. Italy wanted all that was offered in August, 1914—plus much more. Her boundary must be pushed up to the Brenner Pass by the annexation of the Trentino and the Italian Tyrol. In addition, she wanted to control, in one way or another, nearly all of the eastern shore of the Adriatic, from her 1915 boundary to the borders of Greece. She must annex outright Trieste, all of Istria as far as the Quarnero, with Volosca and the offshore islands. She must also annex Dalmatia, from its northern boundary as far south as the Narenta River, and in addition, the islands lying off the entire Dalmatian coast, as well as the peninsula of Sabbioncello, south of the Narenta. Finally, she must annex not only the Albanian port of Valona, with the island of Saseno, but also a strip of Albanian coast from the Voiussa River south to Khimara.

Italy demanded that an abbreviated Moslem

Albanian state remain in existence, and that it retain control of the port of Durazzo and of the coast from the Drin River to the Voiussa. She was willing that the Croatians have the Adriatic coast from Volosca to the northern border of Dalmatia, but without the offshore islands. She was willing that the Serbs and Montenegrins have the coast of Dalmatia south of the Narenta, and the coast of Albania north of the Drin, but without the offshore islands. She was willing that Greece have the short strip of Albanian coast south of Khimara. But she demanded that, of the coast assigned to Serbia and Montenegro, the Bay of Kotor and all the coast south of it, as well as all the coast assigned to Albania and Greece, be neutralized.

In effect, then, Italy was not seeking to deny the South Slavs an exit to the Adriatic. This they would have, in the important ports of Rijeka (Fiume), Dubrovnik (Ragusa), Kotor (Cattaro), Antivari, and San Giovanni di Medua. What she sought to deny them was the possibility of becoming naval Powers. In possession of the offshore islands, she could easily bottle up Rijeka and Dubrovnik. And the most important potential naval base on the Adriatic—Kotor—would be neutralized.

As for the Ottoman Empire, Italy demanded recognition of her rights to the Dodecanese. She also demanded the right to occupy the port of Adalia in southern Anatolia in case other Ottoman territory was occupied, and the right to annex it, in case the Ottoman Empire was partitioned.

Grey assured France and Russia that the offer had been "unsolicited and without any suggestion" on his part. Certain of its conditions seemed to him "excessive," but after all, "considerable offers" had been made by the Germans. Therefore, the offer must not be rejected, but met with a counter-proposal or criticism, and an early answer must be given.[76]

On the day of the delivery of the proposal, Marquis Carlotti had an important conversation with Baron Schilling. While insisting that "the independence and prosperity of Serbia" was a matter of first-rate importance to Italy, he said that Italy was worried by increasing signs that Russia had come to favor a merger of the Serbians and Croatians. For Italy, he frankly de-

The Russian Struggle for Power, 1914-1917

clared, "the creation of a great and strong Yugo-Slav state on the shores of the Adriatic would hardly be acceptable, . . . not only because such a state will compete with Italy herself, but also because it will easily be made into an advance post on the Adriatic of a still stronger power, that is, Russia." Denying direct Russian interest in a Serbo-Croatian merger, Schilling nevertheless conceded that Russia would sympathize with it, if it was desired by the interested parties. At the same time, he warned Carlotti that "excessive Italian claims in the direction of Croatia and Dalmatia can lead Italy on a dangerous path, and put her in the same position in which Austria has found herself up to now, and which is leading the latter before our eyes to destruction." As a matter of fact, by trying to gain Dalmatia, Sonnino was driving the Croatians into the arms of Serbia.[77]

After this conversation, it is not surprising that on March 15 (two days after receipt of the British response to the Straits note), Sazonov recommended to the Tsar that all of the Italian demands except those with respect to Dalmatia be met. The part of that province lying north of the Kerki River, and including the cities of Zara and Šibenik, along with the offshore islands, must be assigned to Croatia, and the rest of Dalmatia, including the offshore islands, to Serbia or Montenegro. Moreover, Russia could not agree to the neutralization of any of the coast assigned to the South Slavs, especially the Bay of Kotor. However, Sazonov predicted, Britain and France would not support this counteroffer, "since for them the interests of the Slavs on the Adriatic seem secondary in comparison with the advantage of attracting Italy to the struggle against Austria-Hungary." Therefore, the part of Dalmatia which Russia wanted Croatia to have might be sacrificed to Italy, but not the rest, including the Bay of Kotor.[78] The Tsar approved this course of action, and Sazonov promptly demanded that Dalmatia be given to Croatia, Serbia, and Montenegro. He also demanded that Kotor, allotted to Montenegro, not be neutralized.[79]

To Sazonov's evident surprise, Grey seemed willing on March 18 to support his objections and asked Italy to review her claims with respect to Dalmatia and, if possible, "to find some means

The Russian Struggle for Power, 1914-1917

of ascertaining the desiderata of the Yugoslav leaders." Delcassé also objected to some features of the Italian proposal, including the provision for an independent Albania, but was anxious not to delay Italy's entrance. Sazonov thereupon suggested that Italy be offered a choice of annexing most of Albania or taking the northern part of Dalmatia.[80]

GREY AND IMPERIALI

Grey and Imperiali began negotiations in London on March 20. Grey presented as strongly as he could the Russian objections to Italy's Dalmatian demands, and Imperiali reported back to Rome. At a second meeting, on March 24, the ambassador insisted that the original demands must be met. Italy's desire "to free herself once and for all from the unbearable position of inferiority in the Adriatic vis-à-vis Austria-Hungary" was one of her main reasons for wanting to intervene in the war. She could achieve her other desiderata without fighting, and in any case, would not fight "merely in order to substitute Slav for Austrian predominance in the Adriatic."[81]

Grey capitulated, and sent to Paris and Petrograd a proposed text of a treaty in which the Italian demands were accepted in full. He explained that he thought Italy was fearful of some hostile power stationing submarines in the Dalmatian islands, and would accept no settlement which did not give her effective control of the Adriatic. Therefore, the Allies must accept her terms or forego her cooperation. He thought Italian cooperation would be the turning point of the war, since it would lead to intervention by Rumania and other neutral states.

To be sure, Grey sugar-coated the pill with three conditions. Italy must join in the agreement of September 5, 1914 and make war on Germany as well as on Austria-Hungary and Turkey. She must sign the alliance immediately, and arrange for the cooperation of her armed forces in consultation with the Allies. Finally, she must agree to make Split (Spalato) a free port for Serbia and any territories acquired by Serbia.

Owing to public discussion of Italy's attitude, Grey feared a new German counter-offer; therefore it was highly desirable that "we should close with Italy." British military authorities were "most strongly in favour of concluding this agreement with Italy without delay."[82]

SAZONOV VERSUS GREY

The Straits Agreement was just ten days old, but Sazonov decided to make some sort of a stand, in hope of yet gaining concessions. He recognized that Italy could draw other states into the war, but thought this did not justify a "complete capitulation." He pointed out that one of the causes of the war was Austria's continuous attempts to "hold up the development of Serbia by depriving her of an outlet to the sea;" therefore, if the Allies wanted a durable peace, they must not put Serbia and Montenegro at Italy's mercy. The absolute limit of his concessions was Italian possession of Dalmatia from Zara to Cape Planca and the independence of Albania. As for the need for haste, the Allies ought to recognize that Italy wanted the negotiations to succeed, since, if Germany and Austria-Hungary learned that they had failed, they would never agree to make any concessions themselves.[83]

On March 15, Delcassé (from whom Sazonov now wanted a stronger affirmation of the Straits Agreement) told Izvolskii that a critical moment in the negotiations had come. He believed that Serbia was gaining as many concessions in Dalmatia as her sacrifices required, and he gave first-rank importance to Italian intervention, which he expected to be followed by that of Rumania, Bulgaria, and Greece. He wanted Grey to decide how much Serbia should get in Dalmatia.[84]

On the same day, to back up his arguments, Rumania made her long-awaited bid for a place in the ranks of the Allies. Grey feared that her attitude depended on that of Italy, and said he thought that "at the present moment the situation is critical, extraordinarily important, and demands great care." However, he now thought that Italy might concede to Serbia Split and the coast to the south, so long as it was neutralized, and Italy kept the offshore islands.[85]

Nevertheless, Sazonov was still stubborn on March 26, and insisted Serbia must have Dalmatia from Cape Planca to the future frontier of Montenegro, including the offshore islands.

The Russian Struggle for Power, 1914-1917

He began to talk of Russian "public opinion" and said Italy would only see a sign of weakness in an "excessively conciliatory attitude."[86]

Further exchanges between Sazonov and Grey took place on March 28, 29 and 30. Grey feared a break-off in negotiations as soon as Italy heard of Russia's views. He thought that Sazonov was not taking account of the defenselessness of the Italian coast before a submarine attack, and of the likelihood that a merger of Serbia, Croatia, and Montenegro would produce a Slavic power stronger than Austria-Hungary. In reply, Sazonov pointed out that Serbia had no fleet in being. However, he was ready with a new compromise: let Italy and Serbia divide Dalmatia, but insist that all of it be neutralized. At the same time, he expressed the view that Italy would be less irreconcilable "if Grey would display more firmness in the negotiations." Later, he suggested that no definite boundaries be established in the disputed area until after the war. At the same time, he pointed out that he was willing to support Britain and France in opposing excessive Italian demands in Asia and Africa and expected a *quid pro quo* in Europe, especially since he was willing to sacrifice Croatian and Slovene interests to Italy. He warned that the Allies were about to alienate the Slavs of Austria-Hungary, by putting them "under the Italian domination, which would be for them only a new yoke, perhaps more severe than the old one."[87]

Grey was not impressed, and insisted that Italy must have the offshore islands, the peninsula of Sabbioncello, and neutralization of the future Serbo-Montenegrin coast. Imperiali had received new instructions which he described as his "last word," and there were rumors that Austria was about to compensate Italy in return for German concessions in Bavaria and Silesia. Grey felt that Serbia had no reason to complain, since she would receive a three-fold increase in territory and an exit to the Adriatic. He could not see why it was necessary to risk prolonging the war in order to give Serbia a small coastal strip and a few offshore islands, and thought the British cabinet was going to have to consider the matter. Later, he argued that he was agreeable to the extension of Serbia at the expense of the Banat of Temesvar, to strengthen Belgrade, and that this was more important than any coastal strip Serbia might receive.[88]

Meanwhile, Delcassé (at that moment fighting for the Straits Agreement before the French cabinet) sent a sizzling message to Petrograd. Its contents may be judged by the fact that on March 30, he told Izvolskii he hoped negotiations would not be broken off over a question "of secondary importance." He insisted that the intervention of Italy would not only be followed by the intervention of Rumania, Bulgaria, and Greece, but would also produce a great moral impression in Austria-Hungary and Germany, and cut the length of the war in half. France, he said, had four million men under arms, and her richest departments were occupied; she would not understand the loss of Italy over a secondary question.[89]

This message brought Sazonov to heel, for on March 31, he agreed that Italy might have four large islands off the future Serbo-Montenegrin coast. However, this concession was conditioned on the neutralization of all Dalmatia and a promise that Italy would attack Austria before the end of April. At the same time, he demanded that Russia, Britain, and France fix the Italo-Serb boundary in Dalmatia. He was very upset and wired Benckendorff that he feared Britain and France were diverting Italian pretensions from Africa and Asia Minor by being conciliatory in Dalmatia. If he had expected that negotiations would be conducted by Grey in this manner, he would never have agreed that they take place in London. He described Grey as "the friendly protector of undivided Italian rule on the Adriatic" and feared that Russian "public opinion" was about to turn against Great Britain.[90]

THE ASQUITH COMPROMISE

After Sazonov's concession of March 31, the negotiations began to move forward, but when Grey left London on April 1 for a short vacation in the country, Delcassé took it as a sign that negotiations were broken off, and became tremendously excited. Pointing out to Izvolskii that Grey was offering Serbia a coast three hundred

The Russian Struggle for Power, 1914–1917

kilometers long, he claimed to fear that Germany was about to reach an agreement with Italy and Rumania over the partition of Austria-Hungary.[91]

However, these fears were unjustified. In Rome, Sonnino was being reasonable. Though he thought it did not comport with Italy's Great Power position to neutralize anything she might acquire, he would agree to neutralize the peninsula of Sabbioncello. At the same time, he gave assurances that Italy did not intend to establish any naval bases or fortifications in Dalmatia or Albania; rather, she proposed to make Pola or one of the Istrian islands her main stronghold for the defense of the Adriatic. At the same time, he pointed out, he was not asking that Rijeka (Fiume) or the Croatian coast as far as Zara be neutralized. Grey was very impressed with this concession, and, in urging that Sazonov accept it, pointed out that Britain and France had agreed to Russian desires relative to Constantinople and the Straits. From London, Benckendorff warned Sazonov of the dangers of being too stubborn, and raised the spectre of the fall of the existing pro-Russian governments in Britain and France.[92]

While Grey was on his week-end vacation, British Prime Minister Asquith handled the negotiations, and on April 2, proposed that Italy agree to neutralize the four islands conceded by Sazonov as well as Sabbioncello, in return for an additional island. Though grateful that Asquith had taken over the negotiations, Sazonov presented an alternative. He was now willing that Italy have five islands, instead of four, and that she not be required to neutralize anything except Sabbioncello. On the other hand, he now wanted only partial neutralization of the Serbian coast and no neutralization of the Montenegrin coast (which would include the great potential naval base of Kotor).[93]

On the same day (April 4), Sonnino was expressing to Sir Rennell Rodd his frank fears that after Russia had acquired Constantinople and the Straits, she would become, as a Mediterranean naval power, a menace to Italy. The reason he was insisting on the neutralization of the Dalmatian islands was the belief that they could be turned into Russian submarine or naval bases, if they were handed over to Serbia and Montenegro. At the same time, Carlotti was telling the Russians that Italy was about to break off negotiations, and Asquith was appealing to Sazonov to find some way out of the dilemma. Sazonov therefore asked the Stavka if he should sacrifice more Serbian interests for Italian military support.[94]

An affirmative reply came from Grand Duke Nikolai on April 5. On the same day, Delcassé came forward with a proposed compromise. Serbia would receive Sabbioncello, and Italy, the disputed islands; Sabbioncello would be neutralized, and Italy not be required to neutralize her coast. In presenting the proposals, Delcassé had warned that a break-off in negotiations would be a "true disaster." At the same time, President Poincaré appealed to Nicholas II, and on April 6, the latter ordered Sazonov to agree to Delcassé's proposal. If it did not work, Sabbioncello might be conceded, provided it was neutralized, and provided Italy intervened no later than the end of April.[95]

However, this concession left the Russians still free to push for the non-neutralization of the Bay of Kotor, and the territory just to the north, which they proceeded to do. There is strong evidence that at this point, they were considering the possibility of using Kotor later as a base for their Navy.[96]

By April 10, Asquith had worked out a general compromise solution which did not meet Russian desires with respect to Kotor, but which was more favorable to Serbia than the original Italian offer. Italy would now receive Dalmatia from Zara to Cape Planca, and all the off-shore islands except one; none of these gains would be neutralized. Serbia would receive the remainder of the Dalmatian coast, plus Sabbioncello and the island of Braz; however, all this must be neutralized except the coast around Dubrovnik (Ragusa). Italy accepted this compromise on April 15, with some minor changes designed to assure that Kotor would indeed be neutralized. However, she now wanted other changes in her original proposals, including firm guarantees of an independent Moslem, Albanian state, and the right to delay her entrance until a month after the signing of the treaty.[97]

Sazonov consented on April 15 to the settlement of the Dalmatian problem, but balked at the proposals regarding Albania. He was willing that a Moslem state exist in central Albania as a virtual Italian protectorate. However, he wanted Greece to have southern Albania; Montenegro, northern Albania, including Scutari, San Giovanni di Medua, and Alessio; and Serbia, enough of eastern Albania to guarantee her a common frontier with Greece. At the same time, he refused to agree to any delay in Italy's entrance.[98]

He repeated his refusal on April 16, but after another appeal from President Poincaré to the Tsar, agreed that Italy might delay her entrance until May 15, provided she adhered to the Allies before May 1. Later, on April 18, he submitted further conditions. The treaty must indicate that Italy had to conquer whatever territories she received. The southern limit of her Dalmatian gains must be mentioned only in general terms. Montenegro's 1914 coast, and the islands near Dubrovnik (Ragusa) must not be neutralized. The rights of the Serbs, Croatians, and Montenegrins, and the existence of the future Moslem Albania, must be guaranteed by the treaty.

None of these stipulations was accepted. Ultimately, on April 19, Sazonov had to agree to let Italy delay entrance for a month after the treaty was signed. However, on April 22, while sending Benckendorff authority to sign the treaty, he produced some new stipulations. There must be a guarantee that the Straits Agreement would not be affected by Italian intervention. Though it appeared that Montenegro had accepted certain restrictions relative to her coast in 1909, no other restrictions must be placed on her 1914 coast. Finally, Russia assumed that all parts of Austria-Hungary's and Albania's coasts and islands not expressly assigned to Italy and the future Moslem Albania were reserved for Croatia, Serbia, Montenegro and Greece.[99]

At the same time, he expressed the belief that the treaty was "in all respects extremely unfortunate" and said he was signing it only "under the insistent pressure of our Allies." Grey's method of conducting the negotiations had left a "painful impression"; the demands of Imperiali had "not once met with a proper rebuff from him"; in fact, he had fortified Imperiali's obstinacy. The articles of the treaty had been worked out by Grey and Paul Cambon, French ambassador in London, and presented to him as *faits accomplis*. If Anglo-Franco-Russian negotiations on the peace terms had taken such a turn, what must be expected from negotiations in which Italy would now join?[100]

Grey defended himself warmly, pointing out that he had gained concessions from Italy for Serbia. Moreover, he had never discussed Constantinople and the Straits with Italy, and was ready to reaffirm the Straits Agreement. He had been willing to make concessions to Italy in African questions, and to sacrifice British interests in Smyrna and Cyprus to win over Greece to the Allies. He had asked nothing for Britain except Egypt, over which Britain had had a protectorate for thirty years. In any case, the concessions in the Adriatic had not been at Russia's expense, and even so, the South Slavic peoples had obtained the greater part of their aspirations.[101]

The Russian Struggle for Power, 1914–1917

THE TREATY OF LONDON AND YUGO-SLAV PROTESTS

Even after April 22, there was still some haggling between Petrograd and London regarding the rights of Montenegro over her 1914 coast. However, by April 26, the Treaty of London was ready to be signed.[102]

For entering the war against the Central Powers, Italy was promised the following: the Trentino, the Cisalpine Tyrol, Trieste, the counties of Gorizia and Gradisca, Istria and the Istrian islands, Dalmatia from its northern boundary to Cape Planca and all the Dalmatian islands except five near Rijeka (Fiume), and seven lying south of Split. She was also promised Saseno, Valona, and the coast of Albania from the Voiussa to Khimara, and the Dodecanese Islands.

The treaty reserved for Croatia, Serbia, and Montenegro the following: the coast from the borders of Istria to those of Dalmatia, all of Dalmatia from Cape Planca southward, the coast of Albania from the mouth of the Drin northward, and the Dalmatian islands not given to Italy. However, all of both the Dalmatian and Albanian coasts assigned to the South Slavs must be neutralized except a small strip around Dubrovnik (Ragusa). All the islands awarded to the South Slavs were to be neutralized.

The treaty considered the possibility of a small Moslem Albanian state being left around Durazzo. If this happened, Italy would not oppose the partition of the rest of the country between Serbia, Greece, and Montenegro. However, whatever became of Albania, all of its coastline except that ceded to Italy must be neutralized. If an Albanian state was left, Italy would be charged with its foreign relations. In turn, Italy conceded that Serbia and Greece must have a common frontier west of Lake Okhrida.

Italy's rights to the province of Adalia in Asia Minor were recognized, in case of the breakup of the Ottoman Empire. She was also promised colonial gains in Africa, in case Britain and France took the German colonies there.[103]

The treaty was signed by Grey, Benckendorff, Imperiali, and Paul Cambon on April 26. On the same day, the same four men created the new

Quadruple Alliance by signing an agreement providing against the conclusion of a separate peace. Its text was the same as that signed by Russia, Britain, and France on September 5, 1914. Finally, Grey, Benckendorff, and Cambon exchanged notes recognizing that all agreements signed by Britain, France, and Russia prior to Italy's adherence to the Allied Powers, remained in effect.[104]

While negotiations were in their final stages, anguished wails of protest reached Petrograd from the centers of Yugoslavism. On April 11, there had taken place in Trieste the first official meeting of sixteen Slovene and Croatian representatives of the largest parties of Trieste, Istria, Gorizia, Carinthia, Croatia, and Slavonia. These leaders, who included members of the Catholic clergy, accepted a program calling for the autonomy of the Croatians and Slovenes under the Crown of Serbia. It was decided that at a suitable time, a proclamation would be issued on the subject. It would state that the Croatians and Slovenes would never exchange the rule of Hungary for that of Italy and would oppose subjection to Italy by force.[105]

The Russian Struggle for Power, 1914-1917

Pashich told Trubetskoi in Nish on April 27 that the question of concessions to the pretensions of Italy was causing increasing concern in Serbia. Prince-Regent Alexander and the cabinet were urging that he go personally to Petrograd to plead the Serb cause, especially since Rumanian pretensions to the Banat of Temesvar were also a matter of concern. On April 28, Pashich wired Sazonov that he had been asked by the leaders of the Serbs, Croatians, and Slovenes under Austro-Hungarian rule to protest the sacrifice of their interests to Italy. They had informed him that they preferred Austro-Hungarian to Italian rule, and that they would fight the Italian army if it entered their country.[106]

However, Sazonov saw no reason to cry over spilt milk, especially since he was now girding his loins for a battle with the Rumanians in behalf of both Serbian and Russian interests. When Pashich complained again to Trubetskoi on April 29, the latter answered sharply that the Serbs presented many requests, and that Russia would do and had done as much as was possible to satisfy them. Pashich was then calmer, and assured the ambassador that the Serbs believed that Russia would not sacrifice them to Italy, nor permit the formation of an independent Croatian kingdom. However, he was concerned about the upcoming negotiations with Rumania. It would appear that despite his protests, he did not know at this time exactly what had been promised to Italy.[107]

V

THE COLLAPSE OF RUSSIAN POWER IN EASTERN EUROPE
(MAY–DECEMBER, 1915)

NEGOTIATIONS ATTENDING the Straits Agreement and the Treaty of London had made it apparent that the Russians were not likely to get all they wanted out of the First World War. After they were concluded, the Russians began to face the sombre prospect of getting nothing out of the war, indeed, of losing something of what they had had in 1914. This was because the Germans started their Gorlice offensive a week after the signing of the Treaty of London, marking the beginning of a series of Russian disasters unequalled since the Crimean War.

All the power, prestige, and authority which a century and a half of diplomacy and war had won for the Tsars in Eastern Europe collapsed, as the German juggernaut pushed eastward to the Western Dvina, the Pripet Marshes, and the headwaters of the Dniester. After that, Bulgaria's adherence to Germany and the crushing of Serbia, Montenegro, and Albania were not only inevitable, but anti-climactic. It was small comfort that any designs the Western Powers may have had on Constantinople and the Straits ended with the failure of the Gallipoli campaign, and that the Italians could not push beyond the Isonzo, much less into Dalmatia. Even so, it was necessary to recognize after the landings in Salonika that the Western Powers had become the surrogates of what was left of Russian influence in the Balkans.

However, despite the sound of Prussian jackboots goose-stepping through Warsaw, Vilna, Belgrade, and Sofia, Sazonov kept up the Russian struggle for power throughout the last seven months of 1915, while weathering a severe internal crisis which foreshadowed either a separate peace by a reactionary Russian government or an internal revolution. Russia might be forced out of Warsaw, but discussion of the future Polish constitution continued. Russia might be forced out of Bukovina, but she kept haggling

The Russian Struggle for Power, 1914-1917

over its division with Rumania. Serbia might be in danger of destruction, but her rights in the Banat of Temesvar and Croatia must be upheld.

Sazonov was right, of course. Germany might win many battles, but what mattered was who won the war. Britain and France had promised Constantinople and the Straits, despite Russia's inability to help in conquering them, and if Germany failed in the West, Russia could still count on realizing her principal war aims. All depended on whether Russia could face up to defeat and see the war through. When the worst seemed over by December, it was possible to breathe a bit easier.

THE POLISH PROJECT OF MARCH 3 AND THE OPENING OF THE GERMAN OFFENSIVE

The dreary Russo-German winter campaign of 1914-15 ended between February 22 and 27 in the important Russian victory of Przasnysz, won between Kovno and Grodno. Now that the Germans were halted, extra exertions on the Southwestern Front were possible, and they led, at long last, to the fall of Przemysl on March 22. The Austrians were wiped out north of the Carpathians, and plans for a trans-Carpathian campaign, ending in Budapest, were eagerly discussed at the Stavka.[1]

It seemed to be time to discuss Poland again, especially since a new, pro-Polish, Governor-General of Warsaw, Prince Engalychev, arrived in the Polish capital in February. Even the rabidly reactionary Count Bobrinskii, Military Governor-General of Galicia, was won over to a pro-Polish position by Professor Stanislaw Grabski of the University of Lvov, destined later to be a Polish Premier. Bobrinskii urged the government to make more definite promises to the Poles (February 12).[2]

The same plea was made to Goremykin by the Grand Duke on February 23, and shortly afterwards, official orders were sent by the Tsar. The Council of Ministers was to "examine again minutely the concluding part of the memorandum of the Council of Ministers on the Polish Question . . . [of November 28, 1914], in order to establish finally the bases of the political system of the future Polish Region, which could then be published to the Polish population by means of a special act, for example, in the form of a

Most Gracious rescript to the Governor-General of Warsaw." The Council was further directed to give to the "so-called Polish Question . . . as much definiteness as is possible under present conditions." Polish public opinion was "to receive a clear answer to its questions on the future fate of the Polish Region."[3]

By March 3, the Council of Ministers had produced a new Polish project which did not differ in any essential respect from its predecessor. However, in discussions regarding it, it was obvious that a new spirit reigned. For example, the Governor-General of Warsaw was to be directed to remove immediately all restrictions on the Roman Catholic Church in Poland, and to introduce immediately a reform of Polish municipalities decreed on June 22, 1914, but suspended owing to the beginning of the war.[4]

The Tsar gave his approval to the March 3 project, and on April 20, ordered the Governor-General of Warsaw to meet him at Baranovichi. Engalychev, upon arriving at the Stavka, was directed to proceed on to Petrograd with certain orders to Goremykin. The latter was to draw up immediately an imperial rescript instituting the March 3 project, and another rescript instituting zemstvo institutions in Russian Poland.[5]

Meanwhile, a debate was going on in Germany between Falkenhayn, who wanted an attempt to reach a decision in France, and Hindenburg, who wanted to try to destroy the Russians in Poland. Hindenburg finally won, to the extent that a whole new army was sent to the Eastern Front. However, though Hindenburg wanted to attack the Russians from East Prussia, it was sent, at Falkenhayn's insistence, to help the hard-pressed Austrians to the south.

On May 3, the Germans and Austrians began an offensive which completely destroyed the Russian position in Galicia. The San River was reached in mid-May, and Przemysl was recaptured in June 3. Sweeping eastward, the Austro-Germans reentered Lvov on June 22. By the end of June, they had advanced a hundred miles and virtually retaken Galicia and Bukovina. Thereafter they paused, since it was feared that Bulgaria was about to join the Allies, and that a Balkan campaign would be necessary in order to save Turkey.[6]

The Russian Struggle for Power, 1914–1917

A Russian proclamation of Polish autonomy during these two ominous months might have helped a little, but the Russian reactionaries were now convinced that the liberation of Poland should be shelved indefinitely. On top of that, pro-Russian Poles insisted that the project of March 3 did not go far enough.

On May 10, possibly emboldened by the German offensive, Count Zygmunt Wielopolski, a Polish member of the Russian State Council, presented to Prince Engalychev a long memorial, deploring the terms of the project of March 3. It failed, he said, to indicate clearly what matters would be handled by the new institutions in Poland. The powers of the Viceroy and of the Polish Council in particular were unclear and indefinite. Moreover, insufficient recognition was given the Polish language; the rights of Poles to public office were still restricted; and the position given the Catholic church in Poland remained less than it ought to be. Only the new plan for Polish schools seemed satisfactory.[7]

These views were echoed in another memorial presented to the Governor-General by Count Wladislaw Wielopolski, brother of Zygmunt, on

June 1. Count Wladislaw insisted that the Galician Poles would suffer a net loss in autonomous rights if the project were pushed through, and demanded "a special legislative organ for questions connected exclusively with the local interests of Poland."[8]

Informed of these objections, the Tsar appointed a "Special Committee on the Question of the Structure of the Polish Region," which held its first meeting on June 3. Its membership consisted of Poles who were members either of the State Council or State Duma, including Zygmunt Wielopolski, I. C. Garusewicz, Roman V. Dmoski, E. E. Dobecki, L. K. Dymsza, and I. A. Szebeko, and of the reactionaries of the Council of Ministers, Goremykin, Maklakov, and Taube. In addition, Prince Engalychev and Professor V. F. Grabski were members.

Just what Nicholas hoped to accomplish by forming such a committee is not clear. Maklakov, along with the reactionary ministers Shcheglovitov and Sabler, opposed the whole idea of the committee. When it finally met, the Russian representatives were wholly unmoved by appeals from the Poles that a strong Poland

The Russian Struggle for Power, 1914-1917

was needed by Russia as a bulwark against German aggression, a somewhat tactless suggestion at the moment.[9]

After some two weeks of this, Maklakov, Shcheglovitov, and Sabler went to the Stavka to have a show-down with the Tsar. They demanded that the idea of Polish self-government be dropped, that a recent recall of the prorogued State Duma be revoked, and that peace be made with Germany. By tying the last of these demands to the first two, they ruined their cause, and by June 18, Maklakov had been dismissed as Minister of Internal Affairs.[10]

In the long run, however, he had achieved a partial triumph. A meeting of the entire Council of Ministers was held at Baranovichi between June 25 and 28. Shcheglovitov and Sabler insisted that autonomy of any part of the Empire was incompatible with the principle of autocracy, and Nicholas finally decided to appoint another committee to study the Polish question. It was headed by Goremykin and contained six Russians and six Poles, and it never seems to have met at all. Perhaps it was just as well, since between July and September, the Poles completely escaped Russian control for the first time in a century, and this made it possible, in the end, to work out a project of Polish autonomy far more generous than would have been accorded in 1914-15.[11]

THE STRAITS CAMPAIGN, GREECE, AND BULGARIA

Meanwhile, things were not going well for the British at the Straits. Naval bombardment of the Dardanelles on February 19 was followed by the occupation of Lemnos on February 23. However, a month later, on March 18, when Admiral de Robeck's squadron tried to force the narrows of the Dardanelles, four ships struck mines and were sunk. De Robeck retreated, somewhat prematurely. By the time the British were able to bring up 75,000 men, under Sir Ian Hamilton, to land on Gallipoli Peninsula (April 25), the Turks, under General Liman von Sanders, were entrenched behind impregnable defenses. The British troops could make no progress, and by May 12, hostile submarines were sinking British ships in the Straits. By early August, it was recognized that the first landings

The Russian Struggle for Power, 1914-1917

had failed, and that others would be necessary before success was in sight.[12]

After the attack was well underway, some consideration was given to calling upon Bulgaria for help, while every inducement was offered to the post-Venizelos government in Greece to cause it to move. It would appear that up to the end of May, the chances of help from both Balkan countries were good.

After the first naval attack on the Dardanelles, Radoslavov announced his intention of remaining neutral in case of a Graeco-Turkish war, unless Bulgaria's frontier was violated. He thought that Russian seizure of the Straits would pose a danger to all the Balkan countries, but nevertheless, predicted on March 6 that if the Allied fleet reached Constantinople, King Ferdinand would be obliged to appoint a pro-Russian cabinet.[13]

Ten days later (March 17), Radoslavov indicated confidentially to the Russian ambassador that he was seeking a rapprochement with Rumania and Greece, and that he intended to ask the latter for the Struma Valley, Kavalla, and Seres. Six months, or even four months before, the Russians would have welcomed such a move, but now all they could do was to suspect that it had something to do with a desire to block their possession of the Straits. Radoslavov hotly denied that it did.[14]

Between March 22 and April 1, a whole series of reports indicated an impending change in the Bulgarian government in favor of Russia. By April 5, a feeler was being sent out from Petrograd, to discover whether Bulgaria was now willing to join the Allies in return for "uncontested" Macedonia and Thrace to the Enos-Midiya line. No response was found in Sofia, but on April 14, the Russian ambassador was reporting that Bulgarian troops were preparing for a campaign in Thrace, and that the pro-Russian leaders gave assurances that their country would eventually join the Allies.[15]

Sazonov was ready on April 18 to reopen Bulgarian negotiations with the usual offer of "uncontested" Macedonia. However, before he could bring Paris and London around, the Bulgarians ruined everything by sending a horde of Macedonian guerrillas into Serbia. The Serbs

The Russian Struggle for Power, 1914-1917

were so incensed that on April 26 (by pure coincidence, the date the Treaty of London was signed), Pashich officially withdrew the offer of the Lakavitsa-Bregalnitsa triangle which he had made back in August, 1914. Sazonov chided him for this step, but it was obviously not a good time to renew the wrangle over Macedonia.[16]

Savinskii reported dolefully from Sofia on May 7 that the situation seemed actually to have changed little over the preceding two months. Opposition leaders pleaded with Radoslavov for immediate intervention, but the latter continued to complain of a lack of specific offers from the Allies, and of the attitude of King Ferdinand. The Bulgarian Premier, moreover, declined to accept the Allied view that he must make the first move towards reopening negotiations.[17]

Meanwhile, the new Greek Minister of Foreign Affairs, Zographos, was telling the Allies on March 13 that the Gounaris government differed from that of Venizelos only on the question of immediate Greek intervention. However, though disturbed about the future of Greek interests in Constantinople, he thought that new conditions might make Greek intervention possible.[18]

Two weeks later (March 27), Zographos announced that Greece would join the Allies after the fulfillment of conditions which would assure "the integrity of our territory and the defense of the rights of Hellenism." Greece was holding back only because of fear of Bulgaria and of the possible fate of the Greek population in Asia Minor. However, if Bulgaria joined the Allies, it was felt that the Anatolian Greeks could be saved by the Greek Army.[19]

The Allies told Zographos on April 4 that they were still willing to offer the Aydin Vilayet for immediate intervention, but the delay in accepting the offer would be fatal. However, they declined to indicate exact boundaries of the territory offered, for fear of offending the Italians, who were known to covet Smyrna.[20]

Zographos was obviously impressed, but on April 20, posed as an absolute condition of immediate Greek intervention an Allied guarantee of territorial integrity. Moreover, Greece could attack Turkey only if she was guaranteed against

The Russian Struggle for Power, 1914–1917

Bulgarian attack by an Allied contingent in the Aegean area.[21]

Finally, on May 4, the Greeks were ready to send their navy against Turkey, so long as their army remained available for use against Bulgaria. By May 12, they were ready to intervene so long as the Allies would promise that they would not be required to cede any territory to Bulgaria. However, it was still Allied policy to demand Kavalla in return for the Aydin Vilayet. Sir Francis Elliott, the British minister in Athens, now thought it time to shift the emphasis in negotiations with the Aegean states to Bulgaria. If she refused to fight Turkey in return for Kavalla and Thrace to the Enos-Midiya line, then the Allies must meet the Greek demand for a guarantee of territorial integrity. Sir Edward Grey agreed, and the stage was set for the last round of Allied negotiations with Bulgaria, which began at the end of May.[22]

THE RUMANIAN NEGOTIATIONS
(MAY–JULY, 1915)

In the meantime, flushed with the triumph of the Treaty of London, the Allies had begun a series of negotiations to bring about Rumanian intervention. The opening of the Dardanelles campaign had the same effect in Bucharest that it had had in Rome, Sofia, and Athens. Bratianu told Poklevskii on March 12 that he hoped Rumanian interests would be taken into account when the Straits were captured, and promised to invade Transylvania if the Russians entered it during their spring offensive. In any case, he said, Rumania would enter the war at the end of the spring, regardless of what Italy did.[23]

In the middle of April, the Rumanians were enquiring in London as to whether the British intended to give Serbia the Banat of Temesvar. When told that Grey wanted Serbia to have a small district north of Belgrade, they insisted that their future western boundary must be the Theiss River, thus extending their demands to include the Banat. Russia was informed by the British of these new demands. Then, on April 21, Poklevskii reported from Bucharest that in addition to the Banat, the Rumanians would probably demand Bukovina south of the Prut, as well as Transylvania.[24]

Meanwhile, in March and April, the Stavka

The Russian Struggle for Power, 1914–1917

continued the campaign it had begun in February for Russian possession of all of Bukovina and a part of Transylvania. The matter was brought to Sazonov's attention by the Grand Duke himself, during a visit of the Foreign Minister to the Stavka (March 15). Later, on March 20, Sazonov and three of his top subordinates discussed the matter in Petrograd with a colonel representing the Grand Duke. The diplomats insisted that future good relations with Rumania required adherence to the terms of the October 1–2, 1914 agreement. Not until after negotiations with Rumania actually began did the Stavka change its mind, mainly because, in the light of the German offensive, it desperately wanted Rumanian military help. The Grand Duke advised Sazonov on May 8 that it was necessary to hasten Rumania's entrance, and on May 11, in a conversation with Neratov at the Stavka, was willing to cede to Rumania Bukovina south of the Suchav (Suceava), provided Serbia received the southwestern corner of the Banat of Temesvar.[25]

The Foreign Ministry had been most disturbed in April by the signs that Rumania was trying to negotiate with the West, rather than with Russia, after the fashion of Italy. Sazonov insisted at this time that any Rumanian negotiations must be handled in Petrograd.[26]

On April 29, three days after the signing of the Treaty of London, the Rumanian ambassador to Russia, Diamandy, arrived in Petrograd after a short visit to Bucharest. He promptly tried to get a promise from Paléologue of French support in the future negotiations with Russia, but his request was turned down, on Delcassé's orders. At the same time, Grey refused to promise to support the Theiss boundary, and advised the Rumanians to consult Russia. Sazonov's complaints against the Treaty of London had had the desired effect.[27]

Having been rebuffed by the French and the British, the Rumanians turned to the Italians, who were willing to oblige. On April 28, Marquis Carlotti told the Russians that Rumania was ready to intervene if she were promised Bukovina to the Prut, Transylvania, and the Banat to the Theiss. Two days later, he urged the Russians to accept these terms, but was told

The Russian Struggle for Power, 1914–1917

that he should follow the example of the British and French ambassadors.[28]

Bratianu made his official offer to intervene on May 1. Carlotti had somewhat overstated his terms, since he actually demanded the Theiss as a western frontier only from its junction with the Danube to Szegedin. From the latter city, he wanted the frontier to bend eastward, away from the river, until it reached the junction of the Theiss and the Somesh (Somesul). On the other hand, all the worst fears of the Russians were confirmed, since Bratianu did want the entire Banat, the Prut frontier in Bukovina, and, what was infinitely worse, sub-Carpathian Ukraine, or Ruthenia (which later became a part of Czechoslovakia from 1918 to 1938, and was ultimately annexed to Russia in 1945). To be sure, Bratianu frankly confessed to Poklevskii that he had thrown in Ruthenia only for bargaining purposes, but swore that Rumania would never intervene unless all her other demands were met. It was the Italian situation all over again. Sir Edward Grey recognized this fact, and firmly insisted to the Rumanians on

May 3 that the whole business was "a question between Russia and Rumania."[29]

On May 2, Sazonov achieved with Buchanan and Paléologue a "reconciliation of views relative to Rumania," *i.e.*, that the "character of an ultimatum" given to Bratianu's demands left little chance of agreement unless there was "substantial rectification." At the same time, Sazonov wired London and Paris that he was taking it upon himself to conduct negotiations, and that he expected "strong support in refusing those of the Rumanian demands which are inacceptable to us."[30]

Diamandy saw Sazonov on May 3, and said that Russia might set the date of Rumania's intervention if she agreed to all of Bratianu's demands. Sazonov replied that it was impossible to agree to the Prut boundary in Bukovina, Rumanian possession of all the Banat, and the annexation of Ruthenia to Rumania. He mentioned the 1914 agreement, in which Rumania had promised to accept an ethnic boundary in Bukovina. Diamandy replied that the 1914 agreement had been a payment for neutrality; as a belligerent, Rumania would expect much

The Russian Struggle for Power, 1914-1917

more. Sazonov reminded him that Russia had not promised Rumania military help in 1914 to realize Rumanian objectives; now such help would be essential. He demanded that Diamandy seek new instructions.[31]

On May 4, Bratianu refused to give way at all, but promised intervention by May 28 if his demands were met. The Russian ambassador in Bucharest thought, however, that there was a chance of concessions in Ruthenia and the Banat. Nevertheless, King Ferdinand I (1914-1927) was supporting Bratianu, and the Rumanians looked upon the Prut boundary as their compensation for the loss of southern Bessarabia to Russia in 1878.[32]

Sazonov insisted again on May 5 on an ethnic frontier in Bukovina, the annexation of Ruthenia to Russia, and satisfaction of Serbia's claims in the Banat. He was willing for the negotiations to fail, if necessary, but consented on May 7, at the urging of Buchanan and Paléologue, to work on a counter-proposal.[33]

Diamandy was still insisting on Rumania's maximum desires on May 12, and the Italian ambassador in Petrograd was telling Baron Schilling that Germany was offering Rumania Bukovina and autonomous status for Transylvania. Thereupon, expecting Carlotti to transmit his words to Diamandy, Schilling threatened that Rumanian intervention on the side of Germany would result in a Russian invitation to Bulgaria to attack Rumania and seize all the Dobrudja, including Constanza.[34]

Bratianu was still unyielding on May 13, and the Russian ambassador in Bucharest suggested a compromise. He thought Bratianu might change his mind and leave the Pančevo district of the Banat to Serbia if Russia would agree to relinquish Chernovets in Bukovina.[35]

Meanwhile, since the beginning of Rumanian negotiations, further agonized wails of protest had come from the Serbs. Two of their leaders who were visiting Petrograd on April 30 complained of the sacrifice of Slavic interests to Italy. They demanded that Pashich be informed of all negotiations affecting Serbia, and spoke openly of the possibility of a separate peace with the Central Powers. On the next day, Pashich himself complained of being ignored, and said his position would become impossible if he were

The Russian Struggle for Power, 1914–1917

not informed of negotiations regarding the Banat. By May 4, Prince-Regent Alexander, fearing that Italy was about to induce the Allies to set up an independent Croatia, thought Pashich should resign.[36]

Pashich officially demanded on May 6 that the Allies not begin to draw new frontiers in the Banat or other parts of Hungary without a preliminary understanding with Serbia. He also wanted a guarantee that the Serbs, Croats, and Slovenes would be "reunited," and that Italy would be restrained from acting "precipitately" in territories that interested them.[37]

None of the major Allies had any intention of admitting Serbia to the Rumanian negotiations, but they were willing to offer Pashich guarantees. Sazonov promised not to oppose a Serbo-Croatian merger and to uphold Serbia's rights in the Banat. Grey went so far as to promise the Serbians Bosnia-Herzegovina and a part of Dalmatia. He also promised that Croatia would have a part of Dalmatia, that he would take account of the coastal interests of Montenegro, and that "Serbian interests on the left bank of the Danube" would be guaranteed. The French gave their approval to Serbo-Croatian union, provided the Croatians were willing, though they seem to have pressed for a treaty of federation which Trubetskoi feared would "weaken the exclusive influence of Russia through Orthodox Serbia, by creating dualism in the latter's midst."[38]

The Serbian complaints undoubtedly influenced the counter-proposal which Sazonov presented to the Rumanians on May 14. He suggested that Rumania accept the line of the Suchav in Bukovina, and the line of the Somesh west of the Carpathians, thus leaving northern Bukovina and Ruthenia for Russia. In addition, he wanted a partition of the Banat between Rumania and Serbia, leaving for the latter the quadrangle bounded by the Theiss, the Danube, Temesvar, and Belaya Tserkov. He insisted that these boundaries would still leave many non-Rumanians in Rumania.[39]

Bratianu complained in reply on May 18 that they gave Rumania only half of the Rumanian Bukovinans and would leave her wedged in a vise between two Slavic states, for whose minor interests major Rumanian interests would be

The Russian Struggle for Power, 1914-1917

sacrificed. He could not, therefore, assume responsibility for recommending war on Austria-Hungary to King Ferdinand, and would content himself with the agreement of 1914. Poklevskii, the Russian ambassador, then raised the question of whether the 1914 agreement was binding, since neither the Rumanian king nor the Western Powers had agreed to it. Bratianu was then more conciliatory. He suggested that Rumania might offer Bulgaria Balchik in return for the latter's giving up her pretensions to Monastir in Macedonia. Thus would Serbia be compensated for her claims to the Banat. In addition, Bratianu would agree to neutralize the Banat opposite Belgrade.[40]

For a time it seemed that the Western Powers would remain content to leave the negotiations in Sazonov's hands, even though it meant their failure. Grey told Benckendorff on May 19 that he thought it necessary to study with care further messages to Bucharest, but added that he was far from willing to surrender to Bratianu's extreme demands. In particular, he thought the extension of Rumania far beyond Transylvania into Hungary proper dangerous. Moreover,

Serbia must not be sacrificed in the Banat, as she had been in Dalmatia, and might be in Macedonia. At the same time, Delcassé was telling Izvolskii that he thought Sazonov had gone as far as he could, and that if Bratianu did not accept the terms now offered, then it could be only because the Rumanians were seeking an excuse not to intervene. Even Sonnino agreed to exert pressure on Bratianu.[41]

However, on May 19, Paléologue appeared before Sazonov and offered a new compromise solution in the most energetic fashion. In Bukovina, it involved extending the Rumanian frontier northward to the Sereth, and in the Banat, leaving Serbia only a tiny area just to the north of Belgrade. Sazonov was annoyed by this intervention, but since he had already decided upon just such a compromise as a last resort, he consented to the plan, provided it was put forward by Rumania, and provided the latter intervened at the same time as Italy, and in any case, no later than May 26.[42]

The French and Italians pushed this plan energetically in Bucharest, and for a time, it seemed that the Rumanians might accept it, provided that in addition, Chernovets were allotted to them. However, by May 22, it became apparent that Bratianu would continue to insist on his May 1 proposals. He was unmoved when the Italians declared war on Austria-Hungary on May 26, since he now felt that the Russian defeats in Galicia would eventually cause the Allies to grant all of his demands. The Russians, meanwhile, had marked the occasion of Italian intervention by telling the Serbs that they would "welcome the merger of the Croatians, Slovenes, and Serbs into one state," and that Russia would not "enter into an agreement with Rumania, if the part of the Banat which is populated principally by Serbs, and which can serve the purposes of the strategic defense of Belgrade, is not guaranteed to Serbia."[43]

By the beginning of June, the good intentions of the Western Powers not to intervene in the negotiations began to evaporate, just as Bratianu had expected. In a very apologetic fashion, Grey approached Sazonov on June 3. Pointing to the Allied defeats in Galicia and Gallipoli, he voiced the opinion that by meeting Rumanian aspirations, the Russians would be able to throw back the Austro-Germans in Galicia and hasten their acquisition of Constantinople and the Straits. He therefore asked that Sazonov grant the line of the Prut in Bukovina and all the Banat except a zone opposite Belgrade, in return for immediate Rumanian intervention and the retrocession of the southern Dobrudja to Bulgaria.[44] Sazonov would not go quite so far, but he did offer Bratianu, on June 3, the line of the Sereth in Bukovina and all the northeastern part of the Banat.[45]

Meanwhile, great nervousness was arising in Paris over the Russian defeats in Galicia. Delcassé was under fire. Insisting that France could not undergo another winter campaign, French politicians were blaming Russian dilatoriness in Rumanian negotiations for the continuation of the war. Though he was very provoked by this attitude, Sazonov asked the Stavka on June 6 whether Rumanian military help would be worth great concessions, in the light of the military situation and the pressures from the Western Powers. Grand Duke Nikolai indicated on June 8 an urgent need for Rumanian assistance, and the Tsar authorized further concessions.[46]

The Russian Struggle for Power, 1914-1917

Pretending that the Tsar had been influenced by the pleas of his cousin, Queen Marie of Rumania, Sazonov offered on June 9 to let Rumania have Chernovets, in addition to the Sereth line, in Bukovina, provided she relinquished all claims to Ruthenia and to the Panchev district of the Banat, opposite Belgrade. Sir Edward Grey was so touched by this gesture that he warmly thanked the Tsar and Sazonov for their "high-minded and generous motives" which had led them thus "to sacrifice the particular interests of Russia to the common cause and general interest of the Allies."[47]

However, Bratianu was not at all touched, and on June 12, still insisted on all his old demands. Moreover, there were increasing signs in Bucharest that the Rumanians did not want to intervene in the war at all, so long as the Russians were being defeated.[48]

Faced with such a situation, Sazonov proposed on June 18 direct negotiations between Rumania and Serbia. The Western Powers, on the other hand, suggested that Serbia might receive a bloc of territory ten kilometers square north of the Danube, or that the whole question be submitted to arbitration. In the interim, they wanted to get busy with negotiation of a military convention, laying territorial questions temporarily aside. However, Bratianu had no intention of negotiating a military convention until all his political demands were met.[49]

Finally, the ground was swept out from under Sazonov completely by a demand from the Stavka on June 20 that Rumanian intervention be purchased at any price. Accordingly, on June 21, Sazonov offered the Prut line in Bukovina and Ruthenia south of the upper Theiss if Rumania would intervene within five weeks. He still wanted a corner of the Banat for Serbia, but thought this question could be worked out by the Serbs and Rumanians under the benevolent auspices of the Allied Powers. Bratianu expressed great happiness over these concessions on June 23, but still wanted his last pound of flesh in the Banat. He was still willing to neutralize the area north of Belgrade, and now also willing to buy the lands of Serbs living north of the Danube and east of the Theiss.[50]

The Russian Struggle for Power, 1914–1917

THE AGREEMENT WITH RUMANIA

Before pursuing the negotiations with Rumania to their sorry end, it would be well at this point to review briefly the highlights of the second phase of the great 1915 Austro-German offensive against Russia. Having retaken Galicia, the Central Powers began on July 1 a great pincers movement designed to squeeze the Russians entirely out of their part of Poland. The northern arm of the pincers had been previously strengthened by a German movement into Kurland (April 26–May 7), which had ended in the capture of Liepaja (Libau). In July, the Germans strengthened their hold on Kurland by seizing Ventspils (Windau) (July 18) and Mitava (Mitau) (August 1). Simultaneously, the Austrians attacked in the south, taking Lublin and Cholm on July 31 and storming Ivangorod on August 4. The Russians now faced the danger of being trapped, and there was nothing to do but evacuate Warsaw, permitting its occupation by the Germans from East Prussia on August 7. After that, the Germans advanced into Lithuania and the remainder of Poland on a wide front, taking Kovno on August 18, Novogeorgievsk on August 20, Brest-Litovsk on August 25, Grodno on September 2, and Vilna on September 19. The Austrians managed to do their part by taking Lutsk on August 31 and Dubno on September 8.

However, the Russians rallied, after the Tsar assumed personal command of the armies, sending Grand Duke Nikolai Nikolaevich off to be Viceroy of Transcaucasia (September 5). This was chiefly because General Alekseev became Chief of Staff at the same time. At the new Stavka in Mogilev, Alekseev directed the establishment of a front along the line Riga-Baranovichi-Pinsk-Dubno-Tarnopol-Chernovets.[51]

Long before the new front was established, it had become apparent that the Rumanians would not now intervene at any price. However, to please the French, negotiations were continued on through July and August, on the theory that the Serbs could be compensated for the loss of the Banat with Allied agreement to the merger of the Serbs, Croats, and Slovenes.

This plan was put forward by Delcassé on June 27, at a time when French politicians were blaming Russia for the failure of the Rumanian negotiations and demanding Delcassé's political head. It was accepted by Russia on June 30, but by July 3, it became apparent that Italy would not agree. By this time, the Rumanian cabinet ministers and generals were already saying that it was useless for them to intervene at a time when their army would only be crushed, although they wanted to go ahead with a political agreement and to start consultations with the Russian Stavka.[52]

Despite their attitude, Grey suggested on July 8 that all Rumania's territorial demands be conceded, provided she guaranteed Serbian interests in the Banat, promised to cede Dobrich and Balchik to Bulgaria, and promised to intervene five weeks after the conclusion of a political agreement. Doubtless, he was most interested in getting Dobrich and Balchik at this point. Sazonov agreed on July 9, provided that in addition, Serbia be guaranteed Croatia, subject to Croatian wishes, and the district of Srem (Syrmia), just west of the Banat, along with the city of Zemun (Zemlin).[53]

Sonnino continued to make difficulties regarding Croatia, claiming there was a chance for a separate peace with Hungary. Therefore, Sazonov proposed that Russia, Britain, and France promise Croatia to Serbia, and try to obtain Italy's consent later.[54] Delcassé was willing to go along with this plan, but the British balked.[55]

Finally, by July 14, Sazonov had lost his patience completely. He told Buchanan and Paléologue that it was becoming clear that no sort of concessions would induce Bratianu to intervene immediately. Russia had sacrificed her own and Serbia's interests only because she expected immediate Rumanian help, and he wanted assurances regarding the time of Rumania's entrance before any more formal offers were made in Bucharest.[56]

The French were much against seeking such preliminary assurances; forced to recognize that Rumania would probably not intervene, they now began to talk about the necessity of countering Austro-German efforts to win Rumania and of gaining Dobrich and Balchik for Bulgaria. However, Grey backed up Sazonov, and on July 23, Bratianu was asked when he expected to enter. He replied that an "examination

The Russian Struggle for Power, 1914–1917

of military conditions" would determine the date of Rumania's entrance.[57]

The British were disgusted with this reply, but Delcassé continued to plead for a political agreement. When it became apparent that his position as Minister of Foreign Affairs was in jeopardy, Grey and Sonnino joined their voices to his (July 27). Sazonov capitulated to these demands on July 29, though he made it plain that he did not consider it "in accord with the dignity of four Great Powers" to satisfy Rumania's political demands completely while leaving her complete freedom as to the time of her intervention. He added that he was giving way only to ease the British campaign on Gallipoli by preventing the passage of military contraband across Rumanian soil.[58]

In notifying Poklevskii of his decision on August 2, Sazonov stipulated that Rumania must agree to Allied inspection of shipments from the Central Powers to Turkey. In addition, a Rumanian officer must be sent to the Russian Stavka to work out a military agreement and set the time of Rumania's entrance. Finally, the political agreement must be worked out by Russia and Rumania and submitted to the Allies for approval.[59]

At this point, the Rumanian pro-Germans intervened and saved Sazonov from the humiliation of signing any formal agreement. At a full-dress Crown Council on August 9 in Bucharest, they persuaded their fellow Councillors to override Bratianu and to agree on a pro-Ally policy not involving signature of any political agreement. Bratianu would have resigned, but for his fear that he would be replaced by a pro-German.[60]

Even Delcassé was now resigned to Rumanian non-intervention. However, after a request from Bratianu on August 11, supported by Grey, Sazonov agreed on August 12 to inform the Rumanians verbally of Allied consent to their territorial demands, on the understanding that they would intervene when the military situation improved, and that they would prevent the shipment of war munitions to Turkey. The appropriate statement was made in Bucharest on August 20.[61]

Thus, all the territorial negotiations for Rumanian intervention were completed in 1915,

The Russian Struggle for Power, 1914-1917

and when the Rumanians actually did intervene in 1916, no further negotiations of this sort were necessary. The settlement achieved in 1915 bore witness to a marked decline of Russian power in eastern Europe, and it is to the credit of Britain and France that at the end of the war, they refused to honor all the pledges which Bratianu exacted by blackmail. Probably Sazonov would have been wiser to have yielded earlier, and later to have found some excuse to do what the Western Powers actually did. However, he was negotiating with bitter memories of the Treaty of London fresh in mind, and determined to maintain Russian prestige, particularly in the eyes of the Serbians. This was, in the long run, more important to him than the actual frontiers, and he failed in his efforts only because Russian military power was not up to the standards he had set for Russian prestige.

THE FINAL ROUND OF BULGARIAN NEGOTIATIONS (MAY–JULY, 1915)

Though the British at first agreed to let Sazonov handle the 1915 Rumanian negotiations, they made no bones in May, 1915, about taking over Bulgarian negotiations themselves. In view of the Gallipoli campaign, this development was only natural. It had become apparent by mid-May that the Greeks would not help in the attack on Turkey until something was done about Bulgaria.

Grey informed Petrograd on May 12 that he had just warned Radoslavov that it was no longer possible for the Allies to continue keeping Bulgarian interests in mind while negotiating with other states. Radoslavov had promptly promised intervention if he received both the "uncontested" and the "contested" zones of Macedonia, as well as Kavalla, Seres, and Drama, thus raising his price; otherwise, he said, he would remain neutral. On the same day, Savinskii indicated to Sazonov that while Bulgaria intended to follow Rumania in joining the Allies, the Russian defeats were having a bad effect.[62]

After indicating to Bulgaria that he saw little hope of her gaining the "contested" zone of Macedonia (which Radoslavov had probably mentioned only for bargaining purposes), Grey proposed to Sazonov and Delcassé that negotiations be begun in Sofia by Bax-Ironside, with support from his Russian and French colleagues. They agreed, but not until the end of May was agreement reached on the text of an offer.

On May 30 the offer was made in Sofia by Bax-Ironside, and was greeted by Radoslavov with surprised pleasure. The Allies made an outright offer of Turkish Thrace to the Enos-Midiya line; Bulgaria might occupy and annex this territory whenever she saw fit. In addition, on the condition that Serbia received equitable compensations in Bosnia-Herzegovina and on the coast of the Adriatic, Bulgaria might have, at the end of the war, that part of Serbian Macedonia south of the Egri-Palanka-Okhrida line, including these two cities and Sopot, Keprülü, and Monastir. In addition, the Allies promised to try to obtain from Greece Kavalla, but pointed out that in order to compensate Greece in Asia Minor, they needed Bulgarian action against Turkey. Finally, the Allies would favor an agreement between Bulgaria and Rumania regarding the Dobrudja, and would give Bulgaria financial aid. For all this, Bulgaria must attack Turkey.[63]

Meanwhile, Sazonov had ordered Trubetskoi

on May 26 to inform Pashich secretly of the proposed statement in Sofia, so that the latter might prepare Serbian public opinion. At the same time, Pashich was told that concessions to Italy had been slight, that Russia favored a Serb-Croat-Slovene merger, and that she would never sacrifice Serbian interests to Rumania. Nevertheless, Pashich refused in the most ardent terms on May 29 to make any concessions. He declared that he would gladly die for Russia himself, but that the parliament and army would not allow the cession of an inch of land. In addition to the old argument that the Serbs and Bulgars could never cooperate, he now said that Italian intervention made Bulgarian intervention unnecessary. On May 30, he threatened to resign.[64]

Greece heard immediately of the Allied offer to Bulgaria, and solemnly protested "the blow thus struck at the independence and territorial integrity of the Kingdom." She insisted that "between Greece and Bulgaria there is not and there could not be any question of discussion on the subject of Kavalla."[65]

The British believed that this protest was sent by the Gounaris government primarily to influence the forthcoming June elections, but decided to offer more specific promises regarding Asia Minor. At the same time, France proposed that Pashich be mollified with exact promises regarding the Adriatic coast, and be told of the efforts being made to save the Banat for Serbia.[66]

After a two weeks' delay, Radoslavov answered the Allied message of May 30, expressing his "profound gratitude" for the evidence of Allied concern for "the legitimate aspirations of the Bulgarian nation." However, he insisted that the Allied note contained "certain points which are not very precise as to the exact meaning and the true interpretation." He wished to know if the part of Macedonia promised by the Allies was the same as the "uncontested zone," and to what degree Serbia must acquire control over her indicated gains in order to give Bulgaria incontestable rights in Macedonia. He also wanted to know how much of Asia Minor Greece must gain in order to make possible the cession of Kavalla, and what hinterland would be included with the latter. Finally, the Allies were asked to state "the principles which ought to serve as a basis for an understanding to be achieved between Rumania and Bulgaria" on the subject of the southern Dobrudja.[67]

The Allied ambassadors in Sofia thought Radoslavov was playing for time so that he might also carry on negotiations with the Central Powers, and that a time limit ought to be set for the acceptance of the offer. They favored promising him the entire "uncontested" zone of Macedonia and Seres and Drama in addition to Kavalla. Serbia's gains should be defined as Bosnia-Herzegovina and an exit to the Adriatic, while Greece's gains need not be defined. Dobrich and Balchik could serve as a basis for Bulgaro-Rumanian talks.[68]

Sazonov acceded to these views, except that he thought Greece's gains should be defined as Smyrna and its hinterland. Grey also acceded, but wanted to add assurances that the Allies, while intending to reward their friends, were concerned over maintaining an even balance among the Balkan nations.[69] Sonnino insisted that Serbia would not keep secrets, and that any accurate definition of future Serbian gains would embarrass him, owing to his failure to gain Rijeka for Italy. Delcassé was opposed to indicating proposed gains for Greece in Asia Minor, to telling Bulgaria that the Allies would not try to gain more than "uncontested" Macedonia from Serbia, and to setting a time-limit on Bulgarian acceptance of the offer. Eventually he withdrew the last of his objections, and Sazonov then accepted his viewpoint. However, by this time, Grey had changed his mind, having become very concerned over the Greek attitude.[70]

It is easy to see from the above paragraph why it was difficult for the Allies to make any progress in the negotiations. As leader in the negotiations, Grey was experiencing what Sazonov had experienced in August–September, 1914. However, cutting through all the objections, he had produced on June 25 a text for the reply to Radoslavov. Bulgaria would be promised "uncontested" Macedonia, in return for Serbia's gaining Bosnia-Herzegovina and "a port on the Adriatic." Radoslavov would be told that the Allies were "unable to lose sight of the ties strengthened by historical association and by actual occupation which bind Greece to a part at any rate of the area in Thrace which is the subject of the Bulgarian claim." Conscious of the aspirations of Greece in Asia Minor, and particularly in the Smyrna regions, the Allies could promise only "to assist to the utmost of their power in the attainment both by Bulgaria and Greece of a reasonable satisfaction of their desires in Thrace and Asia Minor respectively." At the same time, the Allies would consider that the retrocession of Dobrich and Balchik could form the basis of the Bulgaro-Rumanian talks. Finally, the Allied offer would be "open to reconsideration" if Bulgaria did not attack Turkey at "a very early date."[71]

In effect, Grey now wanted to sacrifice Bulgarian and Slavic interests to Greece, just as he had sacrificed Yugo-Slav interests to Italy in March and April, and at a moment when he was asking Sazonov to sacrifice Russian and Serbian interests to Rumania. Despite the serious situation of the Russian armies, Sazonov delivered a strong protest. On June 29, he claimed that this message was even less specific than the one delivered in Sofia in May. At the same time, he deprecated the importance of Greek intervention, and insisted that Serbia was in a worse

The Russian Struggle for Power, 1914-1917

position than Greece, since she could fight Bulgaria only by making peace with Austria-Hungary. On July 1, he took the position that since it was impossible to hope to win over all the Balkan kingdoms at once, the Allies must decide which one would be of most use to them. The profits from an alliance with Greece were problematical, but an attack by Bulgaria on Thrace would make possible the immediate capture of Constantinople by the Allied detachments on Gallipoli. Consequently, Bulgaria should be promised openly Kavalla, with Seres and Drama.[72]

Meanwhile, the Central Powers had come to recognize that a turning point had arrived in the Balkans. By winning over Bulgaria, the Allies were about to nullify the Galician campaign and knock Turkey out of the war. For a time, consideration was given to suspending operations against Russia in order to save Turkey. However, this plan was dropped in favor of what proved to be one of the more brilliant strokes of the war, on a par with despatch of the *Göben* and *Breslau* to Constantinople. This involved persuading Turkey to cede part of Thrace to

Bulgaria, at a time when the Allies were unable to persuade the Serbs to part with any of Macedonia, thus proving that the Austro-Germans had far better command of the situation than did their enemies.

As early as June 20, Radoslavov admitted to Savinskii that the Central Powers were urging him to take Macedonia from Serbia by force, and that Turco-Bulgarian negotiations were in progress at Constantinople to bring about the peaceful cession to Bulgaria of Thrace to the Enos-Midiya line. He argued that such an agreement would help Russia ultimately to realize her Straits ambitions. However, the talks in Constantinople went slowly, since the Turks, like the Serbs, were acting only under pressure and offering less than the Bulgars wanted.[73]

Faced with Sazonov's insistence that concessions must be asked of the Greeks, and with the Turco-Bulgarian talks in Constantinople, the British and French decided on July 8, after a conference in London, on an abrupt change of front towards Bulgaria. They now wanted to tell her that before any further territorial discussions were possible, she must assure them that

The Russian Struggle for Power, 1914–1917

an immediate attack on Turkey would follow any territorial settlement.[74]

However, Sazonov objected, and on July 14, Grey suggested that instead, Bulgaria be asked to indicate the terms on which she would join the Allies. Sazonov also objected to this, since he feared Bulgaria would make sweeping new demands. After that, there was discussion of an Anglo-French occupation of Serbian Macedonia, in order to prove to the Bulgarians Allied good intentions, while protecting it against a Bulgarian attack. Sazonov suggested instead that the Allies occupy Dubrovnik and Split in Dalmatia, and threaten to deny Serbia access to the Adriatic unless she made concession in Macedonia. This alternative was promptly denounced by Delcassé and Sonnino. At the end of July, the Allies were hopelessly divided over the Balkan tangle, and the ground was cut completely from under them on July 22, when, under German pressure, the Turks agreed to cede Bulgaria a strip of territory along the Maritza River. After that, it was probably impossible to expect that Bulgaria would attack Turkey, and the best the Allies could hope for was a guarantee that she would not attack Serbia.[75]

THE FINAL FAILURE OF BULGARIAN NEGOTIATIONS (AUGUST–OCTOBER, 1915)

In the last two of the fourteen months' negotiations in which the Allies tried to save Bulgaria from the fate meted out by the Treaty of Neuilly, Bulgaria ceases to occupy the center of the stage. Perhaps the most important development of these two months was the decision made by Britain and France to take Serbia under their protection. This involved not only the Salonika expedition, which saved the Serbian army, but also a definite decision to make the future aggrandizement of Serbia a war aim, not only of Russia, but of the Western Powers as well. No doubt a strong impelling reason for this decision was disappointment over Italy's performance as a belligerent. In October, 1915, after fighting the third of eleven successive "Battles of the Isonzo," the Italians were still on the Isonzo.

By the end of July, Sir Edward Grey had decided to cut through all the Balkan Gordian

The Russian Struggle for Power, 1914–1917

knots in an effort to save Serbia from Bulgarian attack. On July 30, he demanded that the Allies ask "uncontested" Macedonia of Serbia, in return for a promise that after the war, Serbia, Croatia, or Montenegro would receive all Austro-Hungarian territory west and south of the Drave and Danube as far as the borders of Dalmatia, and, on the Adriatic coast, Rijeka, Split, Dubrovnik, Kotor, and San Giovanni di Medua, subject to the neutralization provisions of the Treaty of London. He also wanted to promise to facilitate the union of Serbia and Croatia.[76]

Within the remarkably short time of four days, Sazonov and Delcassé had given their consent, while, as might have been expected, Sonnino held back. Grey now took a strong tone with Sonnino (August 2), pointing out the very obvious fact that Serbia would never make concessions except on a *quid pro quo* basis, and that the Allies had already partially sacrificed the Yugo-Slavs to Italian ambitions:

> An attitude of opposition on the part of Italy in this matter puts her in an invidious position. Her claims, now recognized, in Istria and Dalmatia have already made our task in the Balkans harder; they

are even now exposing us to possible failure in the Dardanelles . . . If Italy now still further increases our difficulties and compromises our successes in the war by refusing to remove the unfounded Serbian apprehensions, she will incur a heavy responsibility . . ."[77]

After this, Rome gave way, and on August 4, it was possible for the Allies to present *démarches* in both Nish and Sofia. In the first of these, the Allies asked Serbia to cede "uncontested" Macedonia, if Bulgaria joined the Allies; in return, Serbia would receive at the end of the war "huge compensations on the Adriatic Sea, in Bosnia and Herzegovina, and elsewhere, which have already been destined for her"; moreover, the common frontier of Serbia and Greece would be preserved. The message to Bulgaria was in the form of an answer to her queries of May 29. The whole of the "uncontested" zone of Macedonia was promised. Though the Allies could not yet say what would be offered Greece in Asia Minor to induce her to cede Kavalla, nor how much hinterland would be included with the latter, Bulgaria was assured that Greece would gain nothing in Asia

The Russian Struggle for Power, 1914–1917

Minor unless she ceded Kavalla. The offer of Thrace to the Enos-Midiya line was repeated. If Bulgaria accepted, a precise date for her entrance must be set.[78]

In retrospect, it would appear that the August 4 proposals to Bulgaria never had much chance, if any, of bringing the country over to the Allied side. The Turkish concession of July 22, plus the Russian evacuation of Warsaw two weeks later, ruined the Allied cause in Sofia. On the other hand, final arrangements for the cession of the Turkish territory were not complete until late September, and on top of that, the British made a new landing at Suvla Bay on Gallipoli, on the day of the fall of Warsaw (August 7). Not until it was generally recognized at the end of September that the Gallipoli campaign had failed, were the Bulgarians willing to attack Serbia, and then only after the Central Powers were attacking her simultaneously.

Meanwhile, throughout August, the bitter Allied wrangle over what Serbia should be offered for "uncontested" Macedonia went on. On August 4, Pashich insisted that the loss of Macedonia would leave Serbia with an impossible frontier, but on the next day was more resigned to its loss. He now wanted a more accurate definition of Serbian future gains, changes in the 1912 line in Macedonia, and information on the proposed new Graeco-Serbian frontier. Sazonov wanted to comply with his requests (August 6), but Sonnino raised objections, claiming the future Graeco-Serbian frontier could not be defined more accurately.[79]

Pashich, meanwhile, had arranged for a meeting of the Serbian cabinet and the army commanders, under the chairmanship of Prince-Regent Alexander, on August 8. When it was held, no definite decision was made. However, the army commanders were more resigned to concessions, though they wanted changes in the 1912 line in Macedonia, and more accurate definition of Serbia's future gains.[80]

Despite this reasonableness on the part of the Serbs, Sonnino continued to make difficulties. Grey, on the other hand, produced on August 11 a list of "explanations and guarantees" to be made in Nish. Serbia should be promised Bosnia-Herzegovina, the portion of Dalmatia reserved for her by the Treaty of London, and

The Russian Struggle for Power, 1914-1917

"Slavonia and Syrmia up to the line of the Drava and Danube with Semlin and Batchka." She should also be told that the Adriatic coast from Dubrovnik to the Drin was reserved for her or Montenegro; that the coast of Albania from the Drin to the Voiussa was reserved for future settlement, subject to the establishment of a common Serbo-Greek frontier in eastern Albania; that the future of Croatia, with the coast allotted by the Treaty of London, was reserved for future settlement; and that if Rumania did not intervene, the Slavic districts in the southwestern Banat were reserved for future settlement. On the other hand, the Allies could not modify the line of 1912 in Macedonia, nor fix the Serbo-Greek frontier in Albania; moreover, they stipulated the neutralization of the coast from Cape Planca to the Voiussa.[81]

It is worth noting that this proposal violated the spirit, if not the letter, of the Treaty of London, insofar as Albania was concerned, since Italy undoubtedly thought that the future of the coast of that country from the Drin to the Voiussa was a matter for Italy to decide, and not "reserved for future settlement." Moreover, though Grey was pushing Sazonov at this time into a recognition of Rumanian claims in the Banat, he evidently regarded himself as free to make promises to Serbia in that region.

Italy was naturally most unhappy over the British proposal, and by August 13, Sonnino had persuaded Grey to eliminate the reference to the Banat and to make Serbia only a conditional promise of Slavonia. The Italian Foreign Minister wanted other changes, such as a clearer definition of the rights of Montenegro, an exact delimitation of the gains of Greece and Serbia in Albania, etc. He even seems to have been willing to concede to Serbian demands for a rectification of the 1912 line in Macedonia, apparently on the theory that this would make Serbia less demanding with respect to Dalmatia and Croatia. Sazonov, on the other hand, wanted a definite promise of Anglo-Franco-Russian consent to the Serbo-Croatian merger.[82]

Grey proceeded to cut through these objections, and on August 15, delivered his August 11 proposals in Nish, as modified on August 13. Poor Delcassé, whose political neck was threatened, went along with Grey, apparently on the theory that anything was worth winning a diplomatic success in the Balkans. The Italians huffily abstained altogether from the *démarche*. After some soul-searching, the Russians went along, though Trubetskoi privately promised Pashich Croatia, part of Albania, and the Banat, thus going contrary to the promises Sazonov made a short time afterwards to the Rumanians. Later, Sazonov wired Benckendorff that

Grey's haste in acting without gaining the preliminary consent of Russia—the Power most interested in Balkan affairs—has become known here in wide circles, and public opinion blames the deterioration of our foreign policy on England.[83]

However, the day had passed when the British could be threatened with Russian "public opinion." Countries whose armies are in retreat are not in a good position to make demands.

The British meanwhile, had had to allow Pashich one day of temperamental display after the presentation of the August 15 *démarche*. He accused the Allies of treating Serbia like an African colony, and complained that the future Serbo-Greek frontier in Albania would be open to attack by the Albanians and Bulgarians. No assurances, he said, had been given relative to Croatia, and the Slovenes had not been mentioned. He would prefer Macedonia to all the gains offered.[84]

Nevertheless, for the first time, he had a substantial guarantee of post-war gains, and on August 18, was a great deal calmer, though still determined to insist on changes in the 1912 treaty line in Macedonia. Already, a secret session of the Serbian parliament was planned for September 7, in order to shift to it partial responsibility for the cession of Macedonia. As a matter of fact, the Serbian Premier was in fine fettle, and preparing to insist that by the term "Croatia," the British surely meant to include the Slovenes of Carinthia and Styria.[85]

The British had proven themselves masters of the Balkan situation by the August 15 *démarche*, though Sazonov and Delcassé, in its wake, tried to deceive themselves into thinking they still counted by exchanging labored notes about a partition of Albania between Italy, Serbia, and Greece.[86] Then, on August 19, the warning came from Sofia that the Bulgarians intended to turn down the Allies' proposals. On

The Russian Struggle for Power, 1914-1917

August 21, it was learned that King Ferdinand had ordered the removal of all pro-Russian ministers, and that military preparations were in progress. There followed a series of hectic Allied moves, including a promise to Bulgaria by Russia of "uncontested" Macedonia at the end of the war, "whatever the circumstances," a declaration of war on Turkey by Italy (August 22), and Venizelos' return to power as Premier of Greece (August 22), apparently because the Greek court wanted to saddle him with responsibility for the cession of Kavalla, if that became necessary.[87]

The British seem to have been the only one of the major Allies to have kept their heads in the midst of the crisis; realizing that it was hopeless to expect to win over the Bulgarians, they made preparations for the Salonika expedition. Pashich tried at the end of August to enter into direct negotiations with the Bulgarians over Macedonia. When this failed, he at long last, on September 1, gave way to Allied demands regarding Macedonia. To be sure, in agreeing to the cession of "uncontested" Macedonia, he asked for two alterations in the 1912 line. It must be moved south in the vicinity of Skoplje (Uskub) and Ovtche Polje, in order to give these towns a strategic frontier, and the city of Prilep must remain within Serbia. Moreover, there were other conditions in places other than Macedonia. The common Serbo-Greek frontier must start at the crest of the Perister and the Souha Planina, and continue west to a point which would be fixed later. Thus, a little part of the existing Serbo-Greek frontier would be kept, and contact between Bulgarian and Albanian territory avoided. Bulgaria, in order to merit "uncontested" Macedonia, must attack Turkey promptly with all her forces and assist in the conquest of Constantinople and the Dardanelles. The Allies must formally promise that Croatia with Rijeka would be "reunited" with Serbia, that the Slovene territories would be free to decide their fate, and that the western part of the Banat must be "reunited" to Serbia. Serbia must be recognized as an Ally and guaranteed active participation in the future peace conference. She must be guaranteed financial aid of 36 million francs a month for the remainder of the war. She must retain her existing

The Russian Struggle for Power, 1914–1917

railway and port rights giving her access to the Aegean at Salonika. Finally, she must be permitted to settle the question of property rights of Serbs in the ceded area of Macedonia, and be guaranteed the preservation of historic Serbian monuments, churches, and monasteries there.[88]

Pashich's note of September 1, 1915 was unquestionably one of the cleverest strokes of the entire war. Actually, he conceded nothing, since he and nearly everyone else realized at this point that Bulgaria would probably join the Central Powers. However, by conceding, on paper, to the Allied demands for Macedonia, he had laid a firm foundation to demand later the fulfillment of the British promises of August 15, plus much more. The note elevated Pashich to the stature of Bratianu in the ranks of those statesmen able to gain a great deal for nothing at all, or at least, relatively little.

That he had caught the Allied statesmen unawares seems apparent from the two weeks of wrangling which followed the delivery of the note. Grey, Delcassé, Sazonov, and Sonnino continued to bicker over whether further pressure should be exerted in Nish, and over what sort of notification should be given the Bulgarians.[89]

In the meantime, things in Sofia went along on their predestined course. On September 5, the Duke of Mecklenburg-Schwerin arrived in Bulgaria as the special representative of the German Kaiser. Radoslavov began to talk of the danger for Bulgaria in a Russian occupation of Constantinople. The Greeks and Rumanians began to scuttle for cover. Both King Constantine and Bratianu said openly that their countries would not help Serbia if she were attacked by Bulgaria.[90] Radoslavov told the Russian ambassador flatly on September 11 that Bulgaria would not attack Turkey and would not "allow herself the luxury of imitating Belgium" if German troops reached her frontiers. He added frankly that "Bulgaria already now does not fear Russia, which is far away."[91]

At the insistence of Grey, the Allies gave the Bulgarians one last chance when, on September 14, they delivered the following note in Sofia.

> The Four Powers are ready to guarantee to Bulgaria the transfer to her by Serbia at the end of the war of that part of Macedonia which was included

The Russian Struggle for Power, 1914-1917

in the undisputed zone by the Serbo-Bulgarian treaty of 1912.

This guarantee depends on there being made on the part of Bulgaria a statement of her readiness to conclude with the Allies a military agreement relative to opening in a short time action against Turkey. If in the near future a statement of such a nature is not received, the proposal contained in the present note will be considered annulled by mutual consent.[92]

In reply to the note, Radoslavov said grimly that he agreed that the time for a decision had come.

What he meant became apparent on September 19, when the Austro-Germans launched a major attack on the Serbs. Two days later, on September 21, the Turks transferred the right bank of the Maritza River to the Bulgarians, and on the same day, Bulgarian mobilization was announced. Urging the Serbs not to precipitate matters by a preventive attack, Sazonov tried, but failed, to persuade the British to agree on an ultimatum in Sofia. Then, asserting Russia's claims to leadership in the Balkans for the last time, he dispatched a Russian ultimatum to Bulgaria on October 1. Pointing to the existing situation in Bulgaria and to previous warnings against an attack on Serbia, Sazonov indicated that assurances "lavishly given" by Radoslavov were contrary to the facts. Therefore, "the representatives of Russia, which is joined to Bulgaria by the unfaded memory of the latter's liberation from the Turkish yoke, cannot remain in a country in which is being prepared a fratricidal war on the Allied Serbian people." Unless Bulgaria immediately expelled officers of the enemy powers, thus breaking openly "with the enemies of Slavdom and Russia," relations would be broken within twenty-four hours.[93]

Sazonov claimed to be acting thus, without prior consultation in London and Paris, because of Russia's special role as "protectrice" of the Bulgarian people. Despite their annoyance, the British and French associated themselves in his ultimatum on October 4. A day later, on October 5, Radoslavov rejected Sazonov's ultimatum, "with a broken heart." Russo-Bulgarian relations were promptly severed.[94]

However, the Bulgarians waited another whole week, until they were sure of adequate Austro-German help, before launching their attack on Serbia (October 14). The British declared war the next day, and the French, a day later. Not until October 18 did the Russian declaration appear. In it, Bulgaria was accused of committing "an act of treachery against the Slav cause, an act perfidiously contemplated since the very beginning of the war."[95]

THE EFFORT TO SAVE SERBIA: SEPTEMBER AND OCTOBER, 1915

Despite the heavy odds against them, the Allies made heroic efforts to save the Serbians in the fall of 1915. The British were in favor of a large Anglo-French expedition to Salonika, along with efforts to bring about the intervention of Greece and Rumania. The French, or at least, Delcassé, thought that principal reliance must be placed on a Russian expedition into the Balkans, despite the fact that the Russians were barely holding their own in Kurland, Byelorussia, and Ukraine.

It became apparent, immediately after the Bulgarian mobilization, that Venizelos would find it almost impossible to cause Greece to honor the 1913 treaty which promised help to Serbia in the event of a Bulgarian attack, owing to the opposition of King Constantine. Pashich was so concerned that he was ready to cede to Greece a small corner of Macedonia to cause her to honor her treaty obligations. Bratianu, meanwhile, had promised the Austro-Hungarians to remain neutral, though on September 23, he talked of intervening, in case the Russians landed on the Bulgarian coast a detachment equal to that about to be landed at Salonika by the Western Powers.[96]

The decision to despatch the latter was made over the protests of Delcassé, who wanted only a small Western force to be sent to Greece, while main reliance was placed on large Russian forces which he imagined could be spared for a Balkans campaign. Nevertheless, the British overrode these objections, and between September 24 and 29, made arrangements with Venizelos for the Salonika landings. There is no shadow of a doubt that Venizelos was in favor of the landings, even though he indicated his intention to make a purely formal protest.[97]

On October 2, when the first units of the Anglo-French Balkan Expeditionary Force began disembarking in Salonika, Grey made it clear to

Sazonov that thereafter, no more territorial concessions to Bulgaria could be asked of Greece. On the next day, he demanded of the Allies that they promise Greece, in return for the help she was giving Serbia, the preservation of her territorial integrity and Smyrna with its hinterland. Sonnino spared Sazonov the necessity of objecting by opposing the offer of Smyrna, on the ground that Greece might follow Rumania in remaining neutral indefinitely. Grey was impressed by this argument, and agreed to wait until the Greeks asked for Smyrna.[98]

At this point, on October 5, it seemed that the ground was about to be cut out from under the Allies in Greece by the second war-time resignation of Venizelos, following the categorical refusal of King Constantine to honor the 1913 treaty with Serbia. The king's excuse (and it was not without merit) was that the treaty had contemplated Greek help to Serbia only in the event of an attack on the latter by Bulgaria alone, not in the event of a combined Austro-Germano-Bulgarian attack. On the other hand, on the day after Venizelos' fall, Constantine gave firm assurances that no effort would be made to prevent Allied landings in Salonika, or operations therefrom; for many months, he would loyally abide by these pledges.[99]

Nevertheless, the Allies knew that they would never save Serbia without Greek help. Sazonov was forced to agree to Western demands during October that the Greeks be offered Bulgarian Thrace, but since the new Zaimis government showed no interest at all in intervention, this offer was not made in 1915. The British did offer Cyprus on October 20, but again, the Zaimis government was uninterested.[100]

Meanwhile, since the beginning of October, there had been a great hue and cry in France for Russian action in the Balkans. There was talk of a Russian landing at Varna or Burgas and an appeal to the Bulgarian soldiery by the Tsar. In the Chamber of Deputies on October 10, Georges Clemenceau delivered a stinging attack on Delcassé, charging him with too great subjection to Russia in Balkan affairs. Some French politicians were demanding that Russia bring about Rumanian intervention by ceding Bessarabia. On October 12, there were threats that unless Russia took part in the Balkan war,

The Russian Struggle for Power, 1914–1917

the Straits Agreement must be reviewed. On October 15, Delcassé admitted to Izvolskii that his fall as Minister of Foreign Affairs was imminent.

Sazonov's position was none too secure, but by October 11, he had gotten agreement "in principle" from the new Stavka in Mogilev to the sending of a Russian contingent to Salonika via Archangel. However, since it did not arrive until 1916, it was not enough to save Delcassé.[101]

Sir Edward Grey came forward on October 14 with an urgent request to Bratianu to intervene at once. He promised that the Allied Powers would have 200,000 men at Salonika by the end of the year, and that 500,000 British rifles would be sent to Russia to equip troops for a Balkan campaign. Bratianu rejected this proposal on October 17, but on the next day the excited French demanded that the Russians send, or threaten to send, an army into the Balkans, to prevent Rumania's joining the Central Powers.[102]

The new Russian Chief of Staff, General Alekseev, was wholly against any Balkan adventures at all. Determined to concentrate everything on the main front, he went so far as to insist on October 21 that peace must be made with Turkey. Later, apparently after a talk with the Tsar, he ceased to talk along these lines, and consented even to consider a Balkan campaign.[103]

On October 23, Sazonov opened negotiations in Bucharest for the passage of five Russian army corps over Rumanian soil. It is highly probable that in large measure this gesture was mere bluff. In any event, it was a highly useful gesture, from the viewpoint of Russia's relations with the Western Powers. The Rumanians reacted with nervous alarm to the proposals, and talked about fighting Russia in case of an attempted forced transit, and the Germans profited by their mood to offer them on November 1 a large loan, purchase of the Rumanian harvest, and Bukovina and Bessarabia, in return for an attack on Russia. Thereupon, the British and French began to urge that a Russian Balkan campaign not be attempted. The entire project was finally shelved on November 16, following a conference of the Tsar, Alekseev, and Sazonov at the Stavka.[104]

The Russian Struggle for Power, 1914–1917

THE FALL OF DELCASSÉ AND THE THREATENED FALL OF SAZONOV

On October 30, as had been expected, the *union sacrée* French government of August, 1914 was replaced by a new one, headed by Aristide Briand, perennial French Premier throughout the first third of the twentieth century. Delcassé was left entirely out of the new cabinet, and the Premier himself took over the portfolio of the Minister of Foreign Affairs.

Izvolskii lamented to Petrograd that the fall of Delcassé, "almost the greatest of the members of M. Viviani's cabinet, the notable friend of Russia, and the creator of the alliance with England and Italy," had been produced "for reasons and under circumstances which concern us very closely." True, there had been some talk of Delcassé's bad health and of his opposition to the Salonika expedition, but the weight of opinion was that he fell "under the burden of allegedly enormous mistakes, not only his personally, but also the huge ones in the diplomacy of the entire Quadruple Alliance, which led first to the entrance of Turkey, and then to the treachery of Bulgaria, the change in Greece, and the hesitations of Rumania." The Leftists represented him "not only as the friend of Russia, but also as the abject fulfiller of all our desires and yearnings."

It was now said in France that Delcassé had been blind to the real intentions of Turkey, and then, after letting her rearm, had allowed the "insufficiently prepared and ill-conceived" Dardanelles campaign to be launched. Allegedly, Rumania's cooperation had been lost because the right concessions had not been made at the right time. It was claimed that the Straits Question had been raised at the wrong time, and that its decision in favor of Russia had driven away from the Quadruple Alliance Bulgaria, Greece, and Rumania. Finally, Russia was blamed as the originator of "the impossible plan of the re-creation of the Balkan Bloc," whereby, it was alleged, Russia's desire to gratify Bulgaria had led to the sacrifice of the interests of Serbia and Greece, thus preventing the latter's intervention.

Izvolskii feared that with the departure of

The Russian Struggle for Power, 1914–1917

Delcassé, several persons at the Quai d'Orsay who were guided in the question of Constantinople and the Straits by "traditions very near the time of Louis XIV" could "again raise their heads." The military events in Galicia and Poland had not completely shaken French confidence in the Russian Army, nor removed deep sympathies for Russia. Nevertheless, events in the Balkans had caused to be formed the impression that France was playing too passive a role in Allied diplomacy. Briand had reproached Delcassé for having insufficiently laid before Russia the French viewpoint, and would probably exhibit greater independence. Some had been heard to say that since France went to the rescue of the Serbs, she must now assume the leading role in the Balkans. Moreover, it was impossible to forget deeply-rooted French traditions of good-will towards Austria-Hungary, Turkey, and Greece. Finally, there were several Radical Socialists in the new cabinet who were likely to take an anti-Russian position in the matter of Poland and Galicia.[105]

Sazonov almost preceded Delcassé into retirement, not because of popular disapproval of his policies, but because his alignment with the Russian liberals in September enabled the reactionaries to bring down on him the wrath of Empress Alexandra, who was about, at this time, to precipitate her husband's downfall by her fatal interference, under the influence of Rasputin, in affairs of state.

A detailed examination of all the many facets of the last internal crisis of Tsarist Russia, between August, 1915 and March, 1917, is well beyond the scope of this study, but the high points must be indicated. During the retreat from Poland in August, it seemed that Nicholas II was about to succumb to long-standing liberal demands, in an effort to unite the country for winning the war. Most of the reactionaries in ministerial posts at the war's beginning were dismissed. The Duma was so encouraged that on September 7, its "Progressive Bloc" demanded a responsible government and a host of other reforms. The last hope of the reactionaries, Premier Goremykin, promptly recommended to Nicholas that the Duma be prorogued, but for a week, Sazonov led a majority of the Council of Ministers in opposing the move.[106]

Fearing that his colleagues would carry the day, Goremykin appealed to the Tsarina, blaming the opposition to himself on Sazonov. Alexandra lent a ready ear to his entreaties, and as early as August 23, informed her husband that Sazonov was a fool. On September 6, she transmitted a request from the Premier that Sazonov be relieved of his post, but apparently neither she nor Goremykin could think of a good replacement. They feared that Deputy Foreign Affairs Minister Neratov was a creature of Sazonov, and besides, he had never served outside Russia. Izvolskii was "not a very sure man"; nor, for that matter were Benckendorff and Giers (ambassador to Rome). The Empress lamented:

> Where are men I always say, I simply cannot grasp, how in such a big country it happens that we never can find suitable people, with exceptions!

By September 11, Goremykin had given the Empress some new ammunition to use against

Sazonov. In a letter to her husband, she blamed the Foreign Minister as well as "rotten Ferdinand" for the Bulgarians' failure to join Russia. By this time, Goremykin had supplied her with the names of some reactionaries who might supplant Sazonov. One of them she dismissed because he had believed bad stories about Rasputin, but another, an incompetent courtier, Prince Urussov, Marshal of the Horse and an admirer of Rasputin, she approved.[107]

Shortly after, on September 16, Nicholas followed Goremykin's advice and prorogued the Duma; two days later, on September 18, he assumed command of the armies. After this great victory for reaction, the Empress felt a good deal better, and on September 20, was more generous towards Sazonov. She now felt that he was "a very good & honest (but obstinate) man," and that perhaps he might be left in office, so long as there were other changes in the Council of Ministers. Nevertheless, she appears to have renewed her campaign a month later, towards the end of October.[108]

Since Nicholas began at this time to give way

to his wife's advice where other ministries were concerned, he might have let Sazonov go after all, had the reactionaries not overplayed their hand. The rumor around Petrograd at the beginning of November was that the latter had picked a former ambassador to Vienna, N. N. Shebeko, as Sazonov's successor, apparently intending to secure his appointment through Alexandra. The rumor went on, moreover, that Shebeko would be chosen primarily to negotiate a separate peace with the Central Powers, and this fact, apparently, saved Sazonov. Nicholas, seemingly, had determined that his reign would not end without the acquisition of Constantinople and the Straits.

On November 2, Sazonov visited the Tsar at Tsarskoe Selo for the purpose of delivering a routine report. Referring to rumors of his impending dismissal, he asked pointblank when he might expect to be relieved. Nicholas professed not to have heard the rumors, and "with great emphasis, in the most definite way, refuted even the existence of a thought" of relieving Sazonov. Thereafter, apparently, the reactionaries decided to wait for a better day.[109]

The Russian Struggle for Power, 1914–1917

THE COLLAPSE OF SERBIA AND MONTENEGRO
AND THE ITALIAN OCCUPATION OF
ALBANIA

Meanwhile, at long last, the Central Powers were achieving the object for which the First World War had been precipitated, the destruction of Serbia. The main Austro-German attack, under General von Mackensen, was launched on October 6; three days later, Belgrade had fallen. The Bulgarians attacked on October 14, and by October 18, had cut the Nish-Salonika railroad at Vranja. Within another ten days, Uskub (Skoplje) and Pirot were in Bulgaria's hands, and on November 5, Nish, from which the Serbian Government had moved to Scutari, in Albania, was captured. At the end of October, a French relief force moved northward from Salonika across the Serbian frontier. However, it was too weak, and it failed to make contact with the Serbs. By early December, it had been chased back to its base by the Bulgarians.

On November 20, the Austro-Germans occupied Novibazar, and on December 2, Monastir was evacuated by the Serbs. By December 13, the territory of Serbia was entirely in the hands of the enemy.

Determined that the Serbs should not rally in Montenegro or Albania, the Central Powers pushed on into these two countries. The Austrians invaded Montenegro on December 6, and the fall of Cetinje on January 13, 1916 registered the complete collapse of the country.

Since it was apparent that Albania's turn was next, the French occupied Corfu on January 11, over the protests of Greece, as a safer refuge than Albania for the Serbian government and army. Another motive for this step was the probability that the Italians would look askance at any Serbian effort to hold on in Albania.

Back on November 22, Grey had revealed to Sazonov that he was promising both Sonnino and the Albanians the creation of a future autonomous Albania under the protection of Italy, in order to persuade them to help the Serbs. Sazonov was outraged by this step, which seemed to him an effort to extend the concessions made to Italy in the Treaty of London. He complained of the "unconditional undesirability" of Grey's methods, warning that the latter's "one-man *démarches* have had, up to this time, no success, and can, besides, lead to the spread of harmful rumors of the absence of unity among the Allies."[110]

Conceding that he had acted precipitately, Grey denied that he was trying to extend Italy's proposed gains, and said he was only trying to help the Serbs. Benckendorff warned Sazonov not to push Grey too far, and on November 24, the Russian Foreign Minister said he would not continue his opposition if both Britain and France were in favor of the proposal. However, Briand agreed with Sazonov that Italy had been promised enough for any help she might give the Serbs, and on November 27, Grey dropped his proposal.[111]

Nevertheless, when the Austrians invaded Albania on January 23, the Italians moved to stop them. By the end of February, an Austro-Italian front had been established through the middle of the country, and mountain warfare was to go on along it for the remainder of the war. Meanwhile, the Serbian army was being moved from Corfu to Salonika, from which it would operate thereafter.

VI

THE PARTITION OF TURKEY AND THE FALL OF SAZONOV

DURING THE first nine months of 1916 the Russians managed to fight their way back into the ranks of the Great Powers. There can be little doubt that the blows they struck at the Austro-Hungarians in Poland and at the Turks in Transcaucasia gravely weakened these allies of Germany, indeed, made inevitable their later collapse in 1918. As a consequence, the diplomacy of Sazonov began again to have meaning, and he was able to register such triumphs as an Anglo-French promise of the cession of Armenia to Russia, the repelling of French attempts to interfere in the Polish Question, and the first steps towards the intervention of Rumania under circumstances favorable to Russia. Nevertheless, the internal crisis in Russia continued to develop, and in July, 1916, the Foreign Minister who had gotten the British and French to sign the Straits Agreement was replaced by a worthless and incompetent favorite of the Empress and Rasputin.

VICTORY IN ARMENIA

During the Allied débâcle in the Balkans, things began to go very badly for the British in Mesopotamia. On December 7, 1915, the Turks managed to surround General Townshend with 10,000 British troops in the town of Kut-el-Amara, and on April 29, 1916, Townshend would be compelled to surrender with his whole force. Throughout the siege, the Russians loyally tried to help Townshend by creating a diversion across the Zagros Mountains in north-central Persia. However, an even greater diversion was the spectacularly successful campaign they waged against the Turks in Armenia during the winter of 1915-16.

In August, 1915, elated by their defeat of the British at Gallipoli, the Turks had begun a second offensive into Russian Transcaucasia, advancing on Tiflis by way of Aleksandropol. However, they were routed by General Yuden-

The Russian Struggle for Power, 1914-1917

ich a second time, at the Battle of Khalim Pass. Shortly thereafter, the former Supreme High Commander, Grand Duke Nikolai Nikolaevich, arrived in Tiflis as Viceroy of Transcaucasia. In addition to arranging for the British to be helped by a Persian campaign, he also laid plans for an attack on the main front.

In December, all was ready, and the Grand Duke struck. Fierce battles raged in the frozen valleys and on the steep cliffs of the mountains. The Turks fought bravely, but unavailingly, as the Tsar's army surged forward. By January 30, 1916, Yudenich had reached the outskirts of Erzurum. Less than a month later, the city fell, and on February 20, the Grand Duke made a triumphal entry, and was received by the commander in the field. The loss of Erzurum cost the Turks 40,000 casualties, 13,000 prisoners, 323 guns, and nine standards. Meanwhile, the right wing of the advancing Russians was pressing westward along Turkey's Black Sea coast. Eventually, the Byzantine double-eagle was hoisted by the Russians over the ancient Greek city of Trebizond, which had been the last Byzantine fortress to fall to the Turks. The offensive finally ground to a halt in mid-April, and was not to be resumed on a large scale for the remainder of the war. However, until December, 1917, the entire northeastern corner of the Ottoman Empire would be under Russian occupation.[1]

THE DJEMAL PASHA INTRIGUE

While their offensive was in progress the Russians were meditating an effort to effect a palace revolution in Constantinople, through Armenian agents. They did not succeed, but they did arouse the British and French to the possibility that they might be able, without outside help, to bring about a Turkish settlement.

At the end of December, Sazonov informed the British and French that the Russian Armenian, Zavirev, had been able to establish contact with Djemal Pasha, a leading Young Turk. Djemal proposed to depose the reigning Sultan and the Turkish Government, as captives of the Germans, and to declare himself hereditary Sultan of Turkey. If the Allies would furnish him arms, supplies, and artillery, he would wage a campaign against Constantinople. He was re-

The Russian Struggle for Power, 1914-1917

conciled to the loss of Constantinople and the Straits, and obligated himself to save the Armenians at once and to recompense them for their sufferings later. The Allies must promise post-war financial help and the independence and inviolability of Asiatic Turkey. In return, he would set up autonomous states in Syria, Palestine, Mesopotamia, Arabia, Armenia-Cilicia, and Kurdistan.[2]

Sazonov was much in favor of the Allies' negotiating with Djemal. Sonnino expressed unqualified approval, but on December 29, after some wavering, Briand voiced serious objections. After discussing the matter with the French cabinet, Briand pointed out to Izvolskii that under the terms of the proposal, "Russia keeps for herself Constantinople and the Straits, while France must give up the lands secured to her by the agreement with . . . [Russia], *i.e.*, Syria, part of Palestine, and Cilicia." French public opinion would not allow such a sacrifice, any more than Russian public opinion would permit the sacrifice of Constantinople and the Straits. Moreover, it was impossible to forget that Britain planned an independent Arab Khalifate, and was negotiating with the Sherif of Mecca. Therefore, France could agree to the Djemal negotiations only if her rights in Syria, Palestine and Cilicia were stipulated. Izvolskii warned Sazonov that

I cannot hide from You that in the answer of Briand I hear, if not irritation, then at least some dissatisfaction. You know that the agreement on Constantinople and the Straits is not especially popular in parliamentary circles here, and it has served as grounds for reproaching Delcassé, and that some members of the Government are openly unsympathetic to it. Concerning the realization of this agreement, of course, there is no argument by anyone, and we can count fully on its well-advised fulfillment by France, but on our part, we must avoid everything which can give reason for doubts as to our readiness to present France the compensations for which she has spoken.[3]

Later, on January 1, Briand and Izvolskii discussed the possibility of making Syria, Palestine, and Cilicia French protectorates under nominal Turkish sovereignty. Briand did not entirely repel the idea, but it obviously interested him very little.[4]

Meanwhile, on December 30, the British too

were raising objections. After Sir Arthur Nicolson had revealed to Benckendorff that delicate negotiations with the Arabs were in progress, Grey indicated that Britain would make certain definite reservations regarding any talks with Djemal. Britain must have special post-war rights in Basra. The Arabs had asked for a separate state, including Arabia and the Moslem Holy Places, and the British had agreed, subject to the exclusion of Syria, which was coveted by the French. Basra and Baghdad were not to be excluded, but they would form a special province under British control. To be sure, the British had declined to take part in the creation of a Khalifate of Mecca, since they considered this a matter for the Moslems to settle, but they felt bound by their promises to the Arabs, so long as the latter broke with Turkey and made war on her.

Sazonov was not discouraged by the objections of Grey and Briand, and tried throughout January, 1916, to persuade them to agree to negotiate with Djemal in Cairo. However, the British ultimately concluded that their dealings with the Arabs made it impossible for them to deal also with Djemal, though they were willing that the French, Russians and Armenians try their hand. Despite Sazonov's promise "to give France the leading role in all that can affect the fate of Syria," Briand was also unco-operative, and preferred instead efforts to assure that both the Russians and the British recognized the claims of his country, especially since the French had no forces actually operating against the Turks.[5]

THE SYKES-PICOT AGREEMENT

Evidently after a request by Briand, the British sent a Near Eastern expert of the Foreign Office, Sir Mark Sykes, to Paris on February 1, to arrange with M. Georges Picot, a former French Consul-General in Beirut, for a delimitation of Anglo-French interests in the Ottoman Empire. The Russians were told only that Britain and France were negotiating over the formation of an independent Arab kingdom, and that they were not asked to participate because they were less interested in the matter. However, Russia would be informed of the decisions reached, and a final decision would be made

The Russian Struggle for Power, 1914–1917

only if she consented. Apparently, London and Paris did not even bother to inform the Italians, despite the terms of the Treaty of London.[6]

After a week's negotiations, the well-known Sykes-Picot Agreement was reached. It did not, as is sometimes supposed, settle all the questions arising from a partition of Turkey; nor were all its provisions effected after the end of the First World War. However, it was of a sweeping nature, and it proved to be more durable than the various agreements to which Russia was a party, or at least, it was the starting point for an Anglo-French settlement of the Arab world after the war.

The essence of the agreement was the then current expectation that the Arabs, with proper encouragement, would revolt against the Turks in the interests of the Allies if they were promised the creation of an independent Arab state or federation, an expectation clearly stated in the preamble. In case this occurred, Britain retained the right "to establish, in agreement with the Arab state or federation of states, such rule, direct or indirect, or such control" as she desired or considered most suitable in the "Red

Zone," which included ancient Babylonia as far north as a point just beyond Baghdad. France retained the same right with respect to the "Blue Zone," which included Cilicia, the region of the Gulf of Alexandretta, Lebanon, and a strip of territory extending from Cilicia due east to the borders of Persia. In addition, Britain would receive the ports of Akka and Haifa, and promised France not to cede Cyprus to a third power without French consent. Finally, "after discussion with Russia, and also in agreement with the other Allies and the representatives of the Sherif of Mecca," an international regime would be established in the "Brown Zone," which included Palestine, without Akka, Haifa, or the Negev.

There was thus left for the Arab state or federation the regions of northern Mesopotamia, Syria (without any coastline), the Negev, Trans-Jordan, and Arabia proper. In this vast area, there would be two zones, Zone "A" and Zone "B," assigned to France and Britain, respectively, in which these two powers would have exclusive rights of economic exploitation. Zone "A" included Syria and the Mosul region

The Russian Struggle for Power, 1914–1917

of northern Mesopotamia, and Zone "B," all the rest of the Arab state or federation.

There were other provisions in the agreement, mostly of an economic nature. France guaranteed that Zone "B" would receive a definite amount of the water of the Tigris and Euphrates from Zone "A." Alexandretta and Haifa would be free ports for the commerce of both Britain and France. The Baghdad railroad would not be completed between Mosul and Samarra until Aleppo had been joined to Baghdad by a new railroad, and then only by joint Anglo-French action. Britain would be given the right to build a railroad to Zone "B" from Haifa through the international Brown Zone, and retain control over it, including the right to move troops between these two areas. The Turkish tariffs would remain in effect for twenty years in all the territory in question except the Brown Zone, and a customs union between the Red and Blue Zones and Zones "A" and "B" would be established. No third power could acquire territory in the Arabian peninsula or naval bases in the eastern part of the Red Sea. However, the frontiers of Aden would be rectified.[7]

The Russian Struggle for Power, 1914–1917

The treaty undoubtedly represented a definite triumph for the British viewpoint, since the French definitely relinquished their claims to Palestine in favor of an international regime. Moreover, they accepted merely the right to exploit Syria economically, relinquishing their claims to annex that country. In return for these concessions, the British were quite willing for them to make new claims in areas which interested the Armenians and Russians.

It was obvious, therefore, that the consent of Petrograd must be asked. Requests were sent to the Russian capital from Paris (on February 18) and from London (on February 21) that Sykes and Picot be permitted to visit Sazonov and inform him of the arrangements they had made. Sazonov was at once suspicious; he wanted to know the text of the agreement before the visit was made. However, under French pressure, he finally consented that Sykes and Picot should come to Petrograd and inform him personally, without prior notice as to the terms of the agreement. It seems quite obvious that the French hoped in this way to make it more difficult for Sazonov to raise objections.[8]

The Russian Struggle for Power, 1914–1917

THE RUSSIAN REACTION TO THE SYKES-PICOT AGREEMENT

Sykes and Picot journeyed to Petrograd, and they barely missed presenting the text of their agreement to Sazonov on the first anniversary of the Straits Agreement, since their official reception took place at the Ministry of Foreign Affairs on March 9, 1916. The special envoys were introduced to Sazonov by Buchanan and Paléologue, and the revelation of their agreement took place in the presence of the two ambassadors. After the text was read, Sazonov at once expressed surprise over the generous French interpretation of the term "Syria." He could not conceal his surprise, upon looking at a map offered to him, that the territory to which the French laid claim "drove like a long wedge towards the Russo-Persian frontier near Lake Urmia."

Picot lost no time in defending firmly his proposals, dwelling on the natural character of the frontier proposed, and on the necessity for France's including in her future possessions localities where the lasting basis of French influence had been laid by Catholic organizations. According to Baron Schilling, Picot, "who seemed to S.D. Sazonov somewhat narrow in his expressions, with an apparent clerical bias," produced on the Foreign Minister an impression "indefinite and soon negative." Sykes, on the other hand, by his frank manner, "with basic proposals very favorable to Russia" produced "the very best impressions."[9]

On the next day, March 10, Paléologue and Buchanan met Sazonov at their usual daily audience. Paléologue stated, with reference to the Sykes-Picot proposal, that a definite agreement had been reached between Britain and France, and that it must be viewed as a settled matter. Buchanan refused to accept such an interpretation, stating that his instructions had by no means given the project such a character. On the contrary, he had been ordered only to present the proposal for the approval of the Russian government, and had been put under no obligation to insist upon its unqualified acceptance. Later, Sykes and Picot were brought into the conference. Paléologue continued to insist that the project was an *"arrangement fait"* and an *"affaire faite,"* and Buchanan continued to decline to support him.[10]

Sazonov outlined for Nicholas II on March 12 the progress of negotiations over the preceding three days, pointing out that the proposed frontier between French and Russian possessions in the Near East was the matter of greatest interest. According to him, "the appearance on the great extent of our Asiatic frontier, in localities of a mixed and turbulent population, of a great European power, although at the present time allied to us, and its intrusion towards a corner of the Russo-Persian frontier, must be recognized as undesirable." A frontier with some Moslem state, such as an Arab Khalifate or a Turkish Sultanate, was more desirable. In any event, Urmia could not be turned over to France, because of Russian missionary interests among the Christians there.

Recalling that in the Straits Agreement, Russia had promised France only Syria and Cilicia, Sazonov noted that the French were now claiming Diarbekr, which formed part of Mesopotamia. However, he was willing that they make additional gains in Little Armenia, in the region of the Sivas-Kharput-Caesarea triangle, though he thought they must relinquish to Russia their claims to the Urmia region and the Bitlis passes. In general, Russia might state that the extreme southern limit of her interests in eastern Anatolia was the line Amadia-Djezir-ibn-Omar-Diarbekr-Samsat-Marash-Adana (just above the 1923 southern frontiers of Turkey). In addition, Russia must insist that the boundary of Palestine be exactly defined, and that her interests in that country be protected.

In concluding, Sazonov requested that a detailed review of future Russian boundaries in Anatolia be made by a Special Committee, consisting of the Premier, representatives of the War, Navy, and Foreign Ministries, and a representative of the Transcaucasian Viceroy. Nicholas II consented, and issued orders for the formation of the committee on March 14.[11]

On the day after this report, March 13, Paléologue received an audience with the Emperor. At the gates of Tsarskoe Selo, appropriately enough, he arrived at the same time as a party of officers who had come to present Nicholas with Turkish standards captured during the

The Russian Struggle for Power, 1914–1917

Battle of Erzurum. During the interview, he pointed out that Russian victories in Armenia and the simultaneous French victory at Verdun meant that the great diplomatic questions must be settled so that the Allies could impose their solutions when the hour of peace came. He then requested Nicholas to "examine the legitimate claims of the Government of the Republic in the most generous spirit."

Understanding what he meant, Nicholas expressed himself as follows:

It's an exceedingly complicated question. I haven't yet discussed it with my ministers. Personally, I'm not contemplating any conquests in Armenia, with the exception of Erzurum and Trebizond, the possession of which is a strategic necessity for the Caucasus. But I won't hesitate to promise you that my Government will bring to its examination of this question the same friendly spirit which France has displayed towards Russia.

Paléologue then indicated that the matter was urgent:

When peace comes, the hands of the Allies will have been enormously strengthened for dealing with Germany if they have settled in advance all the questions which might possibly divide them. The problems of Constantinople, Persia, the Adriatic and Transylvania have now been solved. We should make haste to solve the problem of Asia Minor.[12]

Nicholas promised to be guided by this consideration in his discussion of the problem with Sazonov on the next day. However, he closed the audience with the warning words, "I hope Asia Minor won't make your Government forget the left bank of the Rhine."[13]

THE SYKES COMPROMISE AND THE RUSSIAN SPECIAL COMMITTEE

Meanwhile, to avoid any Franco-Russian tempest, the British had already come forward with a compromise solution, wherein France would sacrifice to Russia her claims in northern Mesopotamia in return for Russian agreement that France might adopt the role of protector of the Armenians. Though he was not very favorably inclined towards the extension of the French deep into Anatolia, Sir Mark Sykes seems to have concluded, on the basis of conversations with Picot, that such an arrangement would be satisfactory to the French prestige-seekers in Paris.[14]

In a memorandum drawn up for Buchanan, Sykes pointed out that it was impossible for Armenia to remain under Turkish rule. Even an autonomous Armenia under Turkish suzerainty would be unsatisfactory, since it would be only a second Bulgaria, intriguing in the Caucasus and not able to compete with the Kurds. On the other hand, an Armenia under international control would also be an object of intrigues, and might come under German control.

Nevertheless, the complete transfer of Armenia to Russia without preparation would mean the inclusion of more revolutionary elements into the Russian political fabric. Therefore, former Roman or Little Armenia must be transferred to France, while Russia gained all the rest. Russia would thus receive Erzurum, Bitlis, and Van, with a minimum number of Armenians and a large number of Nestorians, Kurds, and Lazes. France would receive Armenia as "Armenia," and the French zone would be the center of Armenian national feeling. This would be all the more favorable to the Russians, in that the Armenians of Little Armenia held clerical and conservative views in contrast to the anarcho-syndicalist Caucasian and eastern Armenians. Thus, Armenian national strivings would issue forth from the peaceful Armenians, who did not want to be involved with the revolutionary anarcho-syndicalists of the Caucasus and Azerbaijan.

French Armenia would include the historic cities of Zeitun, Khadjin, Diarbekr, Meiafarkin, and Sivas, as well as the district ruled by the last Armenian king, who had died an exile in Paris. It would include also the County of Edessa of the Age of the Crusades. These traditions might serve as the true point of Armenian nationalism.[15]

On March 11, all these points were raised by Sykes in a conversation with Sazonov, attended by Buchanan. The essence of his proposal was that the French should relinquish their claims to the Urmia region in northern Mesopotamia in return for the Sivas-Kharput-Caesarea triangle in eastern Anatolia. Sykes sought to put over his ideas by assuring Sazonov that the Russians "must not fear the French too much, since they usually exploit the local population excessively, and are unable to win its sympathy for themselves or the nation."[16]

Sazonov received Sykes again on March 14, in the presence of the top-ranking officials of the Foreign Ministry. The Briton again pointed out that his proposal would remove the French wedge near the Russo-Persian frontier. He added that Russia would receive that part of Armenia once under Persian rule, and would thus gain a population mainly composed of Kurds, Lazes, Kyzylbashes, and other Kochevian tribes, which "from the viewpoint of state security, represent a more hopeful and satisfactory element." Finally, he indicated that Picot seemed disposed to accept his compromise.[17]

It seems likely that there were some heartburnings around the Foreign Ministry and elsewhere at the thought of giving up the role of protector of the Armenians, particularly after the capture of Erzurum and Trebizond. However, the logic of Sykes' views was very impressive, and acceptance of them meant that the Russians could make great territorial gains in eastern Anatolia without bothering with an Armenian autonomous regime. Accordingly, on March 17, Sazonov accepted all provisions of the Sykes-Picot Agreement south of the Amadia-Djezir - ibn - Omar - Diarbekr - Samsat - Marash-Adana line, on condition of the fulfillment of the Straits Agreement. North of the line, he was willing to accept the Sykes compromise. By March 21, Izvolskii was able to report that Briand also accepted the compromise, and was ordering Picot to negotiate accordingly.[18]

Meanwhile, Sazonov was having other problems. During rejoicings over the victories in Turkey, Nicholas II had removed Premier Goremykin and substituted a nominee of the Empress and Rasputin, Boris V. Stürmer (February 1). Even the reactionaries were stupefied, since Stürmer was known to be an ignorant incompetent, and even the most loyal devotee of Throne and Altar winced at his German name and his total subjection to Alexandra Fedorovna. It appears that in March, only urgent prodding by Sazonov made it possible for the new Premier to call together, on March 30, the Special Committee on the Anatolian frontier which the Tsar had decreed.[19]

The Russian Struggle for Power, 1914–1917

Fortunately, Stürmer appears to have sat through the committee sessions without making any trouble, and they were dominated by Sazonov, the Navy Minister, Admiral Griorovich, and the Deputy War Minister, General of Infantry Belyaev. Five officials of the Foreign ministry and another general completed the membership of the committee.

At the March 30 session, Sazonov outlined all that had happened since he had learned of the Sykes-Picot Agreement, and all that he had done was approved. The committee could therefore turn its attention to the question of just how far westward in Anatolia the Russians should expand, in the region to the north of French Armenia. Admiral Grigorovich insisted that the Russians must have Sinope. Sazonov promptly indicated that the French had obtained from the Turks before the war a concession to build a railroad from Sivas to Samsun on the Black Sea, and that Samsun lay on the coast between Trebizond and Sinope. He predicted that it would be difficult to persuade the French to relinquish the concession.

After this, it was suggested that the future

frontier might be drawn from the port of Ordu, which lay between Trebizond and Samsun, and Karakhissar (Shabkaneh). Apparently the generals present favored this proposal, since they thought it would not be possible to gain enough hinterland south of Sinope to guarantee its defense. On the other hand, Grigorovich continued to insist on Sinope. This emboldened one of the diplomatic officials present to protest the proposed division of Armenia between Russia and France, but he was at once squelched by Sazonov. Nevertheless, the Navy's demand for Sinope had created a new problem in relations with France.[20]

THE FRANCO-RUSSIAN ANATOLIAN AGREEMENT OF APRIL 26, 1916

Georges Picot officially notified Sazonov on March 31 that France was willing to relinquish her claims to "the district of Kurdistan" south of Bitlis and Van, provided she received in return the Armenian districts around Caesarea, Zara, Egin, and Kharput. However, she demanded the retention of her railroad conces-

The Russian Struggle for Power, 1914-1917

sions and her religious-educational institutions in Kurdistan.[21]

Negotiations between Picot and Foreign Ministry officials had led the French by April 5 to concede that the retention of existing French rights in Kurdistan could be the subject of friendly negotiations after the war. They also led to an exact definition of the future southern frontier of "Russian Kurdistan," *viz.:*

> ... the boundary of Russian Kurdistan must ... proceed from Mush through Sert, follow the course of the Tigris to Djezir-ibn-Omar, and then on to the east along the line of the mountain ranges which overlook Amadia, reaching the Persian frontier in the region of Mergever. Thither, the boundary of Arabia must follow along the mountain range which now separates Ottoman territory from Persian, with the stipulation, however, that the passes crossing these mountains must be held on the eastern slope by Russian troops, and on the western, remain in the hands of Arab forces under the French protectorate.[22]

Thereafter, Franco-Russian negotiations lagged, because the Russians were still arguing over their future frontier on the west in Anatolia. The Foreign Ministry was willing to draw the line between Trebizond and Ordu, leaving Samsun and Sinope to the Turks, and allowing the French to build a Sivas-Amasia-Samsun Railroad, with a branch line to Erzurum. It was claimed that this proposal would draw the line along the border of the Turkish and Armenian populations.

The Navy Ministry was not impressed by this argument. In a memorandum of April 2, Admiral Grigorovich argued that Turks would probably make better subjects of the Russian Empire than Armenians. Moreover, he saw no objection to letting the French go ahead and build their Sivas-Samsun railroad into Russian territory; in fact, they might even be given a free port in a Russian Samsun. The important thing was to possess Sinope, and thus guarantee the Russian Black Sea Fleet against the Bulgarians and Rumanians, who might be dangerous naval opponents, even after Russia gained Constantinople and the Straits. The admiral claimed that Sinope would be easy to defend if connected to Russian Transcaucasia by a land bridge. For example, Russia could annex the entire coastal strip between the Pontic Taurus and

The Russian Struggle for Power, 1914–1917

the sea, beginning at Kastamun Pass, which connects Ankara to the port of Inebolü, and continuing on to the east and southeast to the neighborhood of Sivas in future French Armenia.[23]

The Army was won over by Grigorovich's arguments, and came to favor annexation of Sinope. However, in a long memorandum to Sazonov on April 6, Deputy War Minister Belyaev urged strongly that France be forced to relinquish the Sivas-Samsun railroad concession, even though Russia had consented to it before the war. He claimed that the integration of Russia's borderlands required that the sphere of contact with the European powers be limited as much as possible. France might decide to give the Armenians independence, "with an ultraliberal administrative social order, not reckoning at all with Russian state interests," leading to demands on the part of the Russian Armenians for autonomy. Indeed, the French would probably try deliberately to wean both the Armenians and the Kurds from Russia.[24]

Eventually, a second meeting of the Special Committee on the future Anatolian frontier was held on April 10. Grigorovich pushed hard for

· 377 ·

the acquisition of Sinope, while Sazonov spoke of the political disadvantages involved, including the fact that the city's population was Turkish, and that the Sivas-Samsun railroad project would give rise to Franco-Russian misunderstandings. Ultimately, however, he promised to do all he could to meet the Navy's wishes.[25]

Accordingly, the question of the Sivas-Samsun railroad project was raised with the French Embassy on April 13, Picot having been recalled to France because of disappointment over his conduct of negotiations. It appeared at once that the reason for his recall was that his concession regarding French rights in the future "Russian Kurdistan" on March 31 had been made without the approval of Paris; this seemed to leave little hope that the French would give up their Sivas-Samsun railroad concession.[26]

Nevertheless, by April 18, Sazonov and Paléologue had agreed to the following compromise on the question:

> The railroad and other concessions presented to the French by the Ottoman Government will be preserved. If the Imperial Government expresses the desire that they be later changed to bring them

The Russian Struggle for Power, 1914–1917

into accord with the laws of the Empire, this change will take place only in agreement with the Government of the Republic.[27]

France promised, in return, to "give the greatest attention" to securing Russian participation in the official organs of the Ottoman Debt.

All obstacles having thus been removed, it became possible for France and Russia to conclude on April 26 a major "secret treaty" in the form of an exchange of notes between Sazonov and Paléologue, partitioning the northeastern part of the Ottoman Empire and complementing the Sykes-Picot Agreement. Sazonov accepted the latter agreement, subject to Russian acquisition of the districts of Erzurum, Trebizond, Van, and Bitlis, "to a point to be defined on the shore of the Black Sea west of Trebizond." Russia also claimed the district of Kurdistan extending south of Van and Bitlis and the province of Mergever. In return, she conceded the rights of France to the Armenian districts of Caesarea, Zara, Egin, and Kharput. Beginning with the province of Mergever, the frontier of the future Arab state would proceed along the line of the mountain tops which separated Ottoman from Persian territory. The arrangements regarding concessions which had been made on April 18 were embodied in the formal agreement.[28]

It remained only to make it apparent to the Armenians that they must now look to the French for the realization of their nationalist strivings. In a letter to the Viceroy of Transcaucasia two months later, on June 27, Sazonov pointed out that the conquest of Armenia Major, and its pending incorporation into Russia, posed the question of its future government. Although raising the question so early might seem premature, it appeared important to discuss general principles, since a project for the military government of the conquered regions had been worked out and would soon be effected.

The Armenian Question, Sazonov went on, was something more than an internal one, owing to Russia's international role in bringing about the 1914 reforms by Turkey, and the fact that Armenia Minor would be ruled in the future by France. Russia might give her Armenians autonomy similar to that gained within the Ottoman Empire in 1914, or she might re-

The Russian Struggle for Power, 1914–1917

duce their political importance to zero. In this connection, it was necessary to remember that the Armenians in the area to be annexed had been reduced to about 25% of the population by the Turkish massacres; hence, to grant the area autonomy as "Armenia" would lead to the subjugation of a majority by a minority.

Of course, it was impossible to allow the Moslems to oppress the Armenians further, and to cause them to cast envious glances towards their kinsmen in the future French Armenia. Therefore, it was best to organize the conquered regions without showing partiality towards any one nationality or religion. However, the most the Armenians could be given was scholastic and ecclesiastical independence, the right to use their language, and the right of municipal and village self-government.[29]

It was a clear indication that despite all the glowing promises made to the Armenians in 1914 and 1915, the Russians intended to extend their Transcaucasian frontiers after the war by sheer right of conquest, fortified by the agreement with France. Of course, it is highly doubtful whether any viable Armenian state was ever a real political possibility, owing to the wide dispersal of the Armenians amongst a host of other nationalities and religious groupings. Moreover, the Armenians of Cilicia had had to be sacrificed to the French as early as March-April, 1915, in order to gain Constantinople and the Straits, and after that, the other concessions to the French followed naturally. In one way or another, the fateful Straits Agreement seemed to affect every other aspect of Russian policy, and to limit severely the ground on which Sazonov could maneuver.

FRANCE RAISES THE POLISH QUESTION

The Russian victories in Transcaucasia in the winter of 1915–16 enabled Sazonov to beat down efforts of the French, in the wake of the German conquest of Russian Poland, to put the Polish Question on the list of those matters which would have to be settled by international discussion. On the other hand, French pressure, plus the fear that the Central Powers would proceed to a reconstitution of Poland, drove Sazonov into new demands that the Russian Government fulfill the promises made by the Polish

The Russian Struggle for Power, 1914–1917

proclamation of August, 1914. In making these demands, Sazonov exhibited a great amount of political courage, since the new Premier, Stürmer, had his eyes on the post of Foreign Minister.

The territory taken from the Russians in 1915 had been divided by the Central Powers into three parts. The Military Government of Ober-Ost, including Kurland, Lithuania, and Suwalki, with headquarters in Kovno, was ruled by the Germans, as was the Government-General of Warsaw, including the northern half of Russian Poland. The Austrians ruled the southern half of Russian Poland, the Government-General of Lublin. The bitterest possible disputes went on between the Germans and Austrians, and among the Germans, as to what permanent disposition should be made of the conquered territories. Only the German liberals, led by Chancellor Theobald von Bethmann-Hollweg, really wanted an independent Poland, as a bulwark against the Russians. The Austrians feared that Galicia would gravitate towards such a state; if it was created, they wanted it to become a third unit of the Hapsburg monarchy, even though the Hungarians were against such a development. Only the Junker landlords wanted the conquered territories annexed outright to Germany, and there was a powerful current in Germany which favored their return to Russia, as the price of a separate peace.[30]

Eventually, largely because they hoped to raise an army in Poland to help solve a critical manpower shortage, the Central Powers did proclaim on November 5, 1916 the existence of a "Kingdom of Poland," limited entirely to former Russian territory. The Austrians consented to this step with great bitterness, and only because by that time, they were wholly dependent on the Germans. In any event, the expected Polish army failed to materialize, and after the Treaty of Brest-Litovsk on March 3, 1918, the Central Powers regarded the question of the future of Poland as still an open one.[31]

Thus, there was never really much chance of the Central Powers' proceeding to a genuine restoration of Poland, which was as dangerous for them as it was for the Russians. However, the French took the position that there was. On January 28, 1916, the influential Louis Barthou said in a public speech that the most important Allied war aims were the "rétablissement" of Belgium and Serbia and "la liberté de la Pologne." This caused Izvolskii to send hysterical telegrams to Petrograd, leading to a cautious reaffirmation by Sazonov of the previously announced Russian policy toward Poland before the Duma in late February.[32]

Paléologue claims in his memoirs that at the beginning of March, 1916, he was losing no opportunity of pointing out to the Russians that they were making a grievous mistake in delaying the proclamation of the autonomy of Poland on a broad basis, since they risked being forestalled by the Teutonic Powers. Sazonov warned him to "Be careful! Poland is a dangerous quarter for an ambassador of France."[33]

Word came from Paris on March 13 that some French radical newspapers felt that the Russian promise of autonomy was insufficient, and had begun to demand the independence of Poland. Warning that the Briand Government depended to a large degree on radical elements which were extremely pro-Polish, Izvolskii recommended that Russia define her attitude very soon.³⁴

On March 15, Jules Cambon, Briand's chief deputy at the *Quai d'Orsay,* broached with Izvolskii the idea of a collective statement by the Allies on the subject of Poland. Izvolskii replied that such a step was "absolutely unacceptable," since Russian "public opinion" would never allow the Polish Question to become a matter for international settlement. He added that "in presenting France complete freedom to decide at her own discretion the question of Alsace and Lorraine, we, for our part, rightfully expect that to us will be given such freedom in the Polish Question." He still remained adamant when Cambon suggested that a formula might be found in which both Alsace-Lorraine and Poland were mentioned.³⁵

Thereupon, Briand appealed directly to Sazonov, with the following note, which was delivered by Paléologue on March 19:

You have notified me of the intention of the Tsar and the Russian Government with regard to Poland. The French Government recognizes and appreciates the liberal feelings of the Emperor of Russia,

The Russian Struggle for Power, 1914–1917

and the declaration made in his name at the beginning of the war. Faced with the clever propaganda of the Germans, and the recent measures by which they have tried to win Polish opinion and to reestablish recruiting to their advantage, we do not doubt that the Russian Government will, on its part, take measures and make statements of a nature to reassure the Polish people and to preserve its fidelity to Russia. We can only recommend to our Ally a care to act with the wisdom and liberalism which the situation requires.[36]

In reply, Sazonov gave assurances that both the Russian Government and people were "moved by the very best intentions in the idea of the satisfaction of the desires of the Poles," and that France could count on their "wisdom and liberality."[37]

Shortly thereafter, on March 27 and 28, there took place in Paris a meeting of top-flight diplomats of the Allied Powers to discuss outstanding political questions. The idea of such a conference had been raised by Briand in November, 1915, and on December 8, Izvolskii had been named Russian representative by the Tsar. However, it required five months to persuade the Italians to attend; hence, the conference did not actually convene until the spring of 1916.

Izvolskii had been provided with explicit instructions by Sazonov. He was to insist that both the Straits Agreement and the Treaty of London remain inviolate. Though believing all hypotheses on future frontiers in Central Europe to be premature at this time, Sazonov felt that "we must hold that we are ready to leave to France and England complete liberty in fixing the western frontiers of Germany, hoping that in their turn, the Allies will leave to us similar freedom in the delimitation of our frontiers with Austria and Germany." Izvolskii must insist that the Polish Question be excluded from international settlements and repulse every effort to put Poland in the future under the guarantee and control of the Powers. Finally, Sazonov felt that Rumania had already been offered all possible political advantages, and that it was useless "to look for new allurements in this domain."[38]

Apparently, Sazonov was unnecessarily concerned, for it appears that the conference, which held four sessions in the Grand Salon de l'Horloge of the *Quai d'Orsay*, was devoted mainly to

The Russian Struggle for Power, 1914-1917

the discussion of military campaigns planned for 1916. However, French radical circles had been able to cause Léon Bourgeois, one of their number, to be included in the French delegation. Izvolskii suspected, probably rightly, that Bourgeois had been introduced primarily to push the matter of Polish independence, or at least to establish the principle that the Polish Question was a matter for international settlement.[39]

However, Briand kept Bourgeois in hand, for the most part. To be sure, the latter wanted the conference, on March 28, to affirm the solemn resolution of the Allies "to consent only to a peace which, by ruining definitely any policy of hegemony and violence, will assure, with the necessary sanctions, respect for treaties and international laws, and will consecrate at the same time the triumph of justice, liberty, and the dignity of peoples." However, at the demand of Izvolskii, Briand persuaded Bourgeois to back down, and to substitute a statement by the conference that it affirmed the Allies' "unshakeable will to pursue the struggle until the victory of the common cause."[40]

Briand's restraint impressed Sazonov, and on April 3, he brought up the problem of Poland with the Emperor at Tsarskoe Selo, in the course of an official report. He felt that more definite statements on the future of Poland were necessary. After mentioning the complexity of the problem and the necessity of caution in dealing with it, Nicholas finally gave his consent that the Ministry of Foreign Affairs work on the problem.

Two weeks later, on April 17, Briand complained to Sazonov of the difficulties being met by his government in suppressing pro-Polish propaganda in France. He asked for definite data on the intentions of Russia. Sazonov replied haughtily that the Polish Question was an internal Russian matter. He even spoke of "the danger for the most friendly mutual relations between Russia and France of any sort of intervention whatsoever of the latter in the present matter." He recalled that France's diplomatic intervention in favor of Poland in 1863 had "played an indubitable role in later events which led France to Sedan."[41]

Nevertheless, work went on in the Foreign

The Russian Struggle for Power, 1914-1917

Ministry, under the direction of Baron Boris Nolde, on a new policy statement on Poland and also a constitutional charter for the future autonomous Polish Kingdom. The two documents were completed and signed by Sazonov on April 30.

Nolde's policy statement pointed to three factors which made necessary a reorientation of Russian thinking on Poland: (1) the evident intention of the Central Powers to change the country's status; (2) favor shown the Poles in Britain and France; and, (3) the necessity of considering public opinion in occupied Poland. In other words, the Polish Question was no longer one of "a private and purely internal question of reforms," but rather "a weapon and an object of the Russo-German struggle." The willingness of the Western Powers to permit Russia to draw new frontiers with Germany in the east would depend on the willingness of Russia to create of the "second Slavic state" a buffer against future aggression. Russia could not, of course, make Poland independent, since that would result only in eventual German control. On the other hand, merely to give Poland the rights enjoyed by Russian provinces would not fulfill promises already made. Hence, autonomous status within the Empire must be given.

The Charter drawn up by Nolde went considerably beyond the projects of 1914 and 1915. Though united to Russia in the person of the King-Emperor, Poland would have her own Council of Ministers and Ministries and a *Sejm*, consisting of a Senate and a Chamber of Deputies. The King-Emperor would be represented in Warsaw by a Viceroy, who would not be subject in any way to any Russian political institution or Minister, but would be guided only by the Sovereign himself. Polish representatives, however, would participate in the Russian State Council and State Duma when "general state matters" were discussed. The latter were enumerated in the charter; everything else was left to the Polish Viceroy, Ministers, and *Sejm*.

The King-Emperor was given a veto over laws passed by the *Sejm*, and the right to appoint the Council of Ministers. The Imperial Senate would arbitrate disputes between the Russian and Polish authorities, but Poles would be represented on that body. The Charter was

The Russian Struggle for Power, 1914–1917

not to be amended except with the consent of both the Russian State Council and Duma and the Polish *Sejm*.[42]

Though accepting both Nolde's policy statement and his charter, Sazonov rightly regarded them as political dynamite. Since early March, Empress Alexandra had begun a new campaign against him, and in May, rumors of his impending dismissal were again making the rounds in Petrograd. Stürmer was accusing him of having liberal ideas and making concessions to the Duma, as well as being too much under the influence of the British and French ambassadors.[43]

It is not surprising, therefore, that for a whole month, Sazonov kept the documents drawn up by Nolde in cold storage, and continued to fend off French efforts to discover his intentions. On May 5, there arrived in Petrograd two French leaders, ex-Premier Réné Viviani and the socialist Minister of Munitions, Albert Thomas. They had come primarily to plead for Russian troops to fill the gaps left in the Western Front by the holocaust of Verdun, but it later became apparent that they also wanted to talk about Poland. However, on May 17, Sazonov insisted in the strongest possible terms that even the most discreet French intervention in the Polish Question might well shake the Franco-Russian alliance. After that, Viviani and Thomas desisted. Not until the new Russian offensive began in June did Sazonov judge the time ripe to unveil the Nolde documents.[44]

RUMANIAN NEGOTIATIONS
(JANUARY–JUNE, 1916)

Meanwhile, in anticipation of a Russian 1916 offensive to recover the lost territories in Europe, a new and prolonged series of negotiations with Rumania was in progress. After completing their conquest of the Balkans, the Germans exerted strong diplomatic pressure in Bucharest at the end of January, but Bratianu and King Ferdinand held firm to their pro-Allied orientation. On February 2, they even consented to receive a Russian military mission in Bucharest, though General Alekseev was very dubious about the wisdom of their intervening.[45]

The general's doubts were strengthened when the Rumanians demanded that, as the price of their attacking Transylvania, Russia

The Russian Struggle for Power, 1914–1917

must allot 250,000 men to oppose any attack by Bulgaria upon Rumania. Disagreements with the Rumanians broke out; the latter seem to have suspected that the Russians had a secret understanding with the Bulgarians. Promptly, the French began to complain; Poincaré and Joffre wrote letters to the Tsar, and Paléologue saw Sazonov. Later, the French wanted Italy to join the Russo-Rumanian talks on military cooperation, but this suggestion was rebuffed in Petrograd.[46]

The slow pace of the military talks caused Sazonov to make threats to the Rumanian ambassador on March 25, and Bratianu retaliated by signing a trade treaty with the Germans. In late April, the Rumanians were demanding more than in February, *i.e.*, that the Russians must reconquer Bukovina before Rumania attacked Transylvania, and afterwards, send an army to conquer the Bulgarian Dobrudja. These demands were made at a time when Bratianu candidly admitted that he intended to negotiate trade treaties with Austria-Hungary and Bulgaria, as well as with Germany. After that, Sazonov decided to wait until the renewal of the

Russian offensive on the main front gave him a better lever for bargaining with Bratianu.[47]

THE BRUSILOV OFFENSIVE, POLAND, AND RUMANIA

On June 4, 1916, the Russians began their great "Brusilov" Offensive, designed to wipe out the shame of the 1915 defeats. It had been preceded by some local attacks against the Germans in March and April, designed primarily to take the pressure off the French at Verdun. It had been planned for June 15, with General Brusilov attacking the Austrians while Joffre attacked the Germans on the Somme in the West. However, Italian appeals for help (the Austrians were attacking in the Trentino) caused the date of the Russian offensive to be advanced.

Brusilov struck in the direction of Kovel on a front three hundred miles wide. The Austrians were taken by surprise and retreated, leaving thousands of prisoners in the hands of the Russians. On June 8, the Russians captured Lutsk; on June 18, they were back in Chernovets, the capital of Bukovina. Between June 11 and 30, heavy fighting took place along the Strypa.

Sazonov judged the time ripe to unveil at last the Nolde project for Poland. Advising Stürmer of his intentions, he went to the Stavka on June 9, and was closeted for two and a half hours with General Alekseev. The latter already knew about the Nolde project, and said he had already mentioned to the Emperor the necessity of attracting the Poles to Russia's side in order to guarantee their support of the new offensive. He promised to support the Nolde project.

A few hours later, the Foreign Minister went to the Governor's Mansion in Mogilev, which served as a temporary residence for the Emperor. Outside the Imperial quarters, he met General Shuvaev, who had just become War Minister. When the latter said he had been discussing Poland with the Emperor, Sazonov was apprehensive, since he knew that Shuvaev held narrow, nationalistic views. He was therefore agreeably surprised and relieved to learn that Shuvaev had urged Nicholas to be generous with Poland. Later, he learned that he had reason to be grateful to Alekseev, who was responsible for this change of attitude.

In the evening, Sazonov discussed the Polish Question with Nicholas in the presence of Alekseev. He stated that he had sought a solution which did not lessen the Emperor's sovereign rights, nor destroy Russian interests, and then read the documents produced by Nolde. Nicholas listened attentively, and then stated that he had thought much over the matter, and had come to be convinced of the justice of Sazonov's arguments. However, he thought the matter must be discussed by the Council of Ministers. Sazonov replied that he expected much opposition from some Ministers, but Nicholas assured him that exceptional significance ought not to be given to their objections. Sazonov and Alekseev then departed, convinced that the Emperor was ready to approve the proposals.[48]

There the matter rested for about a month, while Sazonov dealt with the Rumanians. On June 11, the Rumanian ambassador complained that Russian troops had violated the Rumanian frontier in the course of their offensive, and that Bratianu feared Russia was trying to force him

The Russian Struggle for Power, 1914–1917

into the war. Sazonov haughtily replied that Russia was totally indifferent towards the prospect of Rumanian help. However, the French did not take this attitude. Promising an offensive against Bulgaria from Salonika, they urged that Rumania intervene, and extracted from Bratianu on June 29 a statement that he could no longer remain neutral.[49]

Finally, on July 4, Bratianu told the Russians that he was now ready to intervene as soon as a formal political treaty, guaranteeing the concessions of 1915, was signed, and as soon as a long list of military conditions was satisfied. There was no doubt that this time Bratianu was serious. However, neither Sazonov nor Alekseev were willing to agree to his conditions unless Rumania intervened quickly, and on July 13, Sazonov requested the Western Powers to follow his lead in the coming negotiations, since he had already given way on the major territorial problems. At the same time, the Stavka went to work on the text of a military convention. However, fate had not willed it that Sazonov should participate in the final act of the Rumanian drama.[50]

The Russian Struggle for Power, 1914–1917

THE FALL OF SAZONOV

At the beginning of July, 1916, Petrograd buzzed with rumors that the Emperor would shortly summon the Council of Ministers to Mogilev and settle finally the question of Polish autonomy. Though Stürmer and his followers were more hostile to Sazonov's plans than ever, it was believed that Sazonov, with the help of Alekseev, had an excellent chance of carrying the day.[51]

As had been rumored, the entire Council of Ministers convened in Mogilev on July 11, on the orders of the Emperor. Sazonov at once heard from Alekseev encouraging news. On the previous day, Nicholas had said, "I am coming to the conclusion that the time for the decision of this [the Polish] Question has now indeed come." More encouraging news came from Count Ignatiev, Minister of National Education. The latter had seen Count Wielopolski, who had dined with Nicholas on the preceding day. The Tsar had authorized the Polish leader to announce to his fellow nationals that in the near future a manifesto would be issued granting a new status to Poland.[52]

Sazonov's expectations of success were fulfilled on the next day. On the evening of July 12, after having made his report to the Emperor, he mentioned the words of Count Wielopolski. Nicholas confirmed the news, and asked how, in Sazonov's opinion, it was best to fulfill the promise. Sazonov answered frankly that if the matter of Polish autonomy was turned over to people who did not sympathize with it, Nicholas' decision might be nullified, and "the entire matter corrupted." Although he had at first favored turning over the matter to the Council of Ministers and a committee of Poles, he had come to the conclusion that the drafting of the manifesto should be entrusted to the Foreign Ministry. Nicholas agreed, and ordered that a manifesto be prepared on the basis of the Nolde project.[53]

Sazonov returned to Petrograd on July 13 and prepared to depart for two weeks of much-needed rest in Finland. Before departing, he revealed the good news to Buchanan and Paléologue. Telling them the details of the Nolde project, he added:

The Russian Struggle for Power, 1914-1917

The Emperor has entirely adopted my views—all my views—though I can assure you we had a pretty warm debate! It's all over now! I won all along the line. You should have seen Stürmer and Khvostov storm!

On July 14, he issued orders for the preparation of the Polish manifesto, and on the next day, departed for his Finnish vacation.[54]

Sazonov had underestimated the grip which Alexandra Fedorovna now had on public affairs. For weeks, Rasputin had been prodding the Empress about the dangers of concessions to the Poles, and the news of the *contretemps* at Mogilev was too much for her. Stürmer returned to Petrograd to lay the matter before his patroness, and he and Rasputin convinced Alexandra that it was her duty to save Russia by bringing about the immediate dismissal of Sazonov. Stürmer set out for Mogilev again to ask for the dismissal, and on July 19, the Empress followed, to back up his arguments.[55]

On the next day, July 20, the first inkling of what was about to happen reached Buchanan and Paléologue. At the Ministry of Foreign Affairs, Neratov gravely informed them that "I have serious reason to think we are going to lose

The Russian Struggle for Power, 1914-1917

M. Sazonov." The Deputy Minister had learned further that the excuse for the dismissal would be the alleged bad health of the Minister. When the two ambassadors suggested that their intervention might make a difference, Neratov encouraged them to try this last expedient.[56]

Accordingly, the ambassadors wired the heads of the British and French military missions at the Stavka to see the Minister of the Court immediately. They were asked to impress upon the latter that "a sympathetic word from His Majesty would, no doubt, inspire M. Sazonov to a fresh effort, which would enable him to complete his task," despite the alleged illness. The generals were to add that the ambassadors were greatly perturbed by the thought of the comment which the resignation of the Russian Foreign Minister would not fail to arouse in Germany, and to indicate that "at this decisive moment of the war, anything which could look like a change in the policy of the Allies might have the most disastrous consequences." On July 22, the replies of the generals indicated that this intervention had failed, and that Alexandra Fedorovna had been successful.[57]

On the next day, July 23, there was published an imperial rescript announcing the resignation of Sazonov and the appointment of Stürmer in his stead. Along with it was published a letter from the Emperor to Sazonov, professing to be a reply to a request from the latter that he be relieved because his health had been shattered by overwork. The Emperor "granted" the request, praising Sazonov for his "tireless zeal" as Minister of Foreign Affairs since 1910, and assuring him of his Sovereign's "friendship and sincere gratitude."[58]

About two weeks later, the deposed Sazonov returned to Petrograd from Finland. On August 3, in a confidential chat with Paléologue, he assured the latter that he had not asked to be relieved, but had been removed. He attributed his dismissal entirely to the Empress, and related how he had originally earned her enmity nearly a year before.[59]

From the few shreds of evidence available on this sordid affair, one tends to draw the conclusion that Nicholas II had granted his wife's demands only with the greatest reluctance, and that before sending Stürmer to the Foreign Min-

The Russian Struggle for Power, 1914–1917

istry, he took positive steps to ensure that there would be no real break in Russian Foreign policy. For one thing, Stürmer made only one important personnel change, substituting B.A. Tatishchev for Sazonov's Chief of Chancellery, Baron Schilling. Stürmer conspicuously failed to remove Anatolii A. Neratov, Deputy Minister of Foreign Affairs, despite the fact that the latter was universally regarded as a close friend and confidant of Sazonov. Owing to the fact that many diplomatic dispatches during the remainder of 1916 were addressed directly to Neratov, one strongly suspects that Stürmer had been instructed to follow Neratov's advice without a murmur. It is certain that he was absolutely forbidden to make any change whatsoever in Russia's foreign policy.

On top of this, Nicholas not only loaded Sazonov down with honors on the occasion of his retirement, but ultimately brought him back to a position only slightly less important than the one he had held. In January, 1917, the London Embassy became vacant, following the death of **Count Benckendorff.** Stürmer had been dismissed in disgrace, Rasputin was dead, and the

Empress was trying to communicate with Rasputin's ghost through a spiritualist medium. Therefore, it was possible to appoint Sazonov as the last Imperial Russian ambassador to the Court of St. James, though the revolution of March, 1917 would prevent his assuming the office.

VII

THE ECLIPSE OF RUSSIA AS A GREAT POWER

(JULY, 1916–NOVEMBER, 1917)

GREAT POWERS can withstand a certain amount of defeat in wartime. They can even afford reactionary and totalitarian governments which trample mercilessly on popular rights. But they cannot be ruled by lecherous charlatans like Rasputin, half-demented women like Empress Alexandra, and hopeless incompetents like Boris V. Stürmer, and remain Great Powers, much less wage successful war and achieve sweeping territorial gains and vastly enhanced prestige. Sazonov had not been the greatest Foreign Minister to serve the Tsars, but his dismissal was portentous, for it clearly marked the beginning of an eclipse of Russian power which would not really lift until the signing of the Nazi-Soviet pact in August, 1939.

True, planning for a great future for Russia after the war went on until March, 1917. Even under the Stürmer regime, it was possible to drive another nail into the Austro-Hungarian coffin by signing the August, 1916 treaty with Rumania. After the real end of the reign of Rasputin and the Empress in November, 1916, a new and vigorous Foreign Minister, N. N. Pokrovskii, pushed forward on Sazonov's path. Italy was admitted to the partition of Turkey. France totally abandoned Poland to the tender mercies of Russia.

However, Rasputin and the Empress had retired too late to save Nicholas II. After March, 1917, the only hope for Sazonov's Grand Design lay in the ability of the liberal Kadets, represented by Paul N. Milyukov, to dominate and guide the Russian Revolution. After two months' effort, they had failed, and after May, 1917, Russia drifted aimlessly under the well-meaning but ineffectual leadership of Alexander F. Kerenskii, who hoped for a better Russia and a better world, but had no idea how to bring them into being. By that time, the Messiah of Communism and his prophets were already in the

The Russian Struggle for Power, 1914–1917

wings. On November 7, 1917, Lenin and Trotskii advanced to the center of the stage, and the days of the old Russia were over. So were the dreams of Sazonov and his collaborators, for a whole generation.

STÜRMER IN POWER

There was a brief flurry in the Western capitals when the news of Sazonov's fall came. Was not the unexpected event a sign that the Russian pro-Germans had triumphed, that Stürmer had been chosen to seek a separate peace? It soon became apparent, however, that though the Stürmer appointment was a disaster, it was a disaster of an entirely different type. Later, it did develop that another creature of the Empress and Rasputin, Interior Minister A. D. Protopopov, had talked with some Germans in Stockholm in the spring of 1916. However, he had been in Stockholm accidentally and had not sought the interview, and there is no evidence that he ever mentioned the incident to the Emperor, the Empress, or Stürmer. In the fall of 1916, the liberal Russians talked glibly to Paléologue about Stürmer's "treachery," but when questioned sharply, they could produce not one shred of evidence.[1]

In fact, to cheer up Paris, Paléologue could quote in his despatches lengthy and inane babblings by the new Foreign Minister about his determination to crush Germany and to hold a great peace conference in Moscow. Intoxicated by his new eminence, the pathetic puppet seems to have wanted to confound his Russian critics by being admitted to the counsels of the Allied great and near-great. He went into transports of delight when the British and French decided to hold an Allied conference in Petrograd in the winter of 1916–17, not realizing that they constantly feared he might babble their secrets before German spies in the Russian capital, and that they agreed on the Petrograd conference only in hopes of saving the tottering Russian monarchy.[2]

Britain and France would have known how to deal with a real leader of the Russian reactionaries, who wanted to make a separate peace. But all the intelligent reactionaries were as baffled as everyone else. Their principles required that they obey their anointed Sovereign and fight the Duma and the liberals; however, they

The Russian Struggle for Power, 1914–1917

understood quite well that only the Duma, the liberals, and the socialists, not to speak of Russia's foreign enemies, could profit from the rule of Rasputin and the Empress. They finally killed Rasputin and talked about a palace revolution, but too late. The monarchical system in Russia had been wrecked beyond repair.

However, despite the lowering clouds, portending revolution, the Stürmer interlude at the Russian Foreign Ministry, from July 23 to November 22, 1916, was not without importance from the viewpoint of the conduct of the war. Much of significance occurred during these four months.

THE INTERVENTION OF RUMANIA

In July and August, 1916, the great Brusilov Offensive finally ground to a halt, largely because the Germans transferred fifteen divisions from the Western Front in order to save Austria-Hungary. The Russians had advanced the front from fifteen to seventy-five miles, and they had delivered a blow from which the Hapsburg Empire never recovered. However, they had failed to take either Kovel or Lvov, and they had lost about a million men.

It might have helped some if the Rumanians had intervened in June instead of in August. However, Bratianu ran true to form, and acted only after his assistance had lost its value to the Russians. Nevertheless, by the act of intervening, Rumania committed the Allies once more to the partition of Austria-Hungary already foreseen in the Treaty of London and promised in the exchanges with the Serbs.

On July 27, the Russian Foreign Ministry received from the Stavka a proposed military convention with the Rumanians, setting the date for their entrance as August 14. On the same day, Paléologue and Carlotti appeared at the Ministry to push energetically for the immediate conclusion of an agreement with Rumania. Paléologue said that a failure like that of 1915 would shake the Franco-Russian alliance, since France had exhausted her reserves and saw in Rumania's entrance the last chance of tipping the scales of war.[3]

Though the Stavka was in favor of taking a

The Russian Struggle for Power, 1914–1917

firm tone with the Rumanians, there were additional pressures from the Western Powers at the beginning of August. Therefore, on August 8, the Russian Foreign Ministry forwarded to the Western capitals and to Bucharest a proposed text for a political agreement, and indicated it was willing for the Rumanians to delay their entrance until August 21.

In the first article of the Russian text, the Allies guaranteed the existing frontiers of Rumania, thus assuring her against any later demands for the southern Dobrudja. In the second article, Rumania promised to declare war on Austria-Hungary and to break off all diplomatic and commercial relations with her allies. The third and fourth articles dealt with the future Rumanian frontiers. The Allies guaranteed her annexation of that part of Bukovina south of the Prut. In Hungary, her future frontier would start with the watershed between the Upper Theiss and the small Vizo River. Thence, it would follow along the Theiss to its confluence with the Samosh. From this last point, it would dip down towards the southwest past the city of Debrecsin until it reached the Theiss again just north of

Szegedin. From that point, it would follow the Theiss to its junction with the Danube, and thence along the Danube to the existing frontier with Rumania. Thus, the Serbs were definitely to be sacrificed in the Banat.

However, in the fourth article, Rumania promised not to maintain troops or fortifications opposite Belgrade, and to pay the expenses of those Serbs in the Banat who wished to emigrate. The fifth article promised that neither the Allies nor Rumania would sign a separate peace (which Rumania later did in March, 1918), so long as the territory to be annexed to Rumania, *which had been conquered by Rumania or the Allies,* had been so annexed. In case any of the promised territory had not been conquered by Rumania or the Allies, then it was promised only "to the extent that this seems possible in connection with the general situation after the war." The sixth article promised Rumania an equal status as an Ally, and the seventh guaranteed the secrecy of the agreement.

In submitting this text, the Russians insisted that Rumania must sign it by August 14. If the terms were refused, then all promised advantages would be lost, and Bratianu's domestic opponents informed.[4]

The Western Powers immediately accepted this text, but Bratianu was so outraged by the fifth article that he threatened to resign (August 9). He feared the possibility that Hungary might save herself by signing a separate peace with the Allies. As might have been expected, the French came to Bratianu's rescue, but with a proposal so sophisticated that the Russians at once gave way on the fifth article. Briand pointed out that at the end of the war, either the Allies would be so strong that they could demand a review of all their war-time territorial promises, or they would be so weak that they could not enforce these promises anyway (August 12). This argument from the arsenal of *Realpolitik* so captivated the Russians that they were even willing to give Rumania another week to prepare for her intervention.[5]

On August 17, 1916, the political agreement, minus the fifth article, was signed in Bucharest by Bratianu and the four Allied ambassadors. The Rumanian Premier expressed hope that "a new era of friendship and confidence" between Rumania and Russia had opened.[6]

At the same time, the military convention was signed. It provided that Rumania should attack Austria-Hungary no later than August 28, or within eight days after an Allied offensive had opened from Salonika. Offensive action would begin on the same day as the declaration of war. Russia promised to maintain her offensive in Bukovina, and to guard Constanza from the sea. Russia might use this port, but Russian naval units on the Danube would be under the Rumanian High Command. Russia promised to send two infantry divisions and one cavalry division to the Dobrudja to act against Bulgaria. Rumania would receive at least 300 tons of supplies a day through Russia, as well as nonmilitary supplies and technical personnel.

The General Staffs of Russia and Rumania were to consult each other, but no Allied army would be subject to another. Russian and Rumanian armies would drive across Hungary separately, the Rumanians aiming at Budapest. Russian troops in southern Rumania would be under Rumanian command, unless they ex-

The Russian Struggle for Power, 1914–1917

ceeded Rumanian troops in number. In the latter case, a separate command would be formed when Bulgarian territory was entered. Neither ally would send troops into the territory or conquests of the other except by mutual consent, and railroads would be under the direction and control of the nation owning the railroads in question. Arrangements were made for the division of prisoners and captured war materiel and trophies, and for liaison officers and exchange of information. Disputed questions, a general plan of military activity, and the question of an armistice would be settled by mutual consent. In general, it was not the sort of military agreement negotiated by nations which trust each other; indeed, it seems quite obvious that the Rumanians were very fearful of being enveloped too closely by their new ally.[7]

In any event, Rumania declared war on Austria-Hungary on August 27. Perhaps contrary to Bratianu's expectations, he soon found himself at war with all the Central Powers. Germany declared war on Rumania on August 28, and Bulgaria and Turkey followed suit on August 31. Italy marked the occasion by declaring war on Germany on August 28. The German High Command, which was about to take over complete control of Germany, now decided that Rumania must suffer the fate of Serbia.

THE ANGLO-RUSSIAN AGREEMENT OF SEPTEMBER 16, 1916

The Western Powers breathed a great deal easier after the signing of the agreement with Rumania indicated that the fall of Sazonov did not mark any real change in Russian foreign policy. Indeed, some might argue that Stürmer was even easier to deal with. Additional weight was given to such a view by the settlement in mid-September of a minor, but nagging problem in Anglo-Russian relations.

Back in the spring of 1916, the British had hoped to conclude an agreement with Russia on the partition of Turkey which would round out the Sykes-Picot Agreement and the Franco-Russian Anatolian agreement. That this was a good idea became apparent as early as March 13, when Buchanan revealed to Sazonov that the British were considering a modification of the Sykes-Picot Agreement to the extent of establishing a Jewish national home in Palestine. Grey frankly admitted that he was considering an espousal of Zionism because of the probable political consequences, among which would be "the turning to the side of the Allies of the Jewish elements in the East, in the United States, and in other places, elements at the present time hostilely inclined to a significant degree to the cause of the Allies." However, the establishment of a Jewish national home would require that the British occupy Palestine in order to save the Jews from the Arabs. In such an event, Jerusalem would be internationalized, despite the desires of the Jews to the contrary.[8]

Sazonov raised no objections to Grey's plans, so long as the rights of the Orthodox in Palestine were protected. In general, he did not want to become involved in an Anglo-French squabble over Palestine, and later told the French that he was still agreeable to Palestine's being included in French Syria, if the British did not object, and again, so long as the rights of the Orthodox were protected.[9]

In the meantime, on March 20, another matter had arisen to point up the need of an Anglo-

Russian Near East agreement. Grey asked that the Russians follow the example of the French, in the Sykes-Picot Agreement, and promise that existing tariffs and arrangements for free transit in the Ottoman Empire be preserved in those parts of that Empire acquired by Russia. Sazonov promptly turned down the request, claiming that the economic and commercial interests of the regions to be annexed to Russia were so bound up with those of the latter that it was impossible to erect customs barriers on the 1914 Russian frontiers. Moreover, political considerations would make necessary the complete integration of the annexed territories with the Russian Empire, thus making a special tariff system impossible.[10]

Britain gave up her demand for the preservation of the Ottoman tariffs in the prospective Russian annexations on March 29, but continued to demand the right of free transit of British goods across these annexations. However, the matter was allowed to rest for two months thereafter, until, on May 30, Grey raised with Benckendorff the question of an Anglo-Russian agreement to round out the Sykes-Picot Agree-

The Russian Struggle for Power, 1914–1917

ment and the Franco-Russian Anatolian agreement. He offered a five-point draft which duplicated the second of these agreements, except that Point 4 stated that "in all parts of Ottoman territory thus ceded to Russia, the existing British rights of navigation and development . . . must be preserved." He was willing to offer Russia the same rights in the territories to be annexed by Britain.[11]

On June 3, Sazonov accepted Grey's draft, with the exception of Point 4. Thereupon, the British claimed that the draft was the same as the treaty Russia and France had signed on April 26. Benckendorff objected, but advised Sazonov to be careful, and suggested special negotiations in Petrograd.[12]

When the Arab tribes in Mecca and other places revolted against Turkey on June 12, the British began to urge haste in the signing of an Anglo-Russian Anatolian agreement, so that they could make definite promises to the Arabs. Benckendorff labored to produce a compromise formula on Point 4, but it failed to satisfy either Grey or Sazonov; on June 21, the harried ambassador predicted to Sazonov that further delay would have "unfortunate results."[13]

Finally, on June 23, Sazonov asked Benckendorff to clarify what the British meant by referring to their "existing rights of navigation and development" in the Ottoman territories to be annexed by Russia. On July 4, it was learned that the phrase referred to the right to engage in the Black Sea coastal trade, mining concessions of British subjects near Kersund, and the right of option enjoyed by the British-owned National Spanish Bank to construct ports and wharves in Samsun and Trebizond.[14]

Still, Petrograd did not act to meet the British request made a month before, and on July 10, Benckendorff reported that the Foreign Office was even more concerned about the matter than he had feared. He predicted "unfortunate" results for Russian interests, and again urged direct talks between Sazonov and Buchanan.[15]

However, nothing was done in the remaining two weeks before the fall of Sazonov, and on July 24, Benckendorff brought the matter to Neratov's attention. A few days later, on July 28, there arrived an urgent request from the Viceroy of Transcaucasia in Tiflis, asking if Stürmer shared Sazonov's views regarding the complete incorporation of the districts conquered from Turkey into the Russian Empire.[16]

Stürmer expressed himself as in favor of complete incorporation on August 1, but on the very next day, received from Benckendorff an intimation that the Anglo-Russian Anatolian agreement was still pending and that the new Permanent Undersecretary, Lord Hardinge, was anxious for some settlement. Finally, on August 17, the Foreign Ministry wired Benckendorff that Russian law excluded the possibility of British ships engaging in coastal shipping along the shores of Russia. However, it wanted to proceed with the signing of all the Anatolian agreement except the disputed part of Point 4.[17]

Eventually, on September 16, Benckendorff delivered to Grey a note, bearing the date of September 1, which accepted all points of Grey's note of May 30, but made reservations with respect to Point 4. The record does not disclose what these reservations were; presumably they provided for further discussion of the disputed question. In any event, all three of the major

Allies, Britain, France, and Russia, were now committed to sweeping changes in the Ottoman Empire.[18]

THE QUESTION OF ADMITTING ITALY TO THE PARTITION OF TURKEY

Meanwhile, another legacy of the Sazonov era had begun to bother the Foreign Ministry—the question of admitting Italy to the partition of Turkey. In 1916, the Italians fought the fifth through the ninth battles of the Isonzo series, and achieved only the capture of Gorizia; however, they did successfully repel an Austrian offensive in the Trentino in May and June. This probably explains why they were ignored in the original Anglo-Franco-Russian partition schemes, but it was not likely that they would stand being ignored for too long.

In mid-May, the talkative British Premier, Herbert Asquith, blurted out the fact that Britain, France, and Russia had reached some agreements regarding the partition of Turkey; the Italians were at once indignant. They demanded that they be informed of the agreements, but in late May, were fobbed off with the

The Russian Struggle for Power, 1914–1917

excuse that they had not yet declared war on Germany.[19]

However, on July 17, Tittoni, Italian ambassador in Paris, raised the question again, and said that Italy was interested not only in the Adalia district, but also in Syria and Cilicia. Briand replied testily that Adalia had already been promised in the Treaty of London, and that the other areas mentioned would be in the French sphere. After that, the Italians turned to London, but Grey took a strong tone with them. He refused even to discuss an Anglo-Italian agreement, and insisted that Italy must negotiate in all the major Allied capitals simultaneously; he advised that this not be done until after the Italian declaration of war on Germany.[20]

For another month, the Italians mulled over the situation, and finally declared war on Germany on August 28. Three days later, on August 31, they presented official requests in London, Paris, and Petrograd that they be informed of the Turkish agreements.[21]

Throughout the month of September, messages flew back and forth between London,

Petrograd, and Paris as to the proper answer to be made to this request. Grey was in favor of showing the Italians the texts of both the Straits Agreement and the three treaties regarding Asiatic Turkey, and so were the Russians. In fact the latter were eager to show everything, on the theory that this act would reinforce the binding nature of the agreements. They were willing too to guarantee again the Italian claims in Adalia. Only the French held back, because of Italian interest in Syria and Cilicia. Briand at first wanted a general conference of the Allies in Paris, but the Russians feared this would make it necessary to inform the smaller Allies of the agreements. Then Briand wanted the Allies to inform the Italians, but to insist that the agreements were not subject to change, and that a more precise definition of Italian claims in Adalia must be achieved. Still later, Briand withdrew his consent to showing the Italians anything.[22]

Finally, after Tittoni was told in Paris that there could be no discussion of an Italian zone in Anatolia, Sonnino threatened to resign. These histrionics caused Grey to reveal the Straits

The Russian Struggle for Power, 1914-1917

Agreement to the Italians on his own responsibility (September 22). At the same time, he gave assurances that the Anatolian Question could not be settled until an Italian sphere was defined, and that a new agreement would be reached on this subject. On the other hand, he stated that the boundaries of the Russian and French spheres in Anatolia were settled, from the British viewpoint, although he granted that Italy need not recognize these spheres until her own had been delimited.[23]

Later, Grey exerted pressure on Briand, and persuaded him to agree to inform the Italians of the Anatolian agreements, and to tell them that the Allies were now willing to discuss an Anatolian zone for Italy, within the limits of the Treaty of London. Appropriate notification was then made by Grey on October 12, by which time the Italians were fully informed.[24]

For some three weeks, Sonnino studied the treaty texts with careful attention. That he was about to make new demands became apparent when he made enquiries regarding Smyrna, and was told that the British no longer felt themselves bound by their 1915 promises to Greece.

Finally, on November 4, the expected happened. Sonnino presented in the Allied capitals a memorandum demanding that Italy be awarded almost the whole southern half of Anatolian Turkey, including the vilayets of Konia, Adana, and Aydin. He thus demanded not only Smyrna, already offered so often to the Greeks, but also a part of the projected French sphere in Cilicia, *i.e.*, the towns of Adana and Mersina.

At the same time, the Italian Foreign Minister made a frank bid for Russian support of his demands by forwarding to Petrograd recognition of all Russian claims at Turkey's expense, conditioned on the acceptance of the Italian demands, *viz.*:

The question of Constantinople and the Straits has always been the object of the very lively attention of Italian policy in the Mediterranean Sea, and the Royal Government fully realizes the importance and significance of the new order of things which will be established on this sea as soon as Russia attains her age-old purpose. The Royal Government would be happy to give its agreement to the desire of the Imperial Government, along the lines of the Russian circular telegram of March 4, 1915, on the condition that the war be conducted to

The Russian Struggle for Power, 1914-1917

a victorious end, and that Italy realizes her strivings in the East as in other places. The freedom of transit through the Straits and the establishment of a free port in Constantinople, and also the entire range of privileges which the other Allies will enjoy ... will be equally secured to Italy. The Italian Government also gives its consent, on the recognition of the above conditions, to the territorial gains ... of the Franco-Russian agreement of April 26, 1916. On its part, it expects that the Imperial Government will extend also to Italy, as far as the district of Adana is concerned the principle of its disinterestedness.[25]

Along with these two documents, Sonnino transmitted his second threat to resign unless his demands were met; if he resigned, he would discuss the whole question publicly before his Chamber of Deputies. Rarely has any Power ever demanded so much for so little as did Italy during the First World War.

Sazonov would probably have greeted all this with a great show of indignation, but Stürmer's first reaction was to sound out the British and French. Grey indicated on November 11 that he thought Sonnino's demands impossible, but had not quite decided how to reply to them.

The French were very angry, and were determined to insist on the terms of the Treaty of London. However, Briand finally calmed down enough to express the view that Sonnino was only seeking a good bargaining position for a rounding out of the Adalia Vilayet, already reserved for Italy.[26]

Nevertheless, Sonnino produced another memorandum on November 19, claiming that numerous Italian interests were concentrated in Smyrna and Mersina, and demanding unconditional equality for Italy in the eastern Mediterranean. He added new demands: Italy must have the same rights and privileges in Palestine as the other Allies; Britain must agree not to cede Cyprus to another power without Italy's consent; and Italy must have the same rights in the Arab states as Britain and France.[27]

Stürmer continued to sound out the British and French, while indicating cautiously that he thought the Italian claims excessive. Probably the Russians secretly enjoyed the spectacle of the French going through the experiences of Sazonov in 1915. However, they were now ready to claim that Italy was bound by the 1909

The Russian Struggle for Power, 1914–1917

Racconigi Agreement to recognize Russian possession of the Straits, though they were becoming worried over the possibility that an Italian Smyrna might threaten the Straits. The British and French greeted Sonnino's November 19 demands with new bursts of indignation. Grey feared that acquiescence in the maximum Italian demands would leave the future rump Turkish state insufficient territory to survive.[28]

At this point, Stürmer departed from the Petrograd Foreign Ministry, and two weeks later, Sir Edward Grey departed as British Foreign Secretary. Partly for these reasons, general negotiations regarding the Italian claims were not undertaken until January, 1917.

STÜRMER'S GREEK POLICY

Before his departure from the Foreign Ministry, Stürmer, on the orders of Nicholas II, undertook one fling along a line of foreign policy clearly in the interests of international reaction, by supporting Constantine of Greece and the Greek royalists against Venizelos and the French republican generals at Salonika, despite the pro-Germanism of the former. This incident should not be taken too seriously; Russia had completely lost out in the Balkans in 1915. However, it does point up the internal crisis within Russia.

In May, 1916, a Bulgaro-German force had penetrated Greek soil and occupied Fort Rupel without any resistance from the Greeks. Suspicious of Graeco-German collaboration, the British and French instituted a blockade of Greece in June, and demanded the demobilization of the Greek Army and the holding of new elections. The Greeks complied. Then, in August, to help the Rumanians, the Salonika forces began to attack the Bulgarians. The Allies were pushed back, and in August and September, the Bulgarians occupied Seres, Drama, and Kavalla. The Greek Army still refused to fight; in fact, a whole Greek army corps voluntarily surrendered to the Bulgarians. Thereupon, the Allied commander, General Jacques Sarrail, began to sponsor a pro-Ally movement at Salonika led by Venizelos. On September 29, Venizelos established a Provisional Government in Crete, and on October 9, moved it to Salonika.

Through it all, the Russian ambassador in

The Russian Struggle for Power, 1914–1917

Athens remained on friendly terms with King Constantine. Izvolskii reported to Petrograd on September 18 great dissatisfaction in Paris over this fact, and at the same time revealed that Briand wanted to bring about Constantine's abdication.[29]

Prince Demidov, the ambassador in question, defended himself warmly. He thought that French support of Venizelos was the only thing preventing Constantine from taking a pro-Ally position, and said French policy was "anti-dynastic." He thought it well for Russia to become a patron of Constantine, in order to counterbalance French influence in Greece.[30]

Izvolskii replied as warmly that as long as French support in other matters was needed, Constantine was an insufficient instrument for Russian policy. Moreover, past experience had given little reason to expect gratitude from the Balkan kinglets.[31]

At this point, Alexandra Fedorovna began to plead for "Cousin Tino" in Athens, and Nicholas II ordered Stürmer "to try to modify the fervor of the French Government which inspires General Sarrail and the French Ambassador in

Athens" (October 9). When the British and French demanded the surrender of the Greek fleet on October 10, Nicholas issued stern orders that no Russian naval units take part in assuring the fulfillment of these demands (October 15).[32]

Finally, on October 14, Stürmer warned Briand that the time was coming when Russia would be unable to support the Western Powers in Greece. He accused General Sarrail of being too fascinated by political questions and claimed he was undermining efforts of the British and Russians to reach an agreement with Constantine. He asked that Russia be informed of the scope of Sarrail's instructions.[33]

In reply, the French frankly admitted their intention to support Venizelos and to try to overthrow Constantine. However, they had not yet made up their minds whether to install a Greek Republic. Izvolskii sounded a warning note by predicting that in the end, Britain would support whatever France decided to do. He felt it much wiser for Russia not to support Constantine, but to demand concessions from France in some matter which affected Russian interests.[34]

Stürmer was not unmoved by this advice, but

was terribly upset when he learned that Venizelos was about to ask the Allies for recognition of his government. The Russian Foreign Minister finally decided that he might recognize Venizelos as the civilian authority in the Allied zone of occupation. However, he breathed easier when Briand indicated on October 19 that he had no intention of taking steps against Constantine without prior approval of the Allies.[35]

Finally, on October 25, a common Allied policy towards Greece was worked out. Money would be advanced to Venizelos, and Constantine would be forced to evacuate his army from Thessaly to the Peloponnesus and recognize that a state of war with Bulgaria existed. Shortly thereafter, Grey assured Stürmer that an "antidynastic" policy was excluded.[36]

Nevertheless, this settlement was upset when on November 19, General Sarrail demanded of Constantine the ejection of the representatives of the Central Powers in Athens and the surrender of war materiel. Constantine rejected these demands on November 30; shortly after, Anglo-French units landed at Piraeus and fought a pitched battle with the Greek royalists in the streets.

Briand thereupon demanded (December 5), that Greece be blockaded, Constantine deposed, and the Venizelos Salonika regime recognized. He indicated, however, that the monarchical constitution would be saved. Stürmer was now out of office, but Acting Foreign Minister Neratov pled with the French not to give the Russian opponents of the alliance with the Western Powers a new weapon by deposing Constantine. Finally the British stepped in and persuaded Briand to accept lesser measures than he wanted. Greece was blockaded on December 8, and at the demand of the Allies, Constantine agreed on December 15 to withdraw his army into the Peloponnesus. However, it was only a question of time before the fall of Nicholas II would cause "Cousin Tino" also to lose his throne.[37]

THE FALL OF STÜRMER

Despite the Rumanian intervention in August, 1916, there is no doubt that a serious *malaise* began to affect the morale of those Russians

The Russian Struggle for Power, 1914–1917

most interested in fighting the war through to victory, immediately after Sazonov was dismissed and the Brusilov Offensive ground to a halt. The real pro-Germans (not the Empress, Rasputin, and Stürmer) sensed what was happening, and took advantage of the situation to insinuate assiduously that a separate peace might be had with Germany at the expense of Austria-Hungary and Turkey. The British were so concerned that in mid-August, they had King George V wire Nicholas II and assure him that there was nothing at all to the pro-German rumors that Britain intended to go back on the Straits Agreement.[38]

The Tsar of all the Russias now felt tortured by a burden beyond his ability to bear. He obviously missed the supporting arms of the strong and able men of times past, the Wittes, the Stolypins, and the Sazonovs. His erratic moves became more frequent.

Despite the obvious significance of the dismissal of Sazonov, he had reversed himself on August 10 to the extent of assuring the Russian Poles that he still intended to fulfill the promises of 1914. Such a stand was of course not to Stürmer's liking, but the sycophantic courtier was no Sazonov, and dared not court dismissal by opposing his Sovereign's will. However, he was ready with a counter-proposal. The Russian reactionaries must be satisfied that acquisition of Constantinople and the Straits, rather than the liberation of Poland, was the principal Russian war aim. Therefore, proclamation of Polish autonomy must be preceded by publication of the Straits Agreement. Accordingly, in response to King George's telegram, Nicholas told him that he thought publication of the Straits Agreement would put to rout all pro-German sentiment in Russia. Later, on September 11, it was indicated to both Britain and France that the proclamation of Polish autonomy would follow publication of the Straits Agreement.[39]

The first reaction of the Western Powers, in mid-September, was negative. Grey complained that publication might affect British relations with the Moslems of India, Persia, Afghanistan, and Egypt, and said that the timing of any announcement must be submitted to the British War Council. Briand complained that German propaganda would take full advantage of the publication, although it appears that he most feared the polemics which would follow in the Parisian press. Later, however, Grey seemed to be willing to go along, if France was.[40]

That ended the matter for the time being. In the meantime, Stürmer was becoming the object of a storm of criticism in Russia because of the defeat of Rumania by the Central Powers. On August 31, the ill-equipped and ill-trained Rumanian army had moved across the difficult Hungarian frontier, which was only lightly defended. A few days later, on September 5, the Bulgarians, under the German General von Mackensen, struck across the Danube just south of Bucharest. As things turned out, this first counter-offensive was only a feint, for, after he had succeeded in thoroughly confusing the Rumanians, Mackensen delivered his main blow in the Dobrudja. The Rumanian reserves raced eastward to meet this new threat, just as Mackensen wanted. At the end of September, with the Rumanians thoroughly disorganized, a powerful Austro-Hungaro-German force under the former German Chief of Staff, von Falkenhayn, hit the main Rumanian forces in Transylvania and drove them back across the mountains. Falkenhayn failed to destroy them utterly, but by mid-November, had pushed out into the plains of Wallachia.[41]

All segments of Russian political thought, Right, Center, and Left, blamed the hapless Stürmer for the Rumanian defeats, though he hardly knew what it was all about. Even Paléologue felt it necessary to defend Stürmer before his Russian liberal friends, but they paid no attention. On October 16, Stürmer felt compelled to deny publicly that the Government had the slightest intention of making peace with Germany. Buchanan felt it necessary to visit the Stavka on November 3 to point out to the Tsar the seriousness of the situation.[42]

In a complete reversal of roles, the British and French began to urge the Russian Government in mid-October to publish the Straits Agreement, but Stürmer now held back, fearing that the time was not ripe. Then, on November 5, the Germans helped along the crisis by proclaiming the independence of Poland, and the Western Powers urged Stürmer to reply with a proclamation of Polish autonomy. Finally, it was decided

The Russian Struggle for Power, 1914-1917

that when the Duma met on November 14, Stürmer should try to confound his critics by making an announcement on both Constantinople and the Straits and Poland.[43]

However, Stürmer lost his nerve at the last moment. He and the other ministers appeared before the Duma only during Rodzyanko's opening speech and then withdrew from the chamber. By prearrangement the diplomatic corps followed the example of the ministers. Thus Buchanan and Paléologue missed the famous speech by Milyukov, Mirabeau of the Russian Revolution, accusing Stürmer and the Empress of treason. The press was forbidden to print the speech, but it circulated freely anyway. An eight-day crisis ensued.[44]

There was nothing for Nicholas II to do but dismiss Stürmer or take some drastic counterrevolutionary action. As in the crisis of March, 1917, he consulted his generals, the only strong men left around him, and Alekseev advised that Stürmer be dismissed. Despite the ragings of Alexandra Fedorovna, Nicholas followed this advice, thus bowing to the popular clamor and indicating his own total inadequacy. Stürmer was relieved as both Premier and Minister of Foreign Affairs on November 22. Alexander F. Trepov, the able Minister of Communications who had built the Murmansk-Petrograd Railroad in 1915-16, became Premier immediately. However, not until December 14 was Nikolai N. Pokrovskii, the conscientious but uninspired Minister of Finance, named Minister of Foreign Affairs; Neratov acted as Foreign Minister during the hiatus. Nicholas pacified his wife by leaving Interior Minister A.D. Protopopov in office, and by sending General Alekseev on extended sick leave; General V.I. Gurko acted as Chief of Staff until Nicholas' abdication. Ultimately, Trepov's failure to secure the dismissal of Protopopov led to his resignation on January 10, 1917. He was replaced by Prince Nikolai D. Golytsin.[45]

WAR AIMS ANNOUNCEMENTS

While the game of ministerial musical chairs was being played in Petrograd in November, 1916-January, 1917, it was possible at long last to make to the Russian public announcements about war aims which reaffirmed those already

The Russian Struggle for Power, 1914–1917

made in February, 1915. To put these announcements in the proper perspective, it must be recalled that the great turning point of the First World War had arrived. Not only in Russia, but all over Europe, the war-weary peoples were turning to new leaders with new programs and panaceas. In Britain, on December 7, Asquith and Grey gave way to David Lloyd George and Arthur J. Balfour as Prime Minister and Foreign Secretary, respectively. Almost simultaneously the French replaced Joffre with General Nivelle, only to replace the latter six months later with Pétain. The Briand cabinet fell in March, 1917, and was followed rapidly by Ribot and Painlevé cabinets before Clemenceau came to power in December. There were five Foreign Ministers in 1917: Briand, Painlevé, Ribot, Barthou, and Pichon. Already, in August, 1916, Hindenburg and Ludendorff had taken over the German armed forces and become the real rulers of Germany; in 1916–17, they changed Chancellors twice and Foreign Ministers twice. Franz Josef of Austria-Hungary died on December 14, 1916; the new Emperor, Karl I, changed Premiers and Foreign Ministers frequently. Italy had a complete change of leaders in 1917.

In the meantime, the only uncommitted Great Power, the United States, moved nearer to intervention. Woodrow Wilson received a new mandate from American voters in November, 1916, and was thereafter free to make his effort to end the war with a peace in which right and justice would triumph. It was a time when the old war aims must be given an ideological gloss they had hitherto lacked.

After Stürmer's failure to make his war aims announcement on November 14, the whole question of publication of the Straits Agreement was reviewed again by Russia and her allies. Grey wanted to be sure that any announcement to the Duma made it clear that the agreement had been reached back in March, 1915, and not as a result of the Rumanian defeat. He also wanted both Italy and Japan to be informed prior to publication, and the text of the agreement to be released simultaneously in Paris, London, and Petrograd. Later, he wanted Rumania informed prior to publication. Briand agreed with his views.[46]

The Russian Struggle for Power, 1914-1917

After becoming Russian Premier on November 22, Trepov wanted to make the war aims announcement Stürmer had failed to make as soon as possible. However, Acting Foreign Minister Neratov felt that first, Italy must be persuaded to accede to the Straits Agreement, without prior precise Russian acceptance of her new Anatolian territorial demands, made in November. Between November 26 and December 2, hurried negotiations took place in both Petrograd and Rome. Neratov wanted Sonnino to agree that Italian acceptance of the Straits Agreement changed in no way the 1909 Racconigi Agreement. Sonnino claimed that the earlier agreement had been destroyed when Russia negotiated with Britain and France about Constantinople and the Straits behind Italy's back. However, he finally agreed that "the spirit of the Racconigi Agreement" was not changed, and accepted the Straits Agreement, subject to two stipulations. The Russian announcement must not reveal that Italy was not consulted in the initial negotiations, and Italy must enjoy all privileges guaranteed the British and French by the agreement. However, at the insistence of the British, Sonnino had finally, in his acceptance of the agreement, to indicate that Italy was not consulted when it was first negotiated. On the other hand, the Italian acceptance falsified the date of the original agreement, to make it appear that it was reached before Italy offered herself to the Allies.[47]

Italian acceptance of the Straits Agreement, without previous precise Russian acceptance of Italy's Anatolian claims, became official on December 2, when Sonnino handed the Russian ambassador in Rome the following note:

> The Italian Royal Government gives its consent to the memorandum transmitted by His Excellency the Russian ambassador in Rome to Mr. Sonnino on November 19/December 2 of this year relative to Constantinople and the Straits, on the condition that the war be conducted to a victorious end, that Italy realizes her strivings in the East and in other places, as this is indicated in the Russian memorandum, and that she enjoys all advantages which will be secured to France and Britain.
>
> As far as the Royal Government knows, an identical statement was made *mutatis mutandis* by the Petrograd cabinet to the British and French Governments in February, 1915, and the London and

Paris cabinets expressed their agreement in identical terms.[48]

Sonnino's readiness to meet Neratov's requests no doubt sprang from the conviction that only the Russians were at all likely to accept his maximum Anatolian demands. Nevertheless, Italian acceptance of the Straits Agreement was something of a personal triumph for Sazonov's friend and pupil.

The British were very fearful that Neratov would ignore their request that Rumania be informed before any announcements were made, and an appeal was made direct to the Tsar. Nicholas issued appropriate orders, and on November 28, Bratianu was informed of the Straits Agreement in Iasi, the temporary Rumanian capital. He was assured that Rumania's economic interests would be guaranteed, and that there would be complete freedom of navigation through the Straits for the Rumanian merchant marine and navy. Probably this gave Bratianu a much-needed lift of spirits.[49]

At the last moment, it was decided not to publish the exact text of the Straits Agreement, for fear of the effect on French and Italian public opinion. However, last-minute requests of Grey for assurances regarding the Moslem Holy Places and for mention of the economic clauses of the Straits Agreement were never acted on.[50]

On December 2, Trepov entered the Duma chambers in the Tavricheskii Palace. After rising to speak, he had to leave the tribune three times before making himself heard over shouts of "Down with Protopopov!" Finally he launched into his speech, saying that the war must be fought to the bitter end, and that Russia would shrink from no sacrifice. Then, after a long recital of the perfidy of Turkey, he claimed that Constantinople "ought inevitably to pass under the guardianship of the Power whose development, for centuries, it has cramped and limited by the obstacle which it forms on the road to the open sea, in the narrow defiles of the Bosporus and Dardanelles." Britain, France and Italy had clearly recognized that such a solution was not only just in itself, but that it also served, in general, "the cause of civilization." They had given Russia the definite assurance that "the guardianship over Constantinople and

The Russian Struggle for Power, 1914–1917

over the free access from the Black Sea to the Mediterranean, taken away from Turkey as a result of her hostile bad faith" would pass "by right" to Russia. Trepov then promised to safeguard the rights of Rumania. Fulfilling Stürmer's promises, he confirmed that Poland would be restored within her ethnic frontiers to form an autonomous state. Finally, he invited the Duma to cooperate with him in bringing the war to a successful conclusion.[51]

Despite this announcement, the Duma continued to be more interested in Protopopov than in Poland and the Straits, and the man-in-the-street appears to have greeted the Premier's statement with a shrugging of the shoulders. In Paris, the reaction was one of relief that the Russian pro-Germans seemed to be routed, and some of the sting was taken out of the fall of Bucharest to the Germans on December 6. Sonnino emphasized to the Italian deputies that the Straits Agreement had been concluded long before Italy entered the war, and added vaguely that Italy had later adhered to "the collective recognition of the secular claims of our valiant ally."[52]

Shortly after, in the wake of the fall of Bucharest, Germany judged the time right to forward peace proposals to the Allies through President Wilson (December 12). They contained nothing specific, and were mainly designed to influence American opinion. Two days later, on December 14, the new Russian Foreign Minister, Pokrovskii, appeared before the Duma to deliver a ringing denunciation of Germany's "lying proposals" and "deceitful offers." He assured his audience that Russia would "apply herself with more energy than ever to the realization of the aims proclaimed before you." The Duma responded with an equally ringing resolution in which it declared itself "unanimously in favor of a categorical refusal by the Allied Governments to enter under present conditions into any peace negotiations whatever."[53]

The Allies had planned to present a reply to the German note in very general terms, but after Wilson asked the belligerents to state their peace terms, they decided to be more specific (December 18). On December 23, Briand forwarded to Petrograd a proposed reply to the

The Russian Struggle for Power, 1914-1917

German and American notes. It listed certain "high war aims" which the Allies had made their own. These included the restoration of Belgium, Serbia, and Montenegro, with indemnities; the evacuation of France, Russia, and Rumania, with reparations; "the reorganization of Europe, guaranteed by a stable regime and founded as much upon respect of nationalities and full security and liberty, economic development, which all nations, great or small, possess, as upon territorial conventions and international agreements suitable to guarantee territorial and maritime frontiers against unjustified attacks; the restitution of provinces or territories wrested in the past from the Allies by force or against the will of their populations; the liberation of Italians, of Slavs, of Rumanians and of Czecho-Slovaks from foreign domination; the enfranchisement of populations subject to the bloody tyranny of the Turks; the expulsion from Europe of the Ottoman Empire decidedly foreign to western civilization." Though the Allies wanted to liberate Europe from "the brutal covetousness of Prussian militarism," it had never been their design "to encompass the extermination of the German peoples and their political disappearance."[54]

Briand wanted to include a statement about the reestablishment of Poland, but Pokrovskii objected. Fortunately, however, Nicholas II had just issued, in his capacity as Supreme High Commander, an order of the day to the Russian Army (December 25), which stated that

> The time for peace has not yet come. The enemy has not yet been driven from the occupied territories. Russia has not yet performed the tasks this war has set her, by which I mean the possession of Constantinople and the Straits, as well as the restoration of a free Poland, composed of her three portions.[55]

Consequently, there was finally included in Briand's draft a statement that "the intentions of His Majesty the Emperor of Russia regarding Poland have been clearly indicated in the proclamation which he has just addressed to his armies." After that, the only difficulty was to persuade the Italians to accept a statement which they feared might cause them to lose something guaranteed by the treaty of London.

The Russian Struggle for Power, 1914–1917

They were finally won over, and the Allied reply was delivered to President Wilson on January 10, 1917.

THE LONDON CONFERENCE ON ITALY'S ANATOLIAN CLAIMS

By the beginning of 1917, it was finally possible to settle down to a discussion of the Italian claims in Anatolia. On November 25, 1916, Neratov had made a statement of Russian views to the British and French. Though believing that Anglo-French interests were those most affected by Sonnino's demands, Russia feared that the award of Smyrna to Italy would worsen the position of all the Allies and of Venizelos in Greece. Moreover, Russia did not want the Italians in an area close to their future Straits zone. On the same day, Neratov told Carlotti that it looked as if Turkey was about to share the fate of Poland in 1795, and in that event, Russia must review her own demands. He suggested that Italy be satisfied with an Anatolian zone beginning south of Smyrna near the Gulf of Scala Nuova, which was joined to Konia by a railroad.[56]

Thereafter, negotiations languished while the British made the transition from Grey to Balfour. However, on being installed, the latter suggested a Rome conference on the Italian demands, after Britain, France, and Russia had agreed on a common position (December 14). Briand wanted the conference held in London instead, fearing that Sonnino would increase his demands if he had charge of the conference. By December 18, general consent had been given to a London conference under Balfour's presidency.[57]

The three original Allies then discussed the position they should adopt. Pokrovskii set forth his views in a telegram of instructions to Benckendorff on December 21. Future Russian possession of the Straits and Armenia made it essential to plan for "our further consolidation" in Asia Minor; hence, the installation of any Great Power in Asia Minor was contrary to Russian interests. Russia must try to preserve in Asia Minor as large a Turkey as possible, "gravitating politically and economically towards us." It must contain as many Turks as possible and have an exit to the sea; therefore, neither Smyrna nor any territory to the north should be Italian. In general, Russia would demand that Italy stay south of the Scala Nuova-Konia line; south of it, she would support the position of Britain and France.[58]

It would appear that there was some discussion between London, Paris, and Petrograd on these and other points, but that no common Anglo-Franco-Russian position was ever adopted. In any event, three weeks later, just when Balfour was about to get the conference underway, Count Benckendorff died suddenly and unexpectedly (January 11, 1917). Sazonov was promptly appointed to take his place, but wanted to stay over in Petrograd for the Allied conference scheduled to convene there early in February. Pokrovskii was now much embarrassed, because the Chargé in London, Konstantin Nabokov, was young and inexperienced. Both he and Briand rebuffed a suggestion that the conference site be changed, but Balfour was anxious to proceed, since Sonnino was in political trouble in Italy. After a futile effort to persuade Sonnino to wait, it was finally decided that Nabokov should represent Russia, so long as he accepted all decisions *ad referendum* (January 26). The conference opened on January 29. Balfour represented Britain; Paul Cambon, France; Nabokov, Russia; and Imperiali, Italy.[59]

The meetings began with a long speech by Cambon, in which he accepted the Italian demand for Konia, but insisted that Adana and Mersina must go to France, since they had historic ties with Syria and were its granary. He claimed, moreover, that southwestern Anatolia was more richly endowed with easily exploited resources than the territory claimed by France. Balfour then said that Italy was entitled to a zone equal in value to those assigned the other Allies, but only within the letter and spirit of the Treaty of London. Nabokov then insisted that there must be a viable Turkey in Anatolia, and that it must have Smyrna. Imperiali responded by saying that Italy expected from Russia the same friendly attitude towards her Smyrna claim that she had shown towards Russia's claim for Constantinople and the Straits. Balfour then suggested that the former British ambassador in

The Russian Struggle for Power, 1914–1917

Constantinople, Louis Mallet, draw up a counter-proposal to Imperiali's demands.[60]

A two-week recess in the conference followed. Then, at its second session on February 12, Balfour produced the Mallet counter-proposal. The frontier of the future Italian Anatolia would begin at Scala Nuova and proceed in a straight line to Mount Erjies, whence it would turn south and proceed towards Cape Anamur along the western frontier of the French possessions in Cilicia. Balfour claimed that this proposal filled the requirements of the Treaty of London, and added that it required Britain's giving up the Aydin Railroad, which might arouse protests in Parliament.[61]

Imperiali categorically refused to discuss the Mallet Plan, and it was decided to give him time to seek new instructions. Though Balfour and Cambon were disgusted at his attitude, Nabokov predicted to Pokrovskii that they would soon be putting pressure on Petrograd "to get the negotiations out of the rut" by giving way on Smyrna.[62]

Nabokov was a good prophet. Sonnino was anxious for an agreement by March 12, when the

Italian parliament met, and he tried to enter into private talks with Balfour, Briand, and Lloyd George, only to be rebuffed. Finally, on February 22, he said he would give up his claims to either Mersina or Smyrna, but not both.[63]

Pokrovskii now produced a compromise plan. Smyrna would go to the new Turkish state, but if it failed to show any ability to survive, Italy might have Smyrna, provided she allowed the other Allies a free hand in disposing of the remainder of Turkish territory. However, the plan was not offered at once, because it seemed that Italy might be on the point of accepting the Mallet Plan.[64]

The conference finally convened again on March 6, and Imperiali indicated his willingness to accept the Mallet Plan, provided Smyrna was added to the Italian gains. Obviously, Italy had decided she would have greater success against the Russians than against the French. However, Nabokov rebuffed this new offer. On this sour note, the conference ended, with the British and French voicing anxious concern over Sonnino's domestic situation. However, in its last ten days of existence, the Russian Imperial Government

The Russian Struggle for Power, 1914–1917

took a firm stand. Only after its collapse did Lloyd George and Ribot dare to promise Smyrna to Italy.[65]

THE PETROGRAD CONFERENCE AND THE LAST SECRET TREATY

Appropriately enough, Imperial Russian diplomacy in the First World War started and stopped on the same thorny problem: the Polish Question. In an odd set of circumstances, Imperial Russia, on its deathbed, was able to extract from the French something it had sought in vain during its days of great strength: complete freedom to settle the problem of Poland in any way it saw fit. This was because the French, at the nadir of their fortunes during the First World War, had decided to reach for something offered by the Russians at the beginning of the war but not yet claimed in Paris: control of the German Rhineland.

It should be emphasized that neither the British nor the Italians were partners to the last of the "secret treaties," and that the British, known to be against French Rhineland ambitions, were kept completely in the dark until Trotskii published the secret treaties. However, the treaty is of great importance in understanding French behavior at the Peace Conference and afterwards.

As is now well known, the showy Allied conference held in Petrograd in February, 1917, was a great fiasco. Nicholas II was in mourning for Rasputin, assassinated on December 26, 1916, and Chief of Staff Gurko, Premier Golytsin, and Foreign Minister Pokrovskii were new and untried. No definite decisions on military operations were made, and the Allied representatives left Russia with a profound sense of the downward course of her affairs.[66]

However, the French saw to it that the conference was not all in vain. They sent along with their delegation Gaston Doumergue, then Minister of Colonies in Briand's cabinet, and sometime Minister of Foreign Affairs, Premier, and President of the Republic. He revealed to Paléologue on January 29 that he had been sent to bind the Emperor by a written and detailed agreement to his promises of November, 1914 and March, 1916 that France would have full liberty to decide the fate of Germany west of the Rhine.[67]

Why did Briand want such a treaty? Probably mainly to help prolong the life of his tottering government, but also because all the recent talk of war aims had reminded the French that they did not as yet have any categorical promises that their principal war aim would be fulfilled. They seem to have feared too that if Nicholas II were deposed in a palace revolution, or if the whole Imperial regime fell, it would be well to have something on paper to show any successor or successor regime. Finally, it would always be easier to win Britain and Italy over to something that Russia had approved, especially since they were asking for a great deal more than Alsace-Lorraine, whose retrocession Britain and Italy already approved.[68]

On February 3, Nicholas II received the visiting delegates at Peterhof, and Doumergue used the opportunity to obtain a few moments alone with his Imperial quarry. He then went as far back as the Treaty of Verdun of 843 A.D. to demonstrate the rights of France to the Rhine frontier. Invoking previous promises by the

Emperor, he demanded the annexation of Alsace-Lorraine and other districts directly to France, the complete separation of the remainder of the Rhineland from Germany, and its neutralization, following an extended occupation by French troops. Nicholas promptly gave his unqualified consent. After that, the two men talked about denying the Hohenzollerns the right to speak in the name of Germany when peace was made.[69]

The way having thus been prepared, Paléologue submitted to Pokrovskii on February 12 the formal French request, which is important enough to give here in full:

1. Alsace-Lorraine will be restored to France;
2. Its frontiers ought to be traced at the pleasure of the French Government, in such a way as to take into account the strategic requirements, and to include within French territory all the part of this province which contains deposits of iron as well as the coal basin of the Saar Valley;
3. The other provinces situated on the left bank of the Rhine, and which now form a part of the German state, ought to be separated from it, and freed with respect to it, of all ties of political and economic dependence;

The Russian Struggle for Power, 1914–1917

4. From the provinces which are not included within French territory, an autonomous and neutral state ought to be set up, which will be occupied by French troops until the guarantees required by the Allies for the peace to be solidly assured will have been realized, and in general, so long as the present enemy states have not executed all the conditions of the peace treaty.[70]

The Russians had, in the meantime, realized that here at last was a heaven-sent opportunity to settle definitely the 1916 wrangle with the French on the Polish Question, while gaining the consent of their ally to one of the principal points of Sazonov's exposition of September 14, 1914. Pokrovskii accepted Paléologue's memorandum, but on the same day wired Izvolskii that he intended to recall the viewpoint stated by Sazonov on February 24, 1916, to the effect that "Russia gives France and England a free hand in delimiting the western frontiers of Germany, but she expects in turn that the Allies will grant her the same freedom in the delimitation of her frontiers with Germany and Austria-Hungary." Moreover, France would be asked to consent to the abrogation of the demilitarization of the Aland Islands.[71]

Conversations now began in both Paris and Petrograd regarding the Russian demands for a *quid pro quo*. At first the French were amenable to Pokrovskii's proposals; then there were objections. It was claimed that Russia ought to guarantee the return of Alsace-Lorraine in exchange for the Straits Agreement; Delcassé was blamed for not making such a demand in 1915. Izvolskii replied that the Straits Agreement had been paid for with the agreements partitioning Asiatic Turkey. Ultimately, on February 17, he was able to extract a text of the proposed treaty very favorable to Russia. In it Russia and France promised "to sustain one another in order to guarantee to France the eastern frontiers, and to Russia the western frontiers which . . . are of a nature to give the two countries . . . all the indispensable guarantees of security and economic development."[72]

However, on the next day, the Russian ambassador in Paris learned that Pokrovskii had already consented to Paléologue's February 12 note, and was horrified. He chided his chief bitterly, since he feared that Briand would now go back on some of his concessions. In point of true fact, Briand was under heavy pressure not to give way, and after Doumergue returned to Paris, did insist on some changes in his original text. Ultimately, it was decided that Pokrovskii's acceptance of Paléologue's note of February 12, delivered on February 14, constituted sufficient Russian recognition of French demands, and that the only thing now necessary was a note wherein France recognized the Russian demands. However, Izvolskii's fears, in the long run, were baseless, since Briand gave full consent to Russian desires.[73]

On March 12, 1917, in Paris, the following note was delivered to Izvolskii by Briand:

> The Government of the French Republic, desiring to confirm in all their force the agreements concluded with the Russian Government in 1915 for the purpose of settling at the end of the present war the question of Constantinople and the Straits in conformance with the age-old vows of Russia, and wanting, on the other hand, to facilitate in an equal measure the gaining by its ally of all guarantees desirable from the military, commercial, and industrial viewpoint, so that its security may be assured,

and in order that the economic development of the Empire may be facilitated, recognizes Russia's full freedom in delimiting her western frontiers.[74]

The only thing Briand had not done, and which Izvolskii presumably wanted done, was to link the proposed French gains to the proposed Russian gains, making one dependent on the other. However, in receiving the note, Izvolskii said that he did not doubt that "the Government of His Imperial Majesty will see in it a new proof of the feelings of friendship and reciprocal confidence which exist between Russia and France."[75] He spoke just three days before the abdication of Nicholas II and the advent of the Russian Provisional Government, headed by Prince G. N. Lvov, and including Paul N. Milyukov as Minister of Foreign Affairs. Probably poor Nikolai N. Pokrovskii never even saw his despatch announcing the treaty.

PROVISIONAL GOVERNMENT:
THE MILYUKOV REGIME

This study might well end with the fall of Nicholas II, since in retrospect, there was never any chance after March 15, 1917 that Russia

The Russian Struggle for Power, 1914–1917

would win in the struggle for power on which she had embarked in 1914. The question of war aims ceased almost entirely to be a matter of international negotiation, and became one of domestic politics, and this phase of the question has been adequately covered in many other places. Only the broad outlines of the 1917 debate need be indicated here.

It is perhaps worth noting that throughout the debate there was never any agency in Russia indubitably qualified to express the will of the Russian masses. The ill-fated Constituent Assembly did not meet until January, 1918, and then met for only two days. Naturally, all the competing groups on the Russian scene claimed to speak for the masses, but this need not lead us to accept Trotskii's claim that the Russian soldiers "voted for peace with their feet." Ultimately, the question of whether Russia should continue the struggle for world power begun by the Tsars was settled by the issue of the struggle for power on the domestic scene.

After the fall of Nicholas II, the Russian Right slunk into the shadows, ready to welcome support in the restoration of the old order from

The Russian Struggle for Power, 1914–1917

either the Allies or the Germans, whichever one happened to win. Only the liberal Kadets, led by Milyukov, wanted to carry on business as usual, or at least, to fight the war to victory and realize the advantages already promised to Russia. The Mensheviks and the great body of the Socialist Revolutionaries, led by Kerenskii, Tseretelli, Chkeidze, and Chërnov, wanted basically what President Wilson wanted after American intervention on April 6, 1917, a revision of war aims which would inspire the drooping spirits of the Allied peoples and make the war one "to make the world safe for democracy." The Bolsheviks, led by Lenin and Trotskii, wanted an end to the existing war and a revolutionary struggle of the "oppressed" against the "oppressors" to save the world for Communism. Ultimately, the Bolsheviks won the internal struggle in Russia, but what they achieved was not only the loss of all that had been fought for in the First World War, but a twenty-year eclipse of Russia as a Great Power.

For some two months after the outbreak of the Russian Revolution (March 15-May 18), the Kadets had control of the Ministry of Foreign

The Russian Struggle for Power, 1914-1917

Affairs. From Paul N. Milyukov, the anxious British and French had no difficulty in gaining on March 17 the assurance that the new regime would "remain mindful of the international agreements entered into by the fallen regime" and would "honor Russia's word." On top of this, the Lvov Provisional Government publicly announced on March 20 that it would "sacredly observe the alliances which bind us to other powers," and would "unswervingly carry out the agreements entered into by the Allies." These assurances paved the way for recognition of the Provisional Government by Britain, France and Italy between March 22 and 25.[76]

The Provisional Government further commended itself to the Western Powers by its *Appeal to the Poles*, written by a Pole, A. R. Lednicki, and published on March 29. It promised the creation of "an independent Polish State, the stronghold of all the territories where the Polish people constitute the majority of the population," which would be a "solid rampart against the pressure brought to bear by the Central Powers on the Slav nations." The only conditions were that the new Poland must be "attached to Russia by a free military union," and that the Russian Constituent Assembly must give its approval to the new "fraternal union" and "territorial changes in the Russian State."[77]

On top of this, a new and unaccustomed energy was infused into both the Russian military and diplomatic effort. Milyukov and his likeminded colleague, War Minister A. I. Guchkov, tried unsuccessfully to persuade General Alekseev, who had become Supreme High Commander, to launch an amphibious attack on Constantinople from Trebizond. Milyukov had many friends in Bulgaria, and seems to have undertaken some efforts to detach her from Germany.[78]

To be sure, the new Foreign Minister made some trouble for the Western Powers. He seems to have been as much opposed to Allied sponsorship of the "Greater Greece" movement of Venizelos in the occupied Hellenic Kingdom as the hapless Stürmer had been. He was indignant because the free-wheeling British Prime Minister, Lloyd George, decided at a meeting with the new French Premier, Alexandre Ribot, at

The Russian Struggle for Power, 1914–1917

Folkestone, on April 11, to award Smyrna to the Italians. After the decision was imparted to Sonnino at St. Jean de Maurienne on April 19, it did develop that Russian consent to the decision would be asked, but Milyukov was still indignant. He was even suspicious when Lloyd George sent Balfour to Washington to tell President Wilson about the "secret treaties," following American intervention on April 6.[79]

The reason for this cavalier treatment of Milyukov was that the British and French had concluded by the beginning of April that he had no chance to survive as Foreign Minister. Not only was it a matter of the opposition of all the socialist parties, organized in the Petrograd Soviet, to the policy of "business as usual." In the government itself, the new Justice Minister, Alexander F. Kerenskii, was leading a movement for a revision of war aims. As early as March 19, he publicly proposed internationalization of Constantinople and the Straits and self-government for Poland, Finland, and Armenia, the last of these to be a separate entity from Russian Transcaucasia.[80]

On March 27, the Petrograd Soviet sent out

an appeal to "comrade-proletarians, and toilers of all countries," inviting them to "start a decisive struggle against the grasping ambitions of the governments of all countries," and promising that the Russian democracy would "resist the policy of conquest of its ruling classes." On April 7, the leaders of the Soviet held a joint meeting with the members of the government, and demanded that the latter break officially with the policy of conquest and sponsor a "peace without annexations and indemnities." Milyukov vigorously opposed these demands. Finally, the government produced and published on April 10 a *Declaration of War Aims* which was largely meaningless. In one sentence, it claimed that "the purpose of free Russia is not domination over other nations, or the seizure of their national possessions or forcible occupation of foreign territories, but the establishment of stable peace on the basis of the self-determination of peoples." But in another sentence, it promised not to permit the "fatherland to emerge from this great struggle humiliated," to defend "the rights of our fatherland," and to observe fully "all obligations assumed towards our Allies."[81]

The Russian Struggle for Power, 1914–1917

The Soviet leaders rightly regarded their victory as inconclusive. On April 11, the demand was made that Milyukov transmit the *Declaration of War Aims* to the Allies in the form of a diplomatic note. On April 25, the further demand was made that the government "enter into discussion with the Allies for the purpose of working out a general agreement" whereby there would be "a general renunciation of annexation and indemnity." By this time, the Mensheviks and Socialist Revolutionaries, who dominated the Petrograd Soviet until October, 1917, were themselves subject to pressure. Lenin had returned to Russia on April 18.[82]

The British and French ambassadors had already predicted to their governments that a reconciliation of government and Soviet could be achieved only under the leadership of Kerenskii. Possibly because he saw an opportunity for Britain to escape from the Straits Agreement, Sir George Buchanan established close contact during April with Kerenskii, and with the latter's close friend and supporter, Finance Minister M.I. Tereshchenko, a wealthy young Ukrainian sugar manufacturer. Probably to his disappointment, he discovered that their private views on abandonment of the Straits Agreement and Anatolian treaties were a great deal vaguer than their public announcements. Paléologue, on the other hand, tried as best he could to bolster Milyukov.[83]

Both Lloyd George and Ribot finally decided that the usefulness of Buchanan and Paléologue was hopelessly impaired by their close ties with the fallen Imperial regime. Consequently, special missions headed by patriotic socialists were sent to Petrograd. The first wave of French socialists arrived on April 13, and, to Paléologue's horror talked before the Soviet about a plebiscite in Alsace-Lorraine. A week later, Albert Thomas, the socialist Minister of Munitions in Ribot's cabinet, arrived; he relieved Paléologue on April 23, and, pending the arrival of Joseph Noulens in June, acted temporarily as the French ambassador. However, Buchanan had saved his job by his early friendliness to Kerenskii and Tereshchenko. After arriving in the Russian capital with orders for Buchanan's recall in hand, Labourite Arthur Henderson recommended to London that the experienced ambassador remain, and Lloyd George granted the request.[84]

On April 26, Kerenskii precipitated a crisis by announcing that the government was preparing a note to the Allies in the spirit of the *Declaration of War Aims*. Actually, no such note was being prepared, but Milyukov did finally agree to send the Allies the text of the declaration, so long as he could append an explanatory note. Both declaration and note were sent out on May 1. The latter cancelled the former, since it stated that the Provisional Government "while safeguarding the rights of our own country, will, in every way, observe the obligations assumed towards our Allies," and expressed the view that "the leading democracies, inspired by identical desires, will find the means to obtain those gaurantees and sanctions which are indispensable for the prevention of sanguinary conflicts in the future."[85]

Two days later, on May 3–4, there took place the "April Days," consisting of riots by revolutionary soldiers demanding Milyukov's resignation, and of pro-Milyukov demonstrations organized by the Kadets. The riots were finally stilled after Milyukov had transmitted to the Allies an "explanation" of his May 1 note, defining the words "guarantees and sanctions" as "limitation of armaments, an international tribunal, etc." Nevertheless, some members of the government, as well as the representatives of Britain and France, now felt that Milyukov should resign. After a decent interval, filled with complicated negotiations, a complete reorganization of the Provisional Government took place on May 17–18. Though Prince Lvov remained as Premier, Kerenskii, in his new post of War Minister, became the real head of the government. A merger of government and Soviet leadership was achieved, with the entrance of Tseretelli, Chkeidze, and Chërnov into the government. Tereshchenko became Minister of Foreign Affairs. The Kadets had failed; now the Mensheviks and Socialist Revolutionaries would have their chance.[86]

THE PROVISIONAL GOVERNMENT: THE KERENSKII REGIME

For two months, from May 17 to July 20, it seemed that Kerenskii might save the situation.

The Russian Struggle for Power, 1914–1917

In the aftermath, he was to be almost universally condemned, so it is perhaps worth saying here a word in his favor. He was not quite as stupid and empty-headed as is sometimes supposed; he fully understood that Russia could not go back on all her war-time commitments and hope to retain her Great Power status. He also understood that if she lost her Great Power status, then the revolution, as he understood it, and as all the decent Russians understood it, would be a failure. Indeed, what hope was there for any democratic regime in continental Europe if Germany won the war?

Perhaps Kerenskii's real mistake was to risk everything on an offensive against the Central Powers, at a time when disorganization and desertion had already begun in the army. However, there were sound reasons for the gamble. Kerenskii had come to power on a program of revision of war aims, but was intelligent enough to know that no revision was possible until there was a restoration of Russia's military reputation.

While the offensive was being prepared, Foreign Minister Tereshchenko tried to satisfy the domestic clamor for revision through a few gestures which would not be too strong to alarm the Allies unduly. On May 18, he promised a peace "without annexations and indemnities" and the "taking of preliminary steps towards effecting an understanding with the Allies," while at the same time spurning the idea of a separate peace. The British cooperated by publicly promising on June 8, with regard to the war-time agreements, that "if the Russian Government wants it, the British Government is entirely ready to examine the question with the Allies and, if it is necessary, to revise these agreements." The French were less cooperative, though some private assurances were given by Albert Thomas; however, it was possible to publish on June 4 an official French statement which demanded Alsace-Lorraine, but had a great deal to say about a post-war League of Nations. Sonnino would not cooperate at all, but Italy did not matter much. President Wilson inadvertently made matters worse by a message to the Russian Government on May 26 in which he stated that the demand for revision of war aims stemmed from German propaganda, and that "it was the status quo ante out of which this

The Russian Struggle for Power, 1914–1917

iniquitous war issued forth. . . . That status must be altered in such a fashion as to prevent any such hideous thing from ever happening again." However, few, if any Americans in a position of power seem to have ever really understood the Russian Revolution until long after 1917.[87]

Finally, on June 16, Tereshchenko released for publication a note to the Allies in which, while frankly admitting that the differences of view existed, he expressed the conviction that "the close mutual agreement between Russia and her Allies will ensure complete mutual agreement on all questions." He suggested a conference, to take place "as soon as there are favorable conditions for it." Privately, he explained that "favorable conditions" would come only when "the . . . efforts . . . to reestablish the situation on our front will have been . . . crowned with success." After the offensive finally got underway at the beginning of July, he suggested that the conference might be called in mid-August.[88]

While waiting for Kerenskii's offensive, Tereshchenko tried to prevent the Allies from making the war-aims controversy any worse by opposing any definite grant of Smyrna to Italy. He also opposed, though quite unsuccessfully, the Allies' forcing the abdication of King Constantine and Crown Prince George of Greece on June 11. Despite Russian protests, Prince Alexander became King of Greece, and Venizelos returned to Athens in triumph on June 21, to make the final break with the Central Powers on July 2.[89]

On July 1, Kerenskii's long-awaited offensive began. After some initial successes, it bogged down, and then collapsed completely. An Austro-German counter-offensive began on July 18, and by mid-October, the Russians had been pushed well back of the 1915–17 front. Between July 17 and 19, Petrograd was shaken by bloody riots, and the Bolsheviks made a premature and unsuccessful effort to seize power. After they were routed, a conservative reaction set in. Kerenskii was elevated to the Premiership on July 21, and definitely promised to request an Allied conference in August to discuss Allied foreign policies "in the light of the principles put forward by the Russian Revolution." How-

The Russian Struggle for Power, 1914-1917

ever, the cooperation of the Kadets was now essential, and they resolutely demanded that the government "be guided by the principle of complete union with the Allies" in matters of war and peace. By July 26, it had been decided to delay the war aims conference indefinitely.[90]

Despite the Kadet fidelity to them, the Allies decided in July that Russia would probably eventually leave the war, and became far less considerate than they had been in April and May. Britain and France gave Sonnino an unequivocal promise of Smyrna, though, after Caporetto and Sonnino's fall in October, it was to be promised again to Venizelos. Efforts by Tereshchenko in August to persuade the United States to oppose Italian demands were ineffective. Venizelos began to agitate for Constantinople and the Straits, and the only counteraction Tereshchenko could think of was an effort to bribe the Greek press.[91]

The old question of the publication of the war-time agreements came up again in August and September. Izvolskii had been removed as ambassador to France in May, and so was not on the scene in Paris when a storm arose in July, because the socialists had gotten wind of the Briand-Pokrovskii agreements on German boundaries. Ribot was finally goaded into a July 31 statement in the Chamber of Deputies that the Briand-Pokrovskii agreements would be published. Later, he regretted his rashness, and seized on some mild objections by Tereshchenko to extricate himself, by claiming that the Russians would not permit the agreements to be published. Tereshchenko was indignant, and an angry correspondence took place, in which the question arose as to whether the agreements in question were bound up with those partitioning Turkey. The crisis finally blew over on September 12, when Ribot and his Foreign Minister, Paul Painlevé, exchanged places. However, Tereshchenko did not let the matter drop, and on September 24, stated categorically that "the publication of all the agreements in general, concluded as much before as during the war, does not arouse on the part of Russia any objection if the other interested Allies give their consent."[92]

The British also put Kerenskii and Tereshchenko in an awkward position. In August and

September, international socialism was putting all its hopes in a great socialist congress in Stockholm, which would bring together true believers from all belligerent countries for the first time since 1914. None of the Allied governments wanted their socialists to go; the whole business was regarded as a German propaganda trick. However, none of the governments wanted to be put in the position of opposing the conference, and each wanted some other government to take the onus of being the first to deny passports to its socialists. Finally, the British Government took the lead, and Arthur Henderson was dropped from the cabinet because he wanted to go. Lloyd George then tried to wriggle out of his awkward position by claiming that he had heard from Paris that Kerenskii was opposed to the conference. The Mensheviki and Socialist Revolutionaries promptly showered abuse on their fallen idol.[93]

Kerenskii had had no real program at all since becoming Premier, but in the second week of September, his aimless drifting was finally halted by the Kornilov Affair. Afterwards, the Left was back in the ascendancy in Russia, and the Kadets no longer counted for much in the new government formed on September 15. The Russian Republic was at last proclaimed (September 16), and on October 17, in a moving ceremony in the Bolshoi Theater of Petrograd, an unconditional grant of independence to Poland was made. The Allies were persuaded to promise an Allied Conference in Paris in November. Though they stipulated that there would be no discussion of war aims, Kerenskii announced on October 8 that at the conference, "our delegates will . . . strive to come to an understanding with the Allies on the basic principles laid down by the Russian Revolution."[94]

However, the Russian Left no longer trusted Kerenskii, and early in October, the Bolsheviks were able to get Trotskii elected president of the Petrograd Soviet. That body then proceeded to elect a Menshevik, ex-Minister of Labor Skobelev, as its delegate to the Paris conference. On October 20, it produced a list of war aims which included evacuation of Russia, Belgium, Serbia, Montenegro, and Rumania, plebiscites in Poland, Lithuania, Latvia, Alsace-Lorraine, all disputed Balkan areas, Turkish Armenia, and

The Russian Struggle for Power, 1914–1917

the Italian areas of Austria, return of the German colonies, and the reestablishment of Greece and Persia. All straits giving access to inland seas, and the Suez and Panama Canals, were to be neutralized. War indemnities, economic blockades, separate tariff unions, most-favored-nation treatment, and secret diplomacy were to be abolished. Gradual disarmament of all nations was to be followed by universal adoption of citizen militias. A League of Nations was favored, if all states were put on an equal footing. The Allies should agree to peace negotiations as soon as the Central Powers accepted the above terms, and bind themselves not to begin secret peace negotiations and to admit neutrals to the peace conference. All opposition to the Stockholm Conference must be given up.[95]

Tereshchenko bitterly opposed these proposals in a debate with Skobelev before the "Provisional Council of the Russian Republic" convened by Kerenskii on October 20, and the Allies refused to permit Skobelev to come to Paris. After another bitter debate between Tereshchenko and Skobelev on October 31, the

The Russian Struggle for Power, 1914–1917

latter refused to go to Paris if the former went. However, Kerenskii had persuaded the two men to patch up their quarrel by November 2.[96]

Meanwhile, Lenin had returned to Petrograd, and had begun preparations for the seizure of power. Everyone knew what was going on, and the "Provisional Council of the Russian Republic" blamed Kerenskii on November 5, claiming that he could have averted the situation by "inducing the Allies to publish their conditions and commence negotiations for peace." On November 7, the Bolsheviks struck. Together with the other ministers, Tereshchenko was arrested in the same Winter Palace in which Nicholas II had promised on August 2, 1914 "not to make peace while one of the enemy is on the soil of the fatherland." The road to Brest-Litovsk was now open.

NOTES

CHAPTER ONE

[1] Maurice Paléologue, *La Russie des Tsars pendant la grande guerre*, I, 35–58, 63–65, 83–92. 3 vols. Librairie Plon. Paris: 1921; Sir George Buchanan, *My Mission to Russia and other Diplomatic Memories*, I, 211–214. 2 vols. Little, Brown & Co. Boston: 1923.

[2] N. M. Lapinski, ed., *Russko-Polskie Otnosheniya v period mirovoi voiny*, 57–65. Tsentrarkhiv. Moskva-Leningrad: 1926 g.; *Mezhdunarodnye otnosheniya v epokhu imperializma. Dokumenty iz arkhivov Tsarskogo i Vremmenogo Pravitelstv. 1878–1917 gg.* Seriya III, VI, 1, #338, 334–360. 10 vols. Komissiya pri Prezidiume TsIK Soyuza SSR po izdaniyu dokumentov epokhi imperializma. Gosudarstvennoye Sotsialno-Ekonomicheskoye Izdatelstvo. Moskva-Leningrad: 1931–38 gg.

[3] S. D. Sazonov, *Les anneés fatales. Souvenirs de M. S. Sazonov, Ancien Ministre des Affairs Étrangeres de Russie (1910–1916)*, 320–334. Payot. Paris: 1927.

[4] Paléologue, I, 77–80.

[5] *Vestnik Evropy*, August, 1914.

[6] *Ibid.*, September, 1914. St. Vladimir was Great Prince Vladimir of Kiev (980–1016), who converted Russia to Orthodox Christianity. Yaroslav Osmomysl ("the Wise") was his son, during whose reign (1019–1054), Kievan Russia rose to its highest peak of development. Danilo and Roman were local Russian Princes of Galica who struggled during the 13th and 14th centuries to ward off conquest of their domains by Tatars, Poles, and Hungarians.

Notes

[7] *Ibid.*

[8] *Ibid.*

[9] Youri Danilov, *La Russie dans la guerre mondiale (1914–1917)*, 113–255. Payot. Paris: 1927. See also Albert Pingaud, *L'histoire diplomatique de la France pendant la grande guerre*, I, 49–56. 3 vols. Editions "Alsatia". Paris: 1937–39; Bernard Pares, *The Fall of the Russian Monarchy*, 187–206. Jonathan Cape, Ltd. London: 1939; and B.H. Liddell Hart, *The War In Outline, 1914–1918*, 29–46, 54–58. Random House. New York: 1936.

[10] *Ibid.*

[11] Paléologue, I, 83; *M.O.V.E.I.*, VI, 1, #126, 120–121; Friedrich Stieve, *Iswolski im Weltkrieg*, 64–65. Deutsche Verlagsgesellschaft fur Politik und Geschichte m.G.H. Berlin: 1925; *M.O.V.E.I.*, VI, 1, #132n, 124–125.

[12] "Stavka i Ministerstvo Inostrannykh Del", *Krasnyi Arkhiv*, vols. XXVI–XXX. Moscow: 1928.

[13] A. Popov, "Cheko-Slovatskii Vopros i Tsarskaya Diplomatiya", *Krasnyi Arkhiv*, vols. XXXIV–XXXV, 1929.

[14] Thomas G. Masaryk, *The Making of a State: Memories and Observations, 1914–1918*, 74–77. Frederick A. Stokes Co. New York: 1927; Sazonov, 292–297; *C.V.T.D.*

[15] Masaryk, 141–146; *C.V.T.D.*

[16] Sazonov, 293–294; Masaryk, 11–20, 141–146.

[17] *C.V.T.D.*, Masaryk, 141–146; Sazonov, 292–297.

[18] *Vestnik Evropy*, October, 1914.

[19] *Ibid.*

[20] *C.V.T.D.*, Masaryk, 11–20, 141–146; Sazonov, 292–297.

[21] On the position of Italy and Rumania at the begin-

Notes

ning of the war see Luigi Albertini, *Le origini della guerra del 1914, passim.* 3 vols. Fratelli Bocca. Milano: 1941–43 (English translation in progress).

[22] *Tsarskaya Rossiya v mirovoi voiny*, 149, 235–237. Narodnyi Komissariat Inostrannykh Del. Moskva: 1922 g. On the general subject of the early negotiations with Italy and Rumania, see also Pingaud, I, 42–56, and Paléologue, I, 61–62, 69–71, 77–79.

[23] *T.R.V.M.V.*, 237.

[24] *Ibid.*, 238–242; *M.O.V.E.I.*, VI, 1, ##74, 77, 95, pp. 65–92; *Iswolski im Weltkrieg*, 31–43.

[25] *T.R.V.M.V.*, 243–249; *M.O.V.E.I.*, VI, 1, ##95, 186n, pp. 90–92, 179–180; *Iswolski im Weltkrieg*, 60–95.

[26] *T.R.V.M.V.*, 145–153.

[27] *Iswolski im Weltkrieg*, 28–30; *T.R.V.M.V.*, 153; *M.O.V.E.I.*, VI, 1, #30, 27.

[28] *M.O.V.E.I.*, VI, I, ##37, 43, 53, 59, 75, 78, 79 pp. 33–72; *T.R.V.M.V.*, 154.

[29] *M.O.V.E.I.*, VI, 1, ##82, 237, pp. 76–77, 228; *T.R.V.M.V.*, 22–23, 37, 69, 155–160.

[30] *M.O.V.E.I.*, VI, 1, #266, 259–260; *T.R.V.M.V.*, 159.

[31] Sazonov, 110–114; *T.R.V.M.V.*, 161–164; *M.O.V.-E.I.*, VI, 1, ##284, 288n, 285, 294, pp. 278–288; *Iswolski im Weltkrieg*, 114.

[32] *M.O.V.E.I.*, VI, 1, ##317, 240, 353, pp. 312–313, 341–361; *T.R.V.M.V.*, 164–168.

[33] *M.O.V.E.I.*, VI, 1, ##344, 346, 371, 388, 389, 402, 405, 408, pp. 347–348, 381–415.

[34] *T.R.V.M.V.*, 167–168; *M.O.V.E.I.*, VI, 2, #462, 22–23.

[35] On the immediate pre-war Balkan diplomacy, see Ernst C. Helmreich, *The Diplomacy of the Balkan Wars, 1912–13.* Harvard University Press. Cambridge:

Notes

1938. On war-time Allied diplomacy, see Pingaud, I, 38–42, 151–219. The sections dealing with Balkan diplomacy in Harry N. Howard's *The Partition of Turkey, 1913–1923*, University of Oklahoma Press, Norman, Oklahoma: 1931 are not recommended, since they were written prior to publication of many of the essential documents.

[36] *Ibid.*
[37] T.R.V.M.V., 59–68.
[38] *M.O.V.E.I.*, VI, 1, #2, 4–5.
[39] *Ibid.*, #19, 17–19.
[40] T.R.V.M.V., 63–66; *M.O.V.E.I.*, VI, 1, ##70, 83, 106, pp. 62, 76–77, 104; *Iswolski im Weltkrieg*, 52–53.
[41] *M.O.V.E.I.*, VI, 1, #29, 26–27.
[42] *Iswolski im Weltkrieg*, 41, 48–49; *M.O.V.E.I.*, VI, 1, ##68, 75, pp. 59–67.
[43] *M.O.V.E.I.*, VI, 1, #92, 83; T.R.V.M.V., 69; *Iswolski im Weltkrieg*, 64.
[44] Viscount Grey of Fallodon, *Twenty-Five Years, 1891–1916*, II, 184–186. 2 vols. Frederick A. Stokes Co. New York: 1925. See also *M.O.V.E.I.*, VI, 1, #96, #106, 92–93; 104; and *Iswolski im Weltkrieg*, 65–69.
[45] T.R.V.M.V., 70–71; *Iswolski im Weltkrieg*, 70–72.
[46] *Iswolski im Weltkrieg*, 74–79; T.R.V.M.V., 71.
[47] *M.O.V.E.I.*, VI, 1, #105, #172, 103–104, 162–163; T.R.V.M.V., 71–72; *Iswolski im Weltkrieg*, 82–83.
[48] *Iswolski im Weltkrieg*, 85; T.R.V.M.V., 73.
[49] *M.O.V.E.I.*, VI, 1, #197, #198, #205, 188–197; *Iswolski im Weltkrieg*, 98–100.
[50] *M.O.V.E.I.*, VI, 1, ##206, 212, pp. 199–207; *Iswolski im Weltkrieg*, 101–103.
[51] *M.O.V.E.I.*, VI, 1, ##217, 226, 229, pp. 209–223.
[52] *Ibid.*, ##217, 225, 236, 241, pp. 209–232.
[53] Sazonov, 239–244.

Notes

[54] *Iswolski im Weltkrieg*, 12, 15.
[55] *Ibid.*, 28; *M.O.V.E.I.*, VI, 1, ##201, 208, 215, 218, 220, 224, pp. 193–218; Pingaud, I, 99–105; Grey, II, 163–165.
[56] Paléologue, I, 61–62, 92–94.
[57] *M.O.V.E.I.*, VI, 1, ##256, 257, pp. 247–254; Pingaud, I, 126–131.
[58] *S.I.M.I.D.; M.O.V.E.I.*, VI, ##269, 270, pp. 262–265.
[59] *Ibid.*
[60] *M.O.V.E.I.*, VI, 1, #267, 260–262.
[61] *Ibid.*, #284, #285, 278–279.
[62] *Ibid.*
[63] *M.O.V.E.I.*, VI, 1, #287, 281–282.
[64] *Ibid.*, #372, 381–382.
[65] *Ibid.*, #385, #386, 394–396.
[66] Denmark's "equivocal conduct" was actually nothing more than a resolute determination to remain neutral. See Grey, II, 167.
[67] *M.O.V.E.I.*, VI, 1, #385, #386, 394–392.
[68] Pares, 206–213; Pingaud, I, 116–126; Liddell Hart, 54–58; Danilov, 256–336.
[69] Liddell Hart, 54–58.

CHAPTER TWO

[1] Sidney B. Fay, *The Origins of the World War*, I, 524–546. 2 vols. The Macmillan Co. New York: 1929.
[2] Evgenyi A. Adamov, ed., *Konstantinopol i prolivy*, I, 156–181. 2 vols. Izdaniye Litizdata, Narodnyi Komissariat Inostrannykh Del. Moskva: 1925–26 gg.

Notes

[3] *Ibid.*

[4] *Ibid.*

[5] Fay, I, 524–546.

[6] S. D. Sazonov, *Les années fatales*, 124–156.

[7] *Ibid.; Mezhdunarodnye otnosheniya v epokhu imperializma.* Seriya III. VI, 1, #61, #72, 54, 63–64; *Tsarskaya Rossiya v mirovoi voiny*, 3–7, 20; Harry N. Howard, *The Partition of Turkey, 1913–1923*, 3–115; Ernst Jackh, *The Rising Crescent, Turkey Yesterday, Today, and Tomorrow*, 10–23, 114. Farrar & Rinehart, Inc. New York: 1944.

[8] Albert Pingaud, *L'histoire diplomatique de la France pendant la grande guerre*, I, 126–131.

[9] *M.O.V.E.I.*, VI, 1, #94, 85–90; *T.R.V.M.V.*, 7.

[10] *T.R.V.M.V.*, 11–14.

[11] *Ibid.*, 15–17, 20; *M.O.V.E.I.*, VI, 1, #56, #60, 49–54.

[12] *T.R.V.M.V.*, 20–25; *M.O.V.E.I.*, VI, 1, #72, ##118, 120, 124, pp. 63–64, 114–119; Viscount Grey of Fallodon, *Twenty-Five Years, 1891–1916*, II, 172–173.

[13] Howard, 102–106; Maurice Paléologue, *La Russie des Tsars pendant la grande guerre*, I, 81–83.

[14] *K.I.P.*, I, 155–156.

[15] *T.R.V.M.V.*, 21–30; *M.O.V.E.I.*, VI, 1, ##138, 139, pp. 131–132.

[16] *T.R.V.M.V.*, 30–31; *M.O.V.E.I.*, VI, 1, ##147, 172, 173, 176, 191, pp. 140–141, 163–169, 183–184.

[17] *T.R.V.M.V.*, 36–39; Howard, 96–106.

[18] Jackh, 114–118.

[19] Paléologue, I, 135–136; *K.I.P.*, I, 221–224.

[20] *Ibid.*

[21] Howard, 106–115; Jackh, 116–118.

[22] *K.I.P.*, I, 226–227.

Notes

[23] Howard, 106-115; Jackh, 116-118.
[24] *Vestnik Evropy,* October, 1914.
[25] Paléologue, I, 181-182.
[26] *Ibid.,* 183-184.
[27] Grey, II, 187-188.
[28] A. J. P. Taylor, *The Struggle For Mastery in Europe, 1848-1918, passim.* Oxford University Press. New York: 1954.
[29] *Ibid.*
[30] *M.O.V.E.I.,* VI, 2, #449, 3-4.
[31] *Ibid.,* #450, #471, 4-5, 31-32.
[32] *K.I.P.,* I, 227-229.
[33] *Ibid.,* 230-233.
[34] *Ibid.,* 233-234.
[35] *Ibid.,* 234.
[36] *M.O.V.E.I.,* VI, 1, #338, 334-360; Pingaud, III, 261-284; Paléologue, I, 221-223.
[37] *M.O.V.E.I.,* VI, 1, #412, 423-424.
[38] *Ibid.,* #349, 351-354.
[39] *Russko-Polskiye otnosheniya v period mirovoi voiny,* 9-19.
[40] *Ibid.*
[41] *Ibid.*
[42] *Ibid.*
[43] *R.-P.O.,* 19-23.
[44] *Ibid.,* 23-25.
[45] *M.O.V.E.I.,* VI, 2, #518, 84-86.
[46] *Ibid.*
[47] *Ibid.,* #546, 111-112; Paléologue, I, 197-203.
[48] *Ibid.*
[49] *Ibid.*
[50] *Ibid.*
[51] *M.O.V.E.I.,* VI, 2, #547, 113.
[52] *Ibid.*

Notes

[53] *Ibid.*, #552, 117–119, *K.I.P.*, I, 234–235.
[54] *M.O.V.E.I.*, VI, 2, #562, 127.
[55] *K.I.P.*, I, 156–181.
[56] Sazonov, 269.
[57] *Ibid.*
[58] *M.O.V.E.I.*, VI, 1, #571, 136–137.
[59] *Ibid.*, A. Popov, "Cheko-Slovatskii Vopros i Tsarskaya Diplomatiya."
[60] *M.O.V.E.I.*, VI, 2, #572, 160–161.
[61] *Ibid.*
[62] *Ibid.*, #669, 237.
[63] *Ibid.*
[64] Paléologue, I, 245–247.
[65] *Ibid.*
[66] *Ibid.*, 258.
[67] *M.O.V.E.I.*, VI, 2, #647, 215–217.
[68] *Ibid.*
[69] *Ibid.*
[70] *Ibid.*
[71] *Ibid.*
[72] *K.I.P.*, I, 181–195.
[73] *Ibid.*
[74] *Ibid.*, 11, 3–4.
[75] *Ibid.*, 195–199.
[76] *Ibid.*
[77] *Ibid.*, 8–12.
[78] *Ibid.*, 13.

CHAPTER THREE

[1] *Mezhdunarodnye otnosheniya v epokhu imperializma*. Seriya III. VI, 1, #18, 17; *Tsarskaya Rossiya v mirovoi voiny*, 250–251.
[2] *M.O.V.E.I.*, VI, i, #310, 303–304.
[3] *Ibid.*, #313, 307–309.
[4] *Ibid.*, #351, 356–357.
[5] *T.R.V.M.V.*, 251–252.
[6] *M.O.V.E.I.*, VI, 1, #355, 363–364.
[7] *T.R.V.M.V.*, 252–253.
[8] *M.O.V.E.I.*, VI, i, #368, #385, #386, 377–378, 394–396.
[9] *Ibid.*, #390, 404.
[10] *T.R.V.M.V.*, 253; *M.O.V.E.I.*, VI, 1, #410, 422.
[11] *M.O.V.E.I.*, VI, 1, #430, 443–445.
[12] *Ibid.*, #264, #272, #334, #335, 342, 258, 265–266, 333, 344–346; *T.R.V.M.V.*, 74.
[13] *T.R.V.M.V.*, 75–76.
[14] *M.O.V.E.I.*, VI, 1, #419, #420, #421, #422, #433, #444, 431–435, 447–448, 456–457.
[15] *T.R.V.M.V.*, 77.
[16] *Ibid.*, 168–169; *M.O.V.E.I.*, VI, 2, #453, 7–8.
[17] *T.R.V.M.V.*, 79–81.
[18] *Ibid.*, 79–84; *M.O.V.E.I.*, VI, 2, #454, #462, #463, #466, #479, 8–9, 22–24, 26–28, 38.
[19] *M.O.V.E.I.*, VI, 2, #481, 39–40.
[20] *Ibid.*, #487, 48–49.
[21] *Ibid.*, #496, 57–61.
[22] *Ibid.*, #498, 62–63.
[23] *Ibid.*, #492, #493, 53; *T.R.V.M.V.*, 84–87.

Notes

[24] *M.O.V.E.I.*, VI, 2, #494, 54.
[25] *Ibid.*, #491, #505, 52, 71–72; *T.R.V.M.V.*, 169–170.
[26] *M.O.V.E.I.*, VI, 2, #505, #512, #513, 71–72, 79–81.
[27] *Ibid.*, #515, #516, #519, 81–83, 86.
[28] *T.R.V.M.V.*, 88–89.
[29] *M.O.V.E.I.*, VI, 2, #527, #528, #530, 91–95.
[30] *Ibid.*, #531, #542, 95–96, 108–109.
[31] *Ibid.*, #554, #557, 119, 122.
[32] *T.R.V.M.V.*, 93.
[33] *M.O.V.E.I.*, VI, 2, #561, 126–127.
[34] *Ibid.*, #566, #568, #572, 132, 134, 137–139.
[35] *Ibid.*, #575, #576, #580, #582, #592, 141–142, 145–148, 158–159.
[36] *T.R.V.M.V.*, 93–94.
[37] *M.O.V.E.I.*, VI, 2, #585, #590, #591, #595, #598, 150–166.
[38] *Ibid.*, #605, 169–170.
[39] *Ibid.*, #610, #611, 178–180.
[40] *Ibid.*, #617, #625, 184–185, 193; *T.R.V.M.V.*, 173–178.
[41] *M.O.V.E.I.*, VI, 2, #619, 187–188; *T.R.V.M.V.*, 96.
[42] Grigorii N. Trubetskoi, *Russland als Grossmacht*. Deutsche Verlags-anstalt. Stuttgart und Berlin: 1917.
[43] *M.O.V.E.I.*, VI, 2, #608, 173–174.
[44] *Ibid.*, #658, 226–227.
[45] *Ibid.*, #691, 270–271.
[46] *Ibid.*, #698, 273–274.
[47] *Ibid.*
[48] *Ibid.*, #673, #683, 240, 252.
[49] *Ibid.*, #628, 194–196.
[50] *Ibid.*, #648, 220–221.
[51] *Ibid.*, #661, 229–230.

Notes

[52] *Ibid.*, #671, 238–239; *T.R.V.M.V.*, 175.
[53] *M.O.V.E.I.*, VI, 2, #674, #680, 240–241, 249–250.
[54] *Ibid.*, #688, 259–260.
[55] *Ibid.*, #694, 267.
[56] *Ibid.*, #695, 267–268.
[57] *Ibid.*, #729, #742, #755, #735, 320, 330–331, 336–337, 355–356; *T.R.V.M.V.*, 256–257; Albert Pingaud, *L'histoire diplomatique de la France pendant la grande guerre*, I, 126–131.
[58] *M.O.V.E.I.*, VI, 2, #753, #758, 351, 357–360 and VIII, 1, #3; *T.R.V.M.V.*, 258.
[59] *M.O.V.E.I.*, XXXX VI, 2, #756, #760, 356–357, 363–364.
[60] *Ibid.*, VII, 1, #41, #46, #59, #84, #87, 7–8, 57–59, 66–67, 79–80, 109–110, 117.
[61] *Ibid.*, #13, #14, 19–21.
[62] *Ibid.*, #42, 67–69.
[63] *Ibid.*, XXX #85, 111–114.
[64] *Ibid.*, #202, 263.
[65] *Ibid.*
[66] *Ibid.*, #94, 125–126.
[67] *Ibid.*, #107, #108, #112, #123, 141–144, 149–150, 163–165.
[68] *Ibid.*, #125, #126, #130, #144, 166–168, 170–171, 193–194.
[69] *T.R.V.M.V.*, 102–104.
[70] *Ibid.*, 104–105.
[71] *Ibid.*, 106–107; *M.O.V.E.I.*, VII, 1, #175, #191, 233–234, 251–252.
[72] *T.R.V.M.V.*, 107; *M.O.V.E.I.*, VII, 1, #197, #200, 259–262.
[73] *K.I.P.*, I, 328–330.
[74] *T.R.V.M.V.*, 176.

Notes

[75] *K.I.P.*, I, 331–332.
[76] *Ibid.*, 333–334; *M.O.V.E.I.*, VII, 1, #13, #73, 19–20, 93–94.
[77] *M.O.V.E.I.*, VII, 1, #99, 132.
[78] *Ibid.*, #198, 259–260; *K.I.P.*, I, 337.
[79] *K.I.P.*, I, 305–306.
[80] *M.O.V.E.I.*, VII, 1, #259, 337–338.
[81] *Ibid.*, #210, #378, #401, 277–282, 492–493, 528–529.

CHAPTER FOUR

[1] Lord Grey of Fallodon, *Twenty-Five Years, 1891–1916*, II, 172–173.
[2] Winston Churchill, *The World Crisis*, II, 19–37. 13 vols. Chas. Scribner's Sons. New York: 1923–1927; David Lloyd George, *War Memoirs*, I, 309–455. 6 vols. Little, Brown & Co. Boston: 1933–1937.
[3] Harry N. Howard, *The Partition of Turkey, 1913–1923*, 121.
[4] *Ibid.*, 121–122.
[5] *Ibid.*
[6] *Mezhdunarodnye otnosheniya v epokhu imperializma.* Seriya III. VI, 2, #743, 337–338.
[7] E. A. Adamov, ed., *Razdel Aziatskoi Turtsii*, 106. Narodnyi Komissariat Inostrannykh Del. Moscow: 1924.
[8] *M.O.V.E.I.*, VI, 2, #757, 357.
[9] *R.A.T.*, 107–110.
[10] Sergei D. Sazonov, *Les années fatales*, 274.

Notes

[11] *Konstantinopol i prolivy*, II, 24–25.
[12] *R.A.T.*, 108–110.
[13] *M.O.V.E.I.*, VII, 1, #114, 150–154; *R.A.T.*, 110–112.
[14] *M.O.V.E.I.*, VII, 1, #114, 150–154.
[15] *Ibid.*, #132, 174–175.
[16] *K.I.P.*, I, 237–238.
[17] *Ibid.*, I, 238–240.
[18] Howard, 122–125, 149–150.
[19] *Ibid.*
[20] *Stenographicheskii Otchet. Gosudarstvennaya Duma. Chertvertyi Sozyv. Sessiya III. Zasedanie Pervoe. Vtornik, 27 Yanvarya, 1915 g.*, 1–9. See also Paléologue, I, 290–294.
[21] *K.I.P.*, I, 241–243.
[22] *Ibid.*, 199–200, 241–242.
[23] *Ibid.*, 241–242.
[24] *Ibid.*, 247–248; *M.O.V.E.I.*, VII, 1, #283, 371.
[25] *K.I.P.*, I, 248–249.
[26] *Ibid.*, 249–251.
[27] *Ibid.*
[28] *Ibid.*, I, 256–259.
[29] *Ibid.*, 245–246.
[30] *Ibid.*, 252–253.
[31] *R.A.T.*, 116–117.
[32] *K.I.P.*, I, 255.
[33] *M.O.V.E.I.*, VII, 1, #312, 306.
[34] *K.I.P.*, I, 251–252.
[35] *M.O.V.E.I.*, VII, 1, #321, 416–417.
[36] *K.I.P.*, I, 263–264.
[37] *Ibid.*, 262.
[38] *Ibid.*, 264.
[39] *Ibid.*, 266–267.
[40] *Ibid.*, 267–268.

Notes

[41] *Ibid.*, 268.
[42] *Ibid.*, 277–281.
[43] *Ibid.*, 268–269.
[44] *Ibid.*, 269–271.
[45] *Ibid.*, 270–272, 277–281.
[46] *Ibid.*, 281–282.
[47] *Ibid.*, 267–268.
[48] *Ibid.*, 274–275.
[49] *Ibid.*, 275–277.
[50] *Ibid.*
[51] Sir George Buchanan, *My Mission to Russia and Other Diplomatic Memories*, I, 226–227.
[52] *Ibid.*
[53] *K.I.P.*, I, 284–285.
[54] *R.A.T.*, 127–128.
[55] *Ibid.*, 128–129.
[56] Maurice Paléologue, *La Russie des Tsars pendant la grande guerre*, I, 321–323.
[57] *R.A.T.*, 129–130.
[58] *M.O.V.E.I.*, VII, 1, #381, 495–497.
[59] *Ibid.*, #387, 510; *K.I.P.*, I, 282–288; *R.A.T.*, 130.
[60] *K.I.P.*, I, 288–289, 295.
[61] *Ibid.*, II, 49–95.
[62] *Ibid.*, 295–311.
[63] *Ibid.*, 315–356.
[64] *R.A.T.*, 130–133.
[65] *Ibid.*, 133–136.
[66] *Ibid.*, 135–136.
[67] *Ibid.*, 137–139.
[68] *M.O.V.E.I.*, VII, 1, #275, 364–365.
[69] *Ibid.*, #276, 365.
[70] *K.I.P.*, I, 307–310.
[71] *M.O.V.E.I.*, VII, 1, #281, 368–369.
[72] *K.I.P.*, I, 311.

Notes

[73] *Ibid.*, 311–312.
[74] *Ibid.*, 312–313; *T.R.V.M.V.*, 259–260.
[75] *T.R.V.M.V.*, 259–260; *M.O.V.E.I.*, VII, 1, #348, 446–448; *K.I.P.*, I, 317.
[76] *M.O.V.E.I.*, VII, 1, #348, 446–448.
[77] *Ibid.*, #354, 459–460.
[78] *Ibid.*, #373, #388, 485–488, 510–511.
[79] *Ibid.*, #388, #402, 510–511, 529; *T.R.V.M.V.*, 262–264.
[80] *M.O.V.E.I.*, VII, 1, #393, #401, 518–519, 528–529.
[81] *Ibid.*, #402, 529–530.
[82] *Ibid.*, 2, #417, #418, #419, 3–11.
[83] *T.R.V.M.V.*, 265; *M.O.V.E.I.*, VII, 2, #423, 16–17.
[84] *M.O.V.E.I.*, VII, 2, #426, 20.
[85] *K.I.P.*, I, 373, 375–377; *T.R.V.M.V.*, 266–267; *M.O.V.E.I.*, VII, 2, #439, 34–36.
[86] *M.O.V.E.I.*, VII, 2, #430, 26.
[87] *Ibid.*, #439, #440, #444, 34–38, 43–45; *T.R.V.M.V.*, 267.
[88] *M.O.V.E.I.*, VII, 2, #448, 48–49; *T.R.V.M.V.*, 267–269.
[89] *M.O.V.E.I.*, VII, 2, #453, 56–57.
[90] *T.R.V.M.V.*, 270–271.
[91] *M.O.V.E.I.*, VII, 2, #462, 68–69.
[92] *Ibid.*, #461, #462, 65–69.
[93] *Ibid.*, #462, 68–69, and VII, 1, #373, 281–283; *T.R.V.M.V.*, 272–273.
[94] *M.O.V.E.I.*, VII, 2, #475, #479, 84–86, 90; *T.R.V.M.V.*, 273–274.
[95] *M.O.V.E.I.*, VII, 2, #486, #487, 98–99.
[96] *Ibid.*, #489, #493, 100–103; *T.R.V.M.V.*, 275.
[97] *T.R.V.M.V.*, 275–277.
[98] *Ibid.*, 277–278.

Notes

[99] *Ibid.*, 278–281; *M.O.V.E.I.*, VII, 2, #550, #558, 175–179, 191–192, 204–206; *K.I.P.*, I, 326–327.

[100] *T.R.V.M.V.*, 285–286.

[101] *K.I.P.*, I, 278–279, 329–330, 331–332.

[102] "Dnevnik Ministerstva Inostrannykh Del," April 9/22, 1915, *Krasnyi Arkhiv*, vols. XXXI–XXXII. Moscow: 1929; *M.O.V.E.I.*, VII, 2, #586, 228–229 and VII, 2, #612, 253–258.

[103] *Ibid.*

[104] *M.O.V.E.I.*, VII, 2, ##613–617, 263–266.

[105] *Ibid.*, #560, 193–194.

[106] *Ibid.*, #626, #629, 274–275, 280–281; *T. R. V.-M.V.*, 285–286.

[107] *M.O.V.E.I.*, VII, 2, #632, #642, 283, 295–297.

CHAPTER FIVE

[1] Maurice Paléologue, *La Russie des Tsars pendant la grande guerre*, I, 284–285.

[2] *Russko-Polskiye Otnosheniya v period mirovoi voiny*, 25–40.

[3] *Ibid.*, 25–26, 40–47.

[4] *Ibid.*, 40–47

[5] *Ibid.*, 49.

[6] Youri Danilov, *La Russie dans la guerre mondiale (1914–1917)*, 407–459; B. H. Liddell Hart, *The War in Outline, 1914–1918*, 100–105.

[7] *Ibid.*

[8] *R.-P.O.*, 49–60.

[9] *Ibid.*, 60–77.

Notes

[10] Paléologue, II, 14–15.
[11] *Ibid.*, 20–22.
[12] Liddell Hart, 82–100.
[13] *M.O.V.E.I.*, VII, 1, #316, 410.
[14] *Ibid.*, #390, #410, 515, 542, and VII, 2, #481, #509, #529, 95–96, 122–123, 139–145; *T.R.V.M.V.*, 110–113.
[15] *M.O.V.E.I.*, VII, 2, #602, #618, #636, 246–247, 267–268, 288–289; *T.R.V.M.V.*, 116.
[16] *M.O.V.E.I.*, VII, 2, #703, 375–379.
[17] *Evropeiskie derzhavy i Gretsiya v epokhu mirovoi voiny*, 5–6. Narodnyi Komissariat Inostrannykh Del. Moscow: 1922.
[18] *M.O.V.E.I.*, VII, 2, #432, 27–29.
[19] *Ibid.*, #528, 138–139; *T.R.V.M.V.*, 112.
[20] *M.O.V.E.I.*, VII, 2, #568, 206–208.
[21] *Ibid.*, #678, 542.
[22] *Ibid.*, #735, #736, 411–413.
[23] *K.I.P.*, I, 258, 337; *M.O.V.E.I.*, VII, 2, #359, 464–466.
[24] *M.O.V.E.I.*, VII, 2, #555, 188–189; *T.R.V.M.V.*, 179–180.
[25] *M.O.V.E.I.*, VII, 1, #210, #378, 277–282, 492–493.
[26] *Ibid.*, VII, 2, #584, 227.
[27] *Ibid.*, #637, #643, 291–292, 297; *T.R.V.M.V.*, 182.
[28] *D.M.I.D.*, April 16/29 and April 17/30, 1915.
[29] *T.R.V.M.V.*, 180–182.
[30] *Ibid.*, 182–183; *M.O.V.E.I.*, VII, 2, #660, #667, #673, #676, 323, 331, 337, 339–340; *D.M.I.D.*, April 19/May 2, 1915.
[31] *D.M.I.D.*, April 20/May 3, 1915; *T.R.V.M.V.*, 182–183.
[32] *T.R.V.M.V.*, 184.
[33] *D.M.I.D.*, April 24/May 7, 1915.

Notes

[34] *Ibid.*, April 29/May 12, 1915.

[35] *T.R.V.M.V.*, 86.

[36] *M.O.V.E.I.*, VII, 2, #645, #655, #681, 299–301, 314–315, 346–348.

[37] *Ibid.*, #690, 357–363.

[38] *Ibid.*, #686, #689, #698, 352–353, 356–357, 371, 395–397.

[39] *Ibid.*, #715, #728, #734, 390–392, 405, 410–411; *T.R.V.M.V.*, 186–188.

[40] *D.M.I.D.*, May 4/17, 1915; *T.R.V.M.V.*, 188–190.

[41] *M.O.V.E.I.*, VII, 2, #789, #790, #792, 482–485.

[42] *Ibid.*, #805, 497; *T.R.V.M.V.*, 190, *D.M.I.D.*, May 5/18 and May 6/19, 1915.

[43] *M.O.V.E.I.*, VII, 2, #813, 507–508, and VIII, 1, #11, #20, #24, #31, #36, 13, 22–27, 41–42, 46–47, 52–53; *D.M.I.D.*, May 20/June 2 and May 21/June 3, 1915; *T.R.V.M.V.*, 191.

[44] *M.O.V.E.I.*, VIII, 1, #54, 78–79.

[45] *D.M.I.D.*, May 21/June 3, 1915.

[46] *M.O.V.E.I.*, VIII, 1, #69, #70, 103–105; *D.M.I.D.*, May 26/June 8, 1915.

[47] *M.O.V.E.I.*, VIII, 1, #98, 114–115, 133.

[48] *Ibid.*, #99, 134–136; *T.R.V.M.V.*, 191–192.

[49] *M.O.V.E.I.*, VIII, 1, #127, 161–162; *T.R.V.M.V.*, 192–194.

[50] *M.O.V.E.I.*, VIII, 1, #151, 188–189; *T.R.V.M.V.*, 194–195.

[51] Liddell Hart, 82–100.

[52] *M.O.V.E.I.*, VIII, 1, #214, #230, #235, #237, 253, 277, 283–284, 285, 294–296; *T.R.V.M.V.*, 195–197.

[53] *M.O.V.E.I.*, VIII, 1, 335–337, 345–346.

[54] *Ibid.*, #285, #287, 358–359, 364–365, 368–369.

[55] *Ibid.*, #301, #302, 390–393.

[56] *Ibid.*, #310, 397–398.

Notes

[57] *Ibid.*, #319, #325, #329, #334, #335, #367, 406, 414, 416–417, 421–422, 472–473; *D.M.I.D.*, July 12/25, 1915.

[58] *M.O.V.E.I.*, VIII, 1, #377, #384, #402, 487–488, 496, 518–519.

[59] *T.R.V.M.V.*, 199.

[60] *M.O.V.E.I.*, VIII, 2, #471, 36–37.

[61] *Ibid.*, #477, #490, #503, #552, #553, 43–44, 61–62, 73, 117–118.

[62] *Ibid.*, VII, 2, #736, #744, 412–413, 420–421.

[63] *Ibid.*, #756, #767, #787, #806, 444–445, 459–460, 480–481, and VIII, 1, #1, #37, #38, 5–6, 53–55; *T.R.V.M.V.*, 118–122.

[64] *M.O.V.E.I.*, VIII, 1, #11, #29, #32, #37, #38, 13, 45, 48–49, 53–55; *T.R.V.M.V.*, 121–122.

[65] *M.O.V.E.I.*, VIII, 1, #42, #44, #45, 58–59, 63–65.

[66] *Ibid.*, #49, #50, 70–71.

[67] *Ibid.*, #117, 149–150; *T.R.V.M.V.*, 124.

[68] *T.R.V.M.V.*, 125

[69] *M.O.V.E.I.*, VIII, 1, #136, #142, 170–171, 177–178.

[70] *Ibid.*, #153, #158, 191, 195–196.

[71] *Ibid.*, 217–219.

[72] *Ibid.*, #201, #219, 241–242, 257–258.

[73] *Ibid.*, #144, 180–181, and #190, #191, #238, 232–234, 292–294.

[74] *Ibid.*, 339–340, 347–349.

[75] *Ibid.*, ##332, 333, 337, 357, 358, 364, 369, 373, 375, 414, pp. 400–532; *T.R.V.M.V.*, 125–127.

[76] *M.O.V.E.I.*, VIII, 1, ##406–418, 524–539.

[77] *Ibid.*

[78] *Ibid.*, ##418–433, 537–554.

[79] *Ibid.*, #434, 555–556; VIII, 2, ##437–459, 4–22.

[80] *M.O.V.E.I.*, VIII, 2, #464, 27–29.

Notes

[81] *Ibid.*, #473, #476, 38–39, 41–42.
[82] *Ibid.*, #445, 11–12, and ##487–505, 54–74.
[83] *Ibid.*, ##515–532, 81–98.
[84] *Ibid.*
[85] *Ibid.*, #530, 96–97.
[86] *Ibid.*, #525, #532, 92, 98.
[87] *Ibid.*, ##535–566, 101–152.
[88] *Ibid.*, ##572–618, 136–188.
[89] *Ibid.*, ##627–695, 201–285.
[90] *Ibid.*, #645, #658, #678, 219–220, 241–243, 267.
[91] *T.R.V.M.V.*, 130–131.
[92] *M.O.V.E.I.*, VIII, 2, #704, 294–295; *T.R.V.M.V.*, 132.
[93] *T.R.V.M.V.*, 133–140.
[94] *M.O.V.E.I.*, VIII, 2, #833, #836, #860, 417–418, 421–422, 443–444; *T.R.V.M.V.*, 141.
[95] *T.R.V.M.V.*, 133–139; *M.O.V.E.I.*, VIII, 2, ##704–819, 294–403; Paléologue, II, 81–82, 95–96; Sazonov, 247–256.
[96] *M.O.V.E.I.*, VIII, 2, #747, #748, #770, 338–340, 358–359.
[97] *Ibid.*, ##767–816, 355–399.
[98] *Ibid.*, ##830–847, 414–430.
[99] *Ibid.*, ##860–912, 443–492.
[100] *Ibid.*, #912, 491–492, and IX, 22–23, 30, 37, 59–60, 93; *E.D.I.G.*, 20–24.
[101] *M.O.V.E.I.*, VIII, 2, ##871–917, 451–494.
[102] *Ibid.*, #909, 486–488, and IX, 3–4.
[103] *Ibid.*, IX, 18–19, 40, 86–87, 91–92, 112–113, 116, 131–132, 245–246; *T.R.V.M.V.*, 203; *D.M.I.D.*, October 20/November 2 and November 3/16, 1915.
[104] *K.I.P.*, I, 206–210; *D.M.I.D.*, November 3/16, 1915.
[105] *M.O.V.E.I.*, IX, 104–110; *E.D.I.G.*, 36–37.

Notes

[106] Bernard Pares, *The Fall of the Russian Monarchy*, 214–279.
[107] *Letters of the Tsaritsa to the Tsar, 1914–1916*, 116–182.
[108] *Ibid.*, 198–200.
[109] *D.M.I.D.*, October 20/November 2, 1915.
[110] Pingaud, II, 90–113, 285–340; John C. Adams, *Flight in Winter*. Princeton University Press. Princeton: 1942.
[111] *M.O.V.E.I.*, IX, 305, 308, 338–341, 362.

CHAPTER SIX

[1] Youri Danilov, *La Russie dans la guerre mondiale (1914–1917)*, 457–459.
[2] *Razdel Aziatskoi Turtsii*, 141–143.
[3] *Ibid.*, 144–146.
[4] *Ibid.*, 148–149.
[5] *Ibid.*, 147–151.
[6] *Ibid.*, 151; *D.M.I.D.*, January 25/February 7, 1916.
[7] *R.A.T.*, 154–157.
[8] *Ibid.*, 152–153; *D.M.I.D.*, February 25/March 9, 1916.
[9] *D.M.I.D.*, February 25/March 9, 1916.
[10] *Ibid.*, February 26/March 10, 1916.
[11] *R.A.T.*, 160–161.
[12] Maurice Paléologue, *La Russie des Tsars pendant la grande guerre*, II, 204–206.
[13] *Ibid.*
[14] *R.A.T.*, 158–159.

Notes

15 *Ibid.*
16 *D.M.I.D.*, February 27/March 11, 1916.
17 *Ibid.*, March 1/14, 1916.
18 *Ibid.*, March 4/17, 1916; *R.A.T.*, 163–166.
19 *R.A.T.*, 163–166.
20 *Ibid.*, 172–174.
21 *Ibid.*, 170–171.
22 *Ibid.*, 171–172.
23 *Ibid.*, 175–178.
24 *Ibid.*, 178–182.
25 *Ibid.*, 174–175.
26 *Ibid.*, 183–184.
27 *Ibid.*, 185–188.
28 *Ibid.*
29 *Ibid.*, 207–209.
30 Fritz Hartung, "Germany and Poland During the World War," in Albert Brackmann, ed., *Germany and Poland in Their Historical Relations*, 238–251. R. Oldenbourg. Munich and Berlin: 1934.
31 *Ibid.*
32 *M.O.V.E.I.*, X, 23, 113–114, 198–199.
33 Paléologue, II, 198–199.
34 *M.O.V.E.I.*, X, 398–401.
35 *Ibid.*, 411–412.
36 *Ibid.*, 412–413.
37 *Ibid.*, 428–429, 431.
38 *Ibid.*, IX, 284, 313–314, 372–373; *K.I.P.*, I, 236–237.
39 *Ibid.*, X, 504–525.
40 *Ibid.*, 536–543.
41 *D.M.I.D.*, March 22/April 3 and April 5/18, 1916.
42 *Russko-Polskiye Otnosheniya v period mirovoi voiny*, 84–94.
43 *Letters of the Tsaritsa to the Tsar, 1914–1916*, 304–306; Paléologue, II, 229–230.

Notes

[44] Paléologue, II, 248–249.
[45] *T.R.V.M.V.*, 207–211; *D.M.I.D.*, January 13/26 and January 20/February 2, 1916.
[46] *T.R.V.M.V.*, 212–214; *D.M.I.D.*, February 2/15, 14/27, February 20/March 4, and February 22/March 6, 1916.
[47] *T.R.V.M.V.*, 214–216; *D.M.I.D.*, March 12/25, April 6/19, 1916.
[48] Paléologue, II, 266–267; *D.M.I.D.*, May 27/June 9, 1916.
[49] *D.M.I.D.*, May 30/June 11, 1916; *T.R.V.M.V.*, 217.
[50] *T.R.V.M.V.*, 217–221.
[51] Paléologue, II, 291–292.
[52] *D.M.I.D.*, June 28/July 11, 1916.
[53] *Ibid.*, June 29/July 12, 1916.
[54] Paléologue, II, 297–298; *D.M.I.D.*, July 1/14, July 2/15, 1916.
[55] Paléologue, II, 301–303.
[56] *Ibid.*
[57] *Ibid.*, 303–305.
[58] *Ibid.*
[59] *Ibid.*, 310.

CHAPTER SEVEN

[1] Bernard Pares, *The Fall of the Russian Monarchy*, 279–472; J. Polonsky, ed., *Documents diplomatiques secrets russes, 1914–1917, d'ápres les archives du Ministère des Affaires Étrangeres a Petrograd*. Payot. Paris:

Notes

1928; Maurice Paléologue, *La Russie des Tsars pendant la grande guerre*, II, 305–306.

[2] Paléologue, II, 308, and III, 41–49, 82.

[3] *Tsarskaya Rossiya v mirovoi*, 221–223; "Dnevnik Ministerstva Inostrannykh Del," July 13/26, 1916.

[4] *T.R.V.M.V.*, 223–225.

[5] *Ibid.*, 225–226; *D.M.I.D.*, July 31/August 13, 1916.

[6] *T.R.V.M.V.*, 230–231.

[7] *Ibid.*, 226–230.

[8] *Razdel Aziatskoi Turtsii*, 161–162.

[9] *Ibid.*, 163–169; *D.M.I.D.*, March 1/14, 1916.

[10] *R.A.T.*, 164–169.

[11] *Ibid.*, 170, 199–200.

[12] *Ibid.*, 201–202.

[13] *Ibid.*, 203–206.

[14] *Ibid.*, 206–210.

[15] *Ibid.*, 210.

[16] *Ibid.*, 214–215.

[17] *Ibid.*, 216–218.

[18] *Ibid.*, 226, 235.

[19] *Ibid.*, 189–198.

[20] *Ibid.*, 213–216.

[21] *Ibid.*, 129, 220–221; *D.M.I.D.*, August 18/31 and August 19/September 1, 1916.

[22] *R.A.T.*, 221–232.

[23] *Ibid.*, 236–238.

[24] *D.M.I.D.*, September 18/October 1, 1916; *R.A.T.*, 241–245.

[25] *R.A.T.*, 248–249.

[26] *Ibid.*, 251–252.

[27] *Ibid.*, 253–260.

[28] *Ibid.*, 260–262.

[29] *Evropeiskie derzhavy i Gretsiya*, 98, 109–114.

[30] *Ibid.*, 117–118.

Notes

[31] *Ibid.*, 118–119.
[32] *Ibid.*, 122–127.
[33] *Ibid.*, 133–134.
[34] *Ibid.*, 134–137.
[35] *R.A.T.*, 139.
[36] *Ibid.*, 141–144.
[37] Paléologue, III, 112–113.
[38] *Ibid.*, II, 312–313, 315–318, and III, 11–12; *Konstantinopol i prolivy*, I, 414.
[39] *K.I.P.*, I, 415; *D.M.I.D.*, August 21/September 3, and September 4/17, 1916.
[40] *R.A.T.*, 229–230; *D.M.I.D.*, September 4/17, 1916; *K.I.P.*, II, 416–419.
[41] B. H. Liddell Hart, *The War in Outline*.
[42] Paléologue, III, 41–62, 80–87.
[43] *Ibid.*, 82; *K.I.P.*, I, 421–425; *R.A.T.*, 252.
[44] Paléologue, III, 90–94.
[45] *Ibid.*, 103–109.
[46] *Ibid.*; *K.I.P.*, I, 425–429.
[47] *K.I.P.*, I, 429–433; *R.A.T.*, 267–271.
[48] *R.A.T.*, 272–273.
[49] *K.I.P.*, I, 433–436.
[50] *Ibid.*, 437–444.
[51] Paléologue, III, 112.
[52] *K.I.P.*, I, 445–447.
[53] Paléologue, III, 116; James B. Scott, ed., *Official Statements of War Aims and Peace Proposals, December, 1916 to November, 1918*, 1–11. Carnegie Endowment for International Peace. Washington: 1921.
[54] Paléologue, III, 117; David Lloyd George, *War Memoirs*, III, 50–69. 6 vols. Little, Brown & Co. Boston: 1934; Scott, 12–35.
[55] Paléologue, III, 120–121, 133–134; Lloyd George, III, 50–69; Scott, 35–39.

Notes

[56] R.A.T., 263–264.
[57] Ibid., 274–278.
[58] Ibid., 279–282.
[59] Ibid., 283–285.
[60] Ibid., 285–286.
[61] Ibid., 289–291.
[62] Ibid., 291–298.
[63] Ibid., 298–300.
[64] Ibid., 300–303.
[65] Ibid., 303–308.
[66] Paléologue, III, 177–179.
[67] Ibid.
[68] Albert Pingaud, *L'Histoire diplomatique de la France*, III, 112–114.
[69] Paléologue, III, 181–184.
[70] K.I.P., I, 450–451.
[71] Ibid., 452–453.
[72] Ibid., 453–456.
[73] Ibid., 457–458.
[74] Ibid., 458–460.
[75] Ibid., 460–462.
[76] Ibid., 462–475; Paléologue, III, 243–255; Sir George Buchanan, *My Mission to Russia*, II, 90–91; F. A. Golder, ed., *Documents of Russian History, 1914–1917*, 311–313. The Century Co. New York, 1927; W. H. Chamberlain, *The Russian Revolution*, I, 73–100. 2 vols. The Macmillan Co. New York: 1935; N. Rubenstein, "Vneshnyaya Politika Kerenshchiny," in M. N. Pokrovskii, ed., *Ocherki po istorii Oktyabrskaya Revolyutsii*, II, 356. 2 vols. Gosudarstvennoe Izdatelstvo. Moscow: 1927; A. F. Kerensky, *The Crucifixion of Liberty*, 305. The John Day Co. New York: 1934; Victor Chernov, *The Great Russian Revolution*, 172–173. Yale University Press. New Haven: 1936.

Notes

[77] A. J. Sack, ed., *The Birth of the Russian Democracy*, 251–253. Russian Information Bureau. New York: 1918.

[78] Golder, 334; *K.I.P.*, II, 383–400; Rubenstein, 368–370; Leon Trotsky, *The History of the Russian Revolution*, I, 337–338. 3 vols. Simons & Schuster. New York: 1932; A. I. Denikin, *The Russian Turmoil, Memoirs: Military, Social, and Political*, 144–145. Hutchinson & Co. London: 1923.

[79] *R.A.T.*, 322–329; *E.D.I.G.*, 177–188; Lloyd George, V, 236.

[80] Sir Alfred Knox, *With the Russian Army, 1914–1917. Being Chiefly Extracts from the Diary of a Military Attaché*, II, 366–367, 2 vols. Hutchinson & Co. London: 1921; Buchanan, II, 109; Paléologue, III, 270; *K.I.P.*, II, 463, 473–474.

[81] Golder, 325–331; M. Smilg-Bernario, *Von Kerenski zu Lenin*, 28–29. Amalthea-Verlag. Vienna: 1929; Paul N. Milyukov, *Istoriya vtoroi russkoi revolyutsii*, I, 84–86. Russko-Bulgarskoe Izdatelstvo. Sofia: 1921.

[82] Golder, 331–333; *K.I.P.*, II, 479–480; Buchanan, II, 109.

[83] Buchanan, II, 111–120; Paléologue, III, 281, 295.

[84] Paléologue, III, 299–300.

[85] *Ibid.*, 312–345; Milyukov, I, 92–93.

[86] Chamberlain, I, 142–149; Golder, 334–336.

[87] Kerensky, 187–188, 333–347; Rubenstein, 385–418; Golder, 343–355; *K.I.P.*, II, 490–507; Chernov, 289–299; Milyukov, I, 166–184; Baron R. R. Rosen, *Forty Years of Diplomacy*, 235–237. George Allen and Unwin, Ltd. London: 1922; Alexandre Ribot, *Lettres à un ami. Souvenirs de ma vie politique*, 230–241. Editions Bossard. Paris: 1924; Joseph Noulens, *Mon ambassade en Russie soviétique, 1917–1919*, I, 9–10. Librairie Plon. Paris:

Notes

1933; C. K. Cumming and W. W. Pettit, *Russian-American Relations, March, 1917–March, 1920*, 14–16, 23–25. Harcourt, Brace and Howe. New York: 1920.

[88] Golder, 355–356; *K.I.P.*, I, 373–375 and II, 505–512.

[89] *R.A.T.*, 334; *E.D.I.G.*, 190–212.

[90] Chamberlain, I, 163–190, 223–234; Golder, 467–473; *K.I.P.*, I, 378–379.

[91] Lloyd George, V, 91–94; *K.I.P.*, I, 379–381; *E.D.I.G.*, 204–239.

[92] *K.I.P.*, II, 516–526.

[93] Constantine Nabokoff, *The Ordeal of a Diplomat*, 131–158. Duckworth and Co. London: 1921; Buchanan, II, 163–164; Noulens, I, 55–60.

[94] Noulens, I, 82, 103–106; Golder, 558–560; Buchanan, II, 189–190.

[95] Golder, 646–648.

[96] Buchanan, II, 190–191, 197–205.

BIBLIOGRAPHY

DOCUMENTARY SOURCES

The Russian documents are almost our only important source for the diplomacy of the First World War prior to 1917. The published American documents on the period before American intervention are of only peripheral interest. The published Greek documents are concerned more with the question of the deposition of King Constantine than with the over-all diplomacy of the Allies, and hence cover a very restricted field which was considered only incidentally in this study. Despite the large volume of German documentation for the period 1871–1914, almost nothing has been published of primary material for German and Austro-Hungarian diplomacy in 1914–18. For the subject matter of this study, of course, only the British and French archives could furnish sufficient material to verify or disprove the general picture which emerges from the Russian documents, although the Italian archives would be of considerable value in this regard. The British historians Gooch and Temperly have published British documents on the 1898–1914 period, but did not carry their activity into the period of the war itself. Nor have any considerable number of French documents for the 1914–1918 period been published. It should be added, however, that the diary of the French war-time ambassador to Petrograd, M. Maurice Paléo-

Bibliography

logue, ranks next to the Russian documents in value as a source for this study.

As for the Russian documents, the original "secret treaties" published by People's Commissar of Foreign Affairs Lyov D. Bronstein-Trotskii in 1917–18 can be read in the following translation:

Emile Laloy, *Les documents secrets des archives du Ministère des Affaires Étrangeres de Russie publiés par les Bolsheviks*. Paris: Editions Bossard, 1920.

An English commentary on the originally published Russian documents contains a number of the "secret treaty" texts translated into English. It is:

C. A. McCurdy, *The Truth About the "Secret Treaties."* London: W. H. Smith & Son, 1918.

During the 1920's, M. N. Pokrovskii, E. A. Adamov, and other early Soviet historians published, either in book form or within the covers of the historical journal *Red Archive* (*Krasnyi Arkhiv*) various collections of documents on Russian foreign policy in 1914–17. They include:

Evgenyi A. Adamov, ed., *Evropeiskie derzhavy i Gretsiya v epokhu mirovoi voiny* (*The European Powers and Greece during the World War*). Moscow: People's Commissariat of Foreign Affairs, 1922.

Translated into German as:

Die europaischen mächte und Griechenland während des weltkrieges. Dresden: G. Reissner, 1932.

Evgenyi A. Adamov, ed., *Evropeiskie derzhavy i Turtsiya vo vremya mirovoi voiny, Razdel Aziatskoi Turtsii* (*The European Powers and Turkey During the*

Bibliography

World War. The Partition of Asiatic Turkey). Moscow: People's Commissariat of Foreign Affairs, 1924.

Evgenyi A. Adamov, ed., *Evropeiskie derzhavy i Turtsiya vo vremya mirovoi voiny, Konstantinopol i prolivy (The European Powers and Turkey During the World War. Constantinople and the Straits)*. 2 vols. Moscow: People's Commissariat of Foreign Affairs, 1925.

Translated into German as:

Die europäischen mächte und die Türkei während des weltkrieges: Konstantinopol und die Meerengen. 4 vols. Dresden: C. Reissner, 1930–32.

Also translated into French as:

A. de Lapradelle, L. Eisenmann, B. Mirkine-Guetsevitch, and P. Renouvin, eds., *Constantinople et les Detroits*. 2 vols. Paris: Les Éditions Internationales, 1930.

Tsentrarkhiv (Central Archives), *Tsarskaya Rossiya v mirovoi voiny (Tsarist Russia in the World War)*. Moscow-Leningrad: State Press, 1926.

Translated into German as:

Das zaristische Russland im weltkrieg. Neue dokumente aus den russischen staatarchiven über den eintritt der Türkei, Bulgariens, Rumaniens, und Italiens in den weltkrieg: übersetzung aus dem russischen, mit einem vorwort von Alfred von Wegerer. Berlin: Deutsche verlagsgesellschaft für politik und geschichte, 1927.

Also translated into French, with additional documents drawn from other collections listed above, as:

Bibliography

J. Polonsky, trans., *Documents diplomatiques secrets russes, 1914–1917*. Paris: Payot, 1928.

Articles in *Krasnyi Arkhiv:*

Volume, XIX, 1926.

"Diplomatiya Vremmennogo Pravitelstva v borbu s revolyutsii (Diplomacy of the Provisional Government in the Struggle with the Revolution)."

"Konferentsiya soyuznikov v Petrograda v 1917 godu (Conference of the Allies in Petrograd in 1917)."

Volume XXIII, 1927.

"Inostrannye diplomaty o revolyutsii 1917 g. (Foreign Diplomats on the Revolution of 1917)."

Volumes XXVI–XXX, 1928.

"Stavka i Ministerstvo Inostrannykh Del (General Headquarters and the Ministry of Foreign Affairs)."

Vol. XXVI—August 27/Sept. 9, 1914–Feb. 1/14, 1915.

Vol. XXVIII—Feb. 1/14, 1915–August 28/Sept. 10, 1915.

Vol. XXVIII—Aug. 28/Sept. 10, 1915–June 12/25, 1915.

Vol. XXIX—June 24/July 7, 1916–Dec. 13/26, 1916.

Vol. XXX—Dec. 23/1916/Jan. 5, 1917–May 19/June 1, 1917.

Volumes XXXI and XXXII, 1929.

"Dnevnik Ministerstva Inostrannykh Del za 1915–1916 gg. (Diary of the Ministry of Foreign Affairs for 1915–1916)."

Volumes XXXIV and XXXV, 1929.

"Cheko-Slovatskii Vopros i Tsaristskaya Diplo-

Bibliography

matiya v 1914–17 gg. (The Czecho-Slovak Question and Tsarist Diplomacy in 1914–17)."

While some Soviet scholars were revealing in the above publications the record of Tsarist diplomacy during 1914–17, others were unearthing material on the important question of Russia's attitude towards Poland, mainly a domestic problem, in the same period. The result of their researches is contained in:

N. M. Lapinskii, ed., *Russko-Polskiye otnosheniya v period mirovoi voiny (Russo-Polish Relations During the World War)*. Moscow-Leningrad: Moscow Worker, 1926.

The following volume, which is concerned principally with the pre-war period, contains some documents relating to the early part of the war period:

Materialy po istorii franko-russkikh otnoshenii za 1910–1914 (Materials on the History of Franco-Russian Relations for 1910–1914). Moscow: People's Commissariat of Foreign Affairs, 1922.

Translated into French as:

Réné Marchand, ed., *Un livre noir. Diplomatie d'avant guerre et de guerre. D'ápres les documents des archives russes, 1910–1917*. 3 vols. Paris: Librairie du travail, 1922–1926.

During the 1920's, the indefatigable German scholar, Friedrich Stieve, who seems to have made a career of proving that Izvolskii was responsible for World War I, obtained and published a few documents on the 1914 period from the former Russian Embassy in Paris. They appeared as:

Fredrich Stieve, ed., *Iswolski im Weltkrieg*. Ber-

Bibliography

lin, Deutsche Verlagsgesellschaft für Politik und Geschichte, 1925.

The basic source for this study is the following, which reprints some, but not all, of the material appearing in the preceding collections of documents, and adds yet further material:

Komissiya pri Prezidiume TsIK Soyuza SSR po izdaniyu dokumentov epokhi imperializma, *Mezhdunarodnye otnosheniya v epokhu imperializma. Dokumenty iz arkhivov Tsarskogo i Vremennogo Pravitelstv, 1878–1917 gg.* (Commission attached to the Presidium of the Central Executive Committee of the Union of Soviet Socialist Republics for the Publication of the Documents of the Age of Imperialism, *International Relations in the Age of Imperialism. Documents from the Archives of the Tsarist and Provisional Governments, 1878–1917.*) Moscow-Leningrad: State Social-Economic Press, 1931–1940.

Series I, 1878–1903.

No volumes in this series were ever published.

Series II, 1903–1914.

Volumes covering the period from January 14, 1911 to January 14, 1914 were published in this series between 1938 and 1940.

Series III, 1914–1917.

Between 1931 and 1938, volumes covering the period from January 14, 1914 to April 15, 1916 were published. The following were used in this study:

Volume VI, Part 1; August–November, 1914.

Volume VI, Part 2: November, 1914–January, 1915.

Bibliography

Volume VII, Part 1: January–March, 1915.
Volume VII, Part 2: March–May, 1915.
Volume VIII, Part 1: May–August, 1915.
Volume VIII, Part 2: August–November, 1915.
Volume IX: November, 1915–January, 1916.
Volume X: January–April, 1916.

Translated into German as:

Otto Hoetzsch, ed., *Die Internationale Beziehungen im Zeitalter des Imperialismus. Dokumente aus den Archiven der Zarischen und der Provisorischen Regierung, 1878–1917*. 11 vols. Berlin: Steiniger-Verlage, 1933–1942.

The following collections of documents were useful for the last chapter:

C. K. Cumming and W. W. Pettit, eds., *Russian-American Relations, March, 1917–March, 1920, Documents and Papers*. New York: Harcourt, Brace and Howe, 1920.

F. A. Golder, *Documents of Russian History, 1914–1917*. New York: The Century Company, 1927.

A. J. Sack, *The Birth of the Russian Democracy*. New York: Russian Information Bureau, 1918.

J. B. Scott, ed., *Official Statements of War Aims and Peace Proposals, December 1916 to November 1918*. Washington: Carnegie Endowment of International Peace, 1921.

The official records of the lower legislative chamber of the Russian Empire, the State Duma, which sat between 1906 and 1917, were used on occasion during this study, and are entitled:

Bibliography

Stenographicheskii Otchet. Gosudarstvennaya Duma. Chertvertyi Sozyv. St. Petersburg/Petrograd, 1913–1917.

A few official proclamations quoted in this study were translated from the text as given in a contemporary Russian periodical:

Vestnik Evropy, Petrograd, 1914–1917.

MEMOIR LITERATURE

Bertie, Lord Francis, *The Diary of Lord Bertie.* 2 vols. London: Hodder & Stoughton, 1924.

Buchanan, Sir George, *My Mission to Russia and Other Diplomatic Memories*, 2 vols. Boston: Little, Brown & Co., 1923.

Chernov, V., *The Great Russian Revolution.* Trans. and abridged by Philip E. Moseley. New Haven: Yale University Press, 1936.

Danilov, Youri, *La Russie dans la guerre mondiale (1914–1917).* Paris: Payot, 1927.

Denikin, A. I., *The Russian Turmoil, Memoirs: Military, Social and Political.* London: Hutchinson & Co., 1923.

Grey, Viscount E., of Fallodon, *Twenty-Five Years,* 1891–1916. 2 vols. New York: Frederick A. Stokes Co., 1925.

Gurko, V. I., *Features and Figures of the Past. Government and Opinion in the Reign of Nicholas II.* Stan-

Bibliography

ford University, California: Stanford University Press, 1939.

Kerenskii, A. F., *La revolution russe (1917)*. Paris: Payot, 1928.

———, *The Crucifixion of Liberty*. Trans. by G. A. Kerenskii. New York: The John Day Company, 1934.

Knox, Sir Alfred, *With the Russian Army, 1914–1917, Being Chiefly Extracts from the Diary of a Military Attaché*. 2 vols. London: Hutchinson & Co. 1921.

Lloyd George, David, *War Memoirs*. 6 vols. Boston: Little, Brown & Co., 1934.

Lockhart, R. H. B., *British Agent*, London: G. P. Putnam's Sons, 1933.

Masaryk, T. G., *The Making of a State: Memories and Observations*. New York: F. A. Stokes Co., 1927.

Milyukov, P. N., *Istoriya vtoroi russkoi revolyutsii*. 2 vols. Sofia: Russo-Bulgarian Book Publishers, 1921.

Nabokoff, C., *The Ordeal of a Diplomat*. London: Duckworth and Company, 1921.

Neklyudov, A. V., *Diplomatic Reminiscences Before and During the World War, 1911–1917*. London: Murray, 1920.

Noulens, J., *Mon ambassade en Russie soviétique, 1917–1919*. 2 vols. Paris: Librairie Plon, 1933.

Oxford and Asquith, Earl of (Herbert Asquith), *Memories and Recollections*. 2 vols. Boston: Little, Brown & Co., 1928.

Paléologue, M., *La Russie des Tsars pendant la grande guerre*. 3 vols. Paris: Plon-Nourrit et Cie., 1921.

Radoslavov, Dr. Vasil, *Bulgarien und die Weltkriege*. Berlin: Ullstein, 1923.

Bibliography

Ribot, A., *Lettres à un ami Souvenirs de ma vie politique.* Paris: Editions Bossard, 1924.

Rosen, R. R., *Forty Years of Diplomacy.* 2 vols. London: George Allen & Unwin, Ltd., 1922.

Savinskii, A. A., *Recollections of a Russian Diplomat.* London: Hutchinson & Co., Ltd., 1927.

Sazonov, S. D., *Les années fatales, Souvenirs de M. S. Sazonov, ancien Ministre des Affaires Étrangeres de Russie (1910–1916).* Paris: Payot, 1927.

Trotskii, L. D., *The History of the Russian Revolution.* 3 vols. Trans. by Max Eastman. New York: Simon & Schuster, 1932.

Trubetskoi, Grigorii, *Russland als grossmacht.* Stuttgart und Berlin: Deutsche verlags-anstalt, 1917.

GENERAL

Chamberlain, W. H., *The Russian Revolution.* 2 vols. New York: The Macmillan Co., 1935.

Howard, Harry N., *The Partition of Turkey, 1913–1923.* Norman, Oklahoma: The University of Oklahoma Press, 1931.

Liddell Hart, B. H., *The War in Outline, 1914–1918.* New York: Random House, 1936.

Notovich, F. I., *Poterya Soyuznikami Balkanskogo Poluostrova.* Moscow: Academy of Sciences of the U.S.S.R., 1947.

Bibliography

Pares, Sir Bernard, *The Fall of the Russian Monarchy*. New York: The Macmillan Company, 1939.

Pingaud, A., *L'histoire diplomatique de la France pendant la grande guerre*. 3 vols., Paris: Editions "Alsatia," 1937–40.

Rubenstein, N., "Vneshnyaya Politika Kerenshchiny," in *Ocherki po istorii Oktyabrskoi Revolyutsii*, vol, 2, ed. by M. N. Pokrovskii. Moscow: State Press, 1927.

Smilg-Bernario, M., *Von Kerenski zu Lenin*. Vienna: Amalthea-Verlag, 1929.

INDEX

A

Adalia, 138, 172, 250, 269, 425–426, 430
Adana, 234, 366, 372, 428, 456
Adrianople, 31, 114
Adriatic Sea, 21, 56, 137, 141, 152, 154, 160, 172–174, 186; the Treaty of London, 243–272, 311, 313–315, 319, 322, 325, 368
Aegean Sea, 32, 34, 71, 174, 196, 287, 331
Afghanistan, 231–232, 438
Africa, 59, 257, 260, 267, 269, 327
Akka, 360
Aix-la-Chapelle (Aachen), 106
Aland Islands, 464
Albania, 21, 23, 34; partition first proposed, 35–36, 47–48, 104; turmoil in, 136–137, 139–142; second round of Allied Balkan negotiations (Nov.–Dec., 1914), 142–163, 165; Italy occupies Valona, 169–171; the Treaty of London, 243–272, 274, 325, 327–328; occupied by Austria-Hungary and Italy, 348–350
Aleksandropol, 352
Alekseev, Mikhail, General, 117–119; becomes Chief of Staff (1915), 304; 339–340; Russo-Rumanian negotiations (Jan.–July, 1916), 394–399; the Polish Question and the fall of Sazonov, 397–406; defeat of Rumania and fall of Stürmer, 436–442; Supreme High Commander, 470
Aleppo, 361
Alessio, 265
Alexander, Prince-Regent of Serbia (1914–1918), Prince-Regent of Yugoslavia (1918–1921), King of Yugoslavia (1921–1934). 146–147, 161, 174, 271, 295, 324
Alexander, King of Greece (1917–1920), 480
Alexander I, Emperor of Russia (1801–1825), 4–5, 73
Alexander III, Emperor of Russia (1881–1894), 105
Alexandra Fedorovna (Alix of Hesse-Darmstadt), Empress of Russia, 4, 77; urges dismissal of Sazonov, 344–347, 352, 372, 393; the Polish Question and the fall of Sazonov, 397–406, 407–409, 411; deposition of Constantine of Greece, 431–436; fall of Stürmer, 436–442
Alexandretta (Iskenderun), 238, 242–243, 361
Alexandretta (Iskenderun), Gulf of, 127, 233, 360
Algeciras, 59, 61
Allied Powers (Allies), 44, 52,

· 527 ·

Index

57, 76, 98–100, 137, 140, 151, 154–157, 170, 176–177, 179; the Straits Agreement, 185–243; the Treaty of London, 243–272, 278, 285, 299, 302; final negotiations with Bulgaria, 309–320; Bulgaria joins the Central Powers, 320–335; Anglo-French occupation of Salonica, 335–340, 387, 410; intervention of Rumania, 411–418, 419, 424; Italy's Anatolian demands, 424–481; defeat of Rumania, 436–442; war aims announcements (1916–17), 442–453, 463, 468–469, 472, 475; Kerenskii seeks revision of war aims, 476–486
Alsace-Lorraine, 43, 45, 47, 49, 51, 56, 59, 106, 386; Franco-Russian Agreement on Germany, 459–466, 474, 478, 484
Amadia, 366, 372, 375
Amasia, 376
Anamur, Cape, 457
Anatolia (Asia Minor), 72, 102, 112, 132, 137–138, 172, 182, 192, 194, 197, 211, 215, 220, 228, 235, 238, 245, 250, 260, 269, 286, 311, 313, 315–316, 322–323; Russian aims in Armenia and Anatolia, 363–374; Franco-Russian Anatolian Agreement, 374–382; Anglo-Russian Anatolian Agreement, 418–424; Italy's Anatolian Demands, 424–431, 445–447; London Conference on Anatolia, 453–457; St. Jean de Maurienne Agreement, 470–471, 474
Anglo-Russian Anatolian Agreement, 418–424, 426
Anglo-Russian Convention of 1907, 84, 228–232
Ankara, 103, 377
Antivari, 249
Antony, Metropolitan of Volhynia, 89
"April Days," 475
Arabia, 228, 355–356; Sykes-Picot Agreement, 358–362, 375, 379
Arabs, 357, 375, 419, 430
Archangel, 209, 339
Ardahan, 190
Armenia, 66–67, 71, 75; Russian aims (Nov., 1914), 98, 102–103, 108, 112, 116; question of Russian proclamation, 124–128, 182, 189, 200–203, 205, 220, 233–236, 238, 241–243, 351; Russian campaign of 1915–16, 352–354, 355, 358, 362; Russian aims in Armenia and Anatolia (Mar., 1916), 363–374; Franco-Russian Anatolian Agreement, 374–382, 454, 471, 484
Asia Minor, See Anatolia
Asquith, Herbert, British Prime Minister (1908–1916), 142–143, 260–267, 424–425, 443
Athens, 36, 141, 143–144, 157, 167, 170, 179, 191, 198, 287–288, 433, 435, 480
Austria-Hungary, 3–8; Poles and Ukrainians, 9–12; early defeats, 13–14; Russian

Index

proclamation to peoples of, 18–19; Russian negotiations with Italy and Rumania (Aug.–Oct., 1914), 20–30; Russian negotiations with Serbia and Bulgaria (Aug.–Sept., 1914), 30–41, 42, 45, 48–50, 52, 56–57, 60–62; treaty with Turkey, 67–69, 80, 94–95, 98; war aims of Nicholas II, 100–108; question of separate peace with (1914), 116–124, 129–131, 133, 137–138, 140–141, 143–145; attacks Serbia (1914), 146–147; defeated by Serbs, 158, 162, 164–165, 170–171, 177, 180–181, 189–190, 193, 201–202, 204; the Treaty of London, 243–272, 275–278; Allied Rumanian negotiations (May–Aug., 1915), 288–309, 317, 318; Bulgaria joins, 320–335, 336, 343; fall of Serbia and Montenegro, 348–350, 351; France and the Polish Question, 382–394; Russo-Rumanian negotiations, 394–395, 408; intervention of Rumania, 411–418, 424; defeat of Rumania, 436–442; Allied war aims announcements (1916–17), 442–453, 463, 480, 485

Aydin Railroad, 457
Aydin Vilayet, 195, 286–287, 428
Azerbaijan, 87–88, 370

B

Babylonia, 360
Bachka (Batchka), 325
Baghdad, 241, 357, 360
Baia, 139
Balchik, 150, 167, 297, 305–306, 314, 316
Balfour, Arthur James, British Foreign Secretary (1895–1902, 1916–1920), Prime Minister (1902–1906), 225, 443; London Conference on Anatolia, 453–459, 471
Balkan Peninsula, 23, 26; first round of Macedonian negotiations (Aug.–Sept., 1914), 30–41; Balkan balance, 35, 70, 73, 76, 84, 130; Allied negotiations in (Sept., 1914–Feb., 1915), 135–184; final round of Allied negotiations with Bulgaria (May–July, 1915), 309–320; Bulgaria joins Central Powers, 320–335; Allied efforts to save Serbia, 335–350, 342–343; Central Powers occupy Serbia and Montenegro, 348–350; intervention of Rumania, 411–418, 484
Balkan War, First (1912), 20
Balkan War, Second (1913), 30–31
Baltic Sea, 202
Banat, See Banat of Temesvar
Banat of Temesvar, 29, 138–139; 176, 259, 271, 275, Allied Rumanian negotiations (May–Aug., 1915), 288–309, 313, 325–327, 330, 414
Baranovichi, 13, 232–236, 277, 281, 304
Barthou, Louis, 384–385, 443
Basra, 241, 357

· 529 ·

Index

Batum, 239

Bavaria, 258

Bax-Ironside, British Minister to Bulgaria, 148–149, 151, 310

Bazili, N. A., Russian aims at Straits, 110–116

Beirut, 358

Belaya Tserkov, 296

Belgium, 45, 47–50, 58, 87, 94, 112, 332, 385; Allied war aims announcements (1916–17), 442–453, 484

Belgrade, 116, 139, 158, 160, 259, 274, 288, 297–302, 414

Belyaev, General of Infantry, Russian Deputy War Minister, 373, 377

Benckendorff, Count Alexander, Russian ambassador to Great Britain (1904–1916), British war aims, 54–58, 85–86, 109, 119–120, 142–143, 182; the Straits Agreement, 185–243; the Treaty of London, 243–272, 297, 327, 345, 350, 357, 405; Anglo-Russian Anatolian Agreement, 418–424; dies (1917), 455

Berlin, 30; proposed Russian march on, 53, 62, 68

"Berlin-To-Baghdad" Railroad, 66, 361

Bessarabia, 25–27, 30, 132, 142–143, 183–184, 201, 293, 338, 340

Bethmann-Hollweg, Theobald von, 383

Bitlis, 366, 369, 374, 379

Black Sea, 63, 65, 73, 81, 110–116, 195, 199–200, 202, 205, 213, 373, 379, 422, 449

Black Sea Fleet (Russian), 33, 110–116, 132, 194, 376

"Blue Zone," 360–361

Bobrinskii, Vladimir A., Count, 89–90, 276

Bohemia-Moravia, Kingdom of, 17, 19, 45, 47, 105, 117, 119, 122

See Czech Question and Czechoslovakia

Bolsheviks, 187, 468, 480, 484, 486

Bolshoi Theater, 484

Bompard, 237

Bonar Law, British Prime Minister (1922–23), 225

Bordeaux, 53, 108

Bosnia-Herzegovina, 31, 35, 47, 56, 63, 104, 120, 122, 139, 141, 150–151, 160, 170, 176, 186, 295, 311, 314, 322, 324

Bosporus, 64, 78, 81, 83, 112–113, 130, 132, 190–191, 202, 207, 217, 448

Bourgeois, Léon, 389

Bratianu, Ion, Rumanian Premier, 23–30, second round of Allied Balkan negotiations (Nov.–Dec., 1914), 142–163; Italo-Rumanian bloc, 163–169; Russo-Rumanian coolness, 179–184; negotiations with Allies (May–Aug., 1915), 288–309; 331–332; Allied efforts to save Serbia, 335–340; Russo-Rumanian negotiations (Jan. – July, 1916), 394–395, intervention of Rumania, 411–418

Braz, 264

Brenner Pass, 248

Index

Breslau, 70–71, 76, 79–81, 317
Brest-Litovsk, 304, 384, 486
Briand, Aristide, becomes Premier and Foreign Minister of France (Oct., 1915), 341–343; fall of Serbia and Montenegro, 349–350; Djemal Pasha intrigue, 354–358; Sykes-Picot A g r e e m e n t, 358–362; Franco-Russian Anatolian Agreement, 374–382; France and the Polish Question, 382–394; intervention of Rumania, 411–418; Italy's Anatolian demands, 424–431; deposition of Constantine of Greece, 431–436; fall of Stürmer, 436–442; Allied war aims announcements (1916–17), 442–453; London Conference on Anatolia, 453–459; Franco-Russian Agreement on Germany, 459–466, 482
Britain, 3–8, 19, 24, 37, 39, 43, 45, 38–50; views on Allied war aims, 51–61; and Turkey at beginning of war, 67–69; negotiations with, 71–76, 81; promises Russia Constantinople and the Straits (1914), 81–88, 95, 113, 121, 138, 143, 145, 172, 179, 184; the Straits Agreement, 185–243; the Treaty of London, 243–272, 275; Gallipoli Campaign, 282–287; Rumanian negotiations (May–Aug., 1915), 288–309; final negotiations with Bulgaria (May–July, 1915), 309–320; Bulgaria joins Central Powers, 320–335; Anglo-French occupation of Salonica, 335–340; fall of Serbia and Montenegro, 348–350, 351, 353; Djemal Pasha intrigue, 354–358; Sykes-Picot Agreement, 358–362; Russian aims in Armenia and Anatolia, 363–374, 410; Anglo-Russian Anatolian Agreement, 418–424; deposition of Constantine of Greece, 431–436; defeat of Rumania, 436–442; war aims announcements (1916–17), 442–443; London Conference on Anatolia, 453–459, 461; Russian war aims controversy, 466–476; St. Jean de Maurienne Agreement, 470–471; Kerenskii seeks revision of Allied war aims, 476–486.
Broussa Vilayet, 195
"Brown Zone," 360–361
Brusilov Offensive, 396, 411, 437
Bubnov, A. D., Captain Second Rank, 110–116
Buchanan, Sir George, British ambassador to Russia (1909–1918), 3, 5; military objectives of Allied Powers, 50–54, 78–80, 86–88, 109, 121, 165, 176; Allied Rumanian negotiations (May–A u g ., 1915), 288–309; Russian aims in Armenia and Anatolia, 363–374; fall of Sazonov, 397–406; Anglo-Russian Anatolian Agreement, 418–424, fall of Stürmer,

· 531 ·

Index

436–442; Russian war aims controversy, 466–476
Bucharest, 25, 28, 144, 149, 155, 164–165, 171, 179, 244, 288, 290, 293–294, 297–298, 301, 306, 308, 340, 394, 413, 415, 439, 449
Buckingham Palace, 86
Budapest, 276, 416
Bukovina, 9, 13, 27, 28–29, 42, 56, 102, 120, 168–169, 183–184, 274–275, 278; Allied Rumanian negotiations (May–Aug., 1915), 288–309, 340, 395, 397, 413, 416
Bulgaria, 24–25, 28–29, first round of Macedonian negotiations (Aug.–Sept., 1914), 30–41, 42, 47, 50, 65, 67, 69, 74–75, 103–104, 108, 112–113, 131–133; second round of Allied Balkan negotiations (Nov.–Dec., 1914), 142–163, 166, 170–171; fourth round of Macedonian negotiations, 175–179, 180, 191, 193–194, 207, 228–229, 256, 259, 274, 278; British Gallipoli campaign, 282–287, 294, 300, 306; final negotiations with Allies (May–July, 1915), 309–320; joins Central Powers, 320–335; Allied effort to save Serbia,, 335–340, 342, 346; fall of Serbia and Montenegro, 348–350, 369, 376, 395, 399; intervention of Rumania, 411–418, 432, 435; defeat of Rumania, 436–442; Allied war aims announcements (1916–17), 442–453, 470

Burgas, 145, 338
Buxton, Noel, 191, 194
Buyukdéré, 78
Byelorussia, 13, 335

C

Caesarea (Kaisariyeh), 366, 370, 374
Cairo, 357
Cambon, Jules, 386
Cambon, Paul, 267, 269–270; London Conference on Anatolia, 453–459
Caporetto, 481
Carinthia, 139, 270, 328
Carlotti, Marquis, Italian ambassador to Russia, 21–22, 51, 137, 164–165, 169, 290–291, 294, 412, 453
Carniola, 138
Carol I, Prince of Rumania, 1866–1878, King of Rumania, 1878–1914, 23
Carpathian Mountains, 13, 62, 102, 275–276, 296
Catherine II, Empress of Russia (1762–1796), 73
Catholicos, Armenian, 124
Central Powers, 9, 20, 28–29, 33, 37, 41, 61–62, 68; Turkey joins, 76–82, 100, 140, 196, 200, 268, 294, 303, 307, 314, 317–318; Bulgaria joins, 320–335, 339, 347; occupy Serbia and Montenegro, 348–350, 383–384, 391; intervention of Rumania, 411–418; defeat of Rumania, 436–442; Allied war aims announcements (1916–17), 442–453, 469, 480, 485

Index

Centrists, 201, 204
Četinje, 349
Chamber of Deputies (French), 338, 482
Chamber of Deputies (Italian), 429
Chataldja, 133
Chernov, Victor, war aims controversy with Milyukov, 466–476
Chernovets (Cernauti, Czernowitz), 13, 26, 294, 299, 301, 304, 396
Chios, 67, 70
Chkeidze, Nikolai S., 206; war aims controversy with Milyukov, 466–476
Cholm, 303
Churchill, Winston S., 186–188, 197
Cilicia, 125–126, promised by Russia to France (Mar., 1915), 232–238, 242–243, 355–356; Sykes-Picot Agreement, 358–362; 365, 382, 425–426, 428, 457
Clemenceau, Georges, French Premier (1917–1920), 338
Commons, House of (British), 208–213
Communism, 468
Constantine I, King of Greece (1913–1917 and 1920–1922), 34, 36, 197–198; Anglo-French occupation of Salonika, 335–340; question of deposition (1916), 431–436; abdication, 480
Constantinople, 36; importance to Russia (1908–1914), 63–67, 68, 70–71, 74, 76–81; promised to Russia by Britain, 81–86, 94, 96; France informed of Russian aims, 97–110; definition of Russian aims, 110–116; proposed Russian attack on, 128–134, 137, 141, 167, 181–182; the Straits Agreement, 185–243, 246, 262, 267, 274, 275; British Gallipoli campaign, 282–287, 306, 317, 319, 330, 332, 343, 347, 354–356, 368, 376, 382, 428–429, 438, 441; Allied war aims announcements (1916–17), 442–453, 456, 465; proposed Russian attack on (1917), 470, 471, 481
Constanza, 294, 416
Constituent Assembly (Russian), 467, 470
Corfu, 349–350
Council of Ministers (Russian), future of Poland, 89–96; Polish project of Mar. 3, 1915, 275–282, 345, 398, 400–401
Court of St. James, 406
Crete, 197, 432
Crimea, 67, 79
Crimean War (1854–1856), 84
Croatia, 49, 105, 122–123, 137–139, 172–174; the Treaty of London, 243–272. 275, 295–296, 299, 304–306 312, 321, 325–328, 330
Crusades, 370
Cyprus, 69, 67, 338, 360, 430
"Czechia," See Czech Question
Czecho-Slovak Legion, 16

Index

Czech National Committee, 17, 19
Czecho-Slovakia, 19, 49, 291; Allied war aims announcements (1916–17), 442–453. See Czech Question and Bohemia-Moravia
Czech Question, Russian attitude, 15–20, 42, 105; proposed Russian proclamation, 116–119, 123; Allied war aims announcements (1916–17), 442–453. See Czecho-Slovakia and Bohemia-Moravia
Czechs, See Czech Question

D

Dalmatia, 22, 31, 47, 104, 137, 139, 141, 145, 150, 160, 165, 167, 170, 172–174, 176; the Treaty of London, 243–272, 274, 295, 298, 319, 321, 324, 326
Dalmatian Islands, 141; the Treaty of London, 243–272
Danilo, Prince, 12
Danilov, G. N., General, 110–116, 132–133
Danube River, 123, 132, 138–139, 214, 291, 295–296, 302, 321, 325, 414, 416, 439
Dardanelles, 64, 67, 71–73, 83, 112–113, 130, 178, 189–190, 195, 197–198, 202, 217–218, 228, 244, 246; British Gallipoli Campaign, 282–287, 322, 330, 342, 448
Debrecsin, 413
Declaration of War Aims (Russian Provisional Government), 471–476

Delcassé Théophile, French Foreign Minister (1898–1905, 1914–1915), 23, 38, 40, 51, 53–55; French war aims, 58–61, 74, 82, 97–99, 108–109, 123–124, 140–141; second round of Allied Balkan negotiations, 142–163; fourth round of Macedonian negotiations, 175–179; the Straits Agreement, 185–243; the Treaty of London, 243–272; Rumanian negotiations (May–Aug., 1915), 288–309; final negotiations with Bulgaria (May–July, 1915), 309–320; Bulgaria joins the Central Powers, 320–335; Anglo-French occupation of Salonica, 335–340; ousted, 341–343
Demidov, Prince, Russian ambassador to Greece, 34, 36; British offer of Smyrna to Greece, 191–196; deposition of Constantine of Greece, 431–436
Denmark, 45, 47, 50, 94
Devol River, 154
Diamandy, Rumanian ambassador to Russia, 183; Allied Rumanian negotiations (May–Aug., 1915), 288–309, 314, 316
Diarbekr, 365–366, 370, 372
Djemal Pasha, 354–358
Djezir-ibn-Omar, 366, 372, 375
Dmowski, Roman, 280
Dniester River, 274
Dobecki, E. E., 280

· 534 ·

Index

Dobrich, 150, 167, 305
Dobrudja, 24, 28, 31, 38, 144, 157, 163, 294, 300, 311, 314, 395, 413, 416, 439
Dodecanese Islands, 137, 156, 172, 250, 268
Doiran, 38
Doumergue, Gaston, French Foreign Minister and Minister of Colonies, Italian and Rumanian negotiations (Aug., 1914), 20–30, 37, 42, 71; Franco-Russian Agreements on Germany, 459–466
Drama, 146, 310, 314, 317, 432
Drave River, 321, 325
Dreikaiserbund, 216
Drin River, 248–249, 268, 325
Druzhina, Czech, 16, 118. See Czecho-Slovak Legion
Dubno, 304
Dubrovnik (Ragusa), 137, 141, 249, 264–265, 269, 319, 321, 325
Duma, Fourth State (1912–1917), 6–7, 93, 96, 183; discussion of Russian war aims, 198–207, 208, 219, 344–346, 385, 392–393, 410–411; fall of Stürmer, 436–442, 444; war aims announcements, 448–449, 450
Durazzo, 154, 249, 269
Dvina River (Western), 274
Dymsza, 280

E

Eastern Front, 278
Edessa, County of, 370
Egin, 374, 379
Egri, 311
Egypt, 57, 84; British annexation of, 108, 267, 438
Elliott, Sir Francis, 190, 194, 197
Engalychev, Prince, 276, 279–280
England, See Britain
Enos-Midiya Line, 74, 103, 114, 143, 151, 155, 207, 210, 217, 284, 287, 311, 318, 323
Enver Pasha, 67; offers Allies Turkish help, 69–70, 79, 116, 189
Epirus, 165
Ergene, 114
Erjies, Mount, 457
Erzurum, 127, 189; captured by Russians, 353, 367, 369, 371, 376, 378
Ethiopia, 138
Euphrates River, 361

F

von Falkenhayn, General, 278, 439–440
Feodosiya, 79
Ferdinand I, King of Rumania (1914–1927), 293, 297, 394
Ferdinand I, Prince of Bulgaria (1888–1908), King (Tsar) of Bulgaria (1908–1918), 30, 32, 40, 143, 177, 283, 285, 329, 346
Finland, 401–402, 404, 471
Folkestone, 471
Foreign Office (British), 188, 358, 422
Fourteen Points, 46

Index

France, 3–8, 9, 13–14, 19, 24, 37–39, 43, 47–50; war aims, 51–61, 62; negotiations with Turkey, 71–76, 81, 83, 94–95; Straits Question, 97–110, 113, 121, 138, 145, 172; the Straits Agreement, 185–243; the Treaty of London, 243–272, 275; Rumanian negotiations (May–Aug., 1915), 288–309; final negotiations with Bulgaria (May-July, 1915), 309–320; Bulgaria joins Central Powers, 320–335; Anglo-French occupation of Salonika, 335–340; ouster of Delcassé, 341–343; fall of Serbia and Montenegro, 348–350, 351; Djemal Pasha intrigue, 354–358; Sykes-Picot Agreement, 358–362; Russian aims in Armenia and Anatolia, 363–374; Franco-Russian Anatolian Agreement, 374–382; France and the Polish Question, 382–394; Russo-Rumanian negotiations (Jan.-July, 1916), 394–399, 410; intervention of Rumania, 411–418, 419, 421, 424; Italy's Anatolian demands, 424–431; deposition of Constantine of Greece, 431–436; defeat of Rumania, 436–442; war aims announcements (1916–17), 442–453; London Conference on Anatolia, 453–459; Franco-Russian Agreement on Germany, 459–466; Russian war aims controversy, 466–476; St. Jean de Maurienne Agreement, 470–471; Kerenskii seeks revision of war aims, 476–486

Francis Joseph, See Franz Josef.

Franco-Russian agreement on Germany, 459–466

Franco-Russian Alliance of 1891–93, 43–44, 394, 412

Franco-Russian Anatolian Agreement (April, 1916), 374–382, 418, 421, 426, 429

Franz Josef, Emperor of Austria, King of Hungary (1848–1916), 104, 120, 122, 443

Frisia, 56

G

Galata, 420

Galicia, 9, 11–13; Russian invasion (1914), 13–14, 42, 47, 56, 82; Russian occupation of, 89–90, 92, 102, 120, 122, 199, 201, 276, 278, 280, 297, 300, 317, 343, 383

Gallipoli Peninsula, 113–114; origins of British campaign, 186–190, 220, 241, 274; British campaign, 282–287, 299, 307, 310, 317, 323, 352

Garusewicz, I. C., 280

George, Crown Prince of Greece (King George II, 1922–23, 1935–41, 1946–47), 480

George V, King of Great Britain (1910–1936), 86–87, 437

Georgia, 206

Gepetskii, Nikolai E., 201

Index

German Colonies, 45, 48–49, 55–56, 60, 138, 269, 485
German Navy, 58
Germany, 3–8, 13–14; Russian war aims concerning, 43–50, 52; British war aims concerning, 59–60, 62, 65–67; alliance with Turkey, 70–71, 73–74, 80, 86, 88, 94–95, 98; Russian war aims concerning, 100–108, 112, 116, 119–120, 131, 133–134, 165, 187–189, 193, 195, 201–202, 204, 218, 244, 246–247, 254–255, 259, 273–275; 1915 offensive against Russia, 275–282, 303–304, 289, 294, 300, 318, 351; Bulgaria joins, 320–335, 337, 340, 354, 367, 369; France and the Polish Question, 382–394; Russo-Rumanian negotiations (Jan.-July, 1916), 394–399, 403, 409–410, intervention of Rumania, 411–418, 425, 431–432; Allied war aims announcements (1916–17), 442–453; Franco-Russian Agreement on Germany, 459–466, 470, 477–478, 480, 482–483
Gibraltar, Straits of, 214
Giers, A. A., 137, 345
Göben, 70–71, 76, 79–81, 317
Golden Horn, 240
Golytsin Nikolai D., Russian Premier (1917), 442, 460
Goremykin, Ivan L., Russian Premier (1914–1916), 6, 10, 90–91, 96; Russian war aims, 199–200; Polish project of March 3, 1915, 275–282; urges dismissal of Sazonov, 344–347; removed, 372
Gorizia, 268, 270, 424
Gorlice Offensive, 273–274
Gounaris, Greek Premier, 198, 285, 312
Grabski, Stanislaw, 276, 280
Gradisca, 268
Great Britain, See Britain
Greece, 23; first round of Macedonian negotiations, 30–41, 42, 48, 50, 67, 69, 72–104, 112–113, 133, 137, 140; second round of Allied Balkan negotiations, 142–163, 165–167; reaction to Italian occupation of Valona, 169–175, 176, 179–180, 182; Britain offers Smyrna, 190–198, 201, 208, 228, 231, 238, 248–249, 256, 259, 265–267, 269; British Gallipoli campaign, 282–287; final Allied negotiations with Bulgaria (May–July, 1915), 309–320; Bulgaria joins Central Powers, 320–335; Anglo-French occupation of Salonika, 335–340, 342–343; fall of Serbia and Montenegro, 348–350, 427–428; deposition of King Constantine, 431–436; London Conference on Anatolia, 453–459, 470; joins Allies, 480, 481, 485
Grey, Sir Edward, British Foreign Secretary (1906–1916), Italian and Rumanian negotiations (Aug.-Oct., 1914),

· 537 ·

Index

20–30; first round of Macedonian negotiations, 30–41; formation of Allied Powers, 43–44, 53; British war aims, 54–56, 61, 72, 74, 80; promises Russia Constantinople and the Straits, 81–88, 96, 108–109, 119–120, 140; second round of Balkan negotiations, 142–163; fourth round of Macedonian negotiations, 175–179; the Straits Agreement, 185–243; the Treaty of London, 243–272; Gallipoli campaign, 309; final negotiations with Bulgaria, 309–320; Bulgaria joins the Central Powers, 320–335; Anglo-French occupation of Salonika, 335–340; fall of Serbia and Montenegro, 349–350; Djemal Pasha intrigue, 354–358; Sykes-Picot Agreement, 358–362; Anglo-Russian Anatolian Agreement, 418–424; Italy's Anatolian demands, 424–431; deposition of Constantine of Greece, 431–436; fall of Stürmer, 436–442; Allied war aims announcements (1916–17), 442–453; resigns, 454

Grigorovich, Admiral, Russian Naval Minister, 373–374, 376–377

Grodno, 275, 304

Guchkov, A. I., Russian War Minister, 470

Guise, Duc de, 177

Guesde, Jules, 54, 222

Gulkevich, 125–128

Gurko, V. I., General, Russian Acting Chief of Staff (1916–17), 442, 460

H

Haifa, 360–361
Hamilton, Sir Ian, 282
Hanover, 45, 47, 49, 59, 95, 106
Hapsburg Monarchy, 19, 42, 49, 107–108, 383, 411
Hardinge, Lord, 423
Hellenism, 195, 286
Henderson, Arthur, 474, 483
Hesse-Nassau, 95
Hindenburg, Paul von, Marshal, 62, 278, 443
Hohenzollern Dynasty, 107, 462
Holy Places (Christian), 234–235
Holy Places (Moslem), 221; 228, 231, 357, 448

I

Iasi, 447
Ignatiev, Count, Minister of Education, 400
Igor, 206
Imbros, 113, 217
Imperiali, Marquis, Italian ambassador to Great Britain; the Treaty of London, 247–272; London conference on Anatolia, 453–459
India, 69, 84, 438
Iran, See Persia
Iraq, See Mesopotamia
Ishtib, 32
Isonzo River, 274, 320, 424
Ispahan, 231

Index

Istria, 137, 139–140, 141; the Treaty of London, 243–272, 321
Italia Irredenta, 244
Italy, Allied negotiations with (Aug.–Sept., 1914), 20–23, 35, 48, 50, 56–57, 75, 104, 122, 133; Serb vs. Italian ambitions (Sept.–Oct., 1914), 136–142, 150, 152, 154, 162; Italo-Rumanian bloc, 163–169; occupation of Valona and aftermath, 169–175, 179, 182, 185, 201, 221; the Treaty of London, 243–272, 274; Rumanian negotiations (May–Aug., 1915), 287–309; final Allied negotiations with Bulgaria (May–July, 1915), 309–320; Bulgaria joins Central Powers, 320–335; occupies southern Albania, 348–350, 359, 388, 395–396, 417; Anatolian demands, 424–431; war aims announcements (1916–17), 442–443; London conference on Anatolia, 453–459, 461; Russian war aims controversy, 466–476; St. Jean de Maurienne Agreement, 470–471; Kerenskii seeks revision of Allied war aims, 476–486; promised Smyrna, 481
Inebolü, 377
Ivangorod, 303
Ivan Kalita, Great Prince, 12
Izmid, Gulf of, 217
Izmir, See Smyrna
Izvolskii, Alexander Petrovich, Russian ambassador to France (1910–1917), 53, 55; French war aims, 58–61; and the Straits (1908), 63–64, 120, 140–141; the Straits Agreement, 185–243, 246, 256, 259–260, 298, 339; ouster of Delcassé, 341–343, 345, 355–356, 372; France and the Polish Question, 382–394; deposition of Constantine of Greece, 431–436; Franco-Russian Agreement on Germany, 459–466; removed, 481

J

Japan, 45, 48, 444
Jerusalem, 234, 419
Jews, 89–90, 418–419
Joffre, General, 51–58; 395–396, 443
Junkers, 384

K

Kadets (Constitutional Democrats), 203, 205, 408; Russian war aims controversy, 466–476, 481, 484
Karakhissar (Shabkaneh), 374
Karl I, Emperor of Austria, King of Hungary (1916–1918), 443
Kastamun Pass, 377
Kastoria, 37
Kavaia, 154
Kavalla, 31, 34, 36, 41, 146, 153–154, 191, 194, 283, 287, 310, 311–314, 317, 322–323, 329, 432
Keprülü, 311
Kerbela, 85

Index

Kerenskii, Alexander F., Russian Minister of Justice, War Minister, and Premier, 206–207, 408; war aims controversy with Milyukov, 466–476; seeks revision of Allied war aims, 476–486
Kerki River, 252
Kersund, 422
Khadjin, 370
Khalifate, 231, 241–242, 355–356, 357; Sykes-Picot Agreement, 358–362, 365
Khalim Pass, 353
Kharput, 366, 370, 374, 379
Khimara, 248–249, 268
Khvostov, 402
Kiel Canal, 55, 108
Kiev, 16
Kochana, 32
Kochevian tribes, 371
Kolubara, Battle of, 158
Konia, 103, 428, 453, 455–456
Korea, 113
Kornilov Affair, 483
Kotor (Cattaro), Bay of, 249–250, 252, 262, 264, 321
Kovalevskii, Evgraf P., 201–202
Kovel, 396, 412
Kovno, 275, 304, 383
Kraguevats, 161
Kramar, Karel, 15
Kremlin, 7–8
Krivoshein, A. V., 77–78, 91
Kudashev, A. A., Prince, 118
Kurdistan (Kurds), 75, 125, 128, 243, 355; Sykes-Picot Agreement, 358–362, 369, 371, 374–375, 377–379
Kurland, 303, 335, 383
Kut-el-Amara, 352

Kutuzov, Mikhail, 4
Kyzylbashes, 371

L

Labor Party (Trudoviks), 206
Lakavitsa-Bregalnitsa Triangle, 33, 38, 285
Landsdowne, Lord, British Foreign Secretary (1902–1906), 225
Latvia, 484
Lazes, 367, 371
League of Nations, 478, 485
Lebanon, 260
Lemnos, 67, 70, 72, 113–114, 282
Lenin (Ulyanov), Vladimir I., 408–409, 468, 473, 486
Lesbos, 67, 70
Liman von Saunders, General, 66, 282
Lithuania, 92, 303, 383, 484
Livadia, 67
Lloyd George, David, British Prime Minister (1916–1922), 186, 197, 212; Allied war aims announcements (1916–17), 442–453, 458; St. Jean de Maurienne Agreement (1917), 470–471, 474; Kerenskii seeks revision of Allied war aims, 476–486
London, 22, 44, 61, 170, 182, 212, 214, 221, 247, 268, 288, 292, 318, 359, 362, 405, 425, 444, 455
London Balkan Committee, 191
London, Treaty of, 185–186; negotiated, 243–272, 273, 285, 287, 290, 300, 321,

Index

324-325, 349, 359, 388, 412, 425, 427, 430, 452, 456-457
Louis XIV, King of France (1643-1715), 343
Lublin, 303, 383
Ludendorff, Erich von, General, 443
Lule Burgas, 114
Lutsk, 304, 396
Luxembourg, 56, 94
Lvov (Lemberg), 13, 89, 276, 278, 412
Lvov, G. N., Prince, Russian Premier (1917), 466, 469
Lvov, V. N., 204-205

M

Macedonia, first round of negotiations concerning, 30-41, 47, 104; second round of negotiations concerning, 143-163; third round of negotiations concerning, 171, 174; fourth round of negotiations concerning, 175-179, 284-285, 297-298; final round of Allied negotiations with Bulgaria, 309-320; Bulgaria joins Central Powers, 320-335, 336
Mackensen, von, General, 348, 439
Maklakov, V. A., Minister of Internal Affairs, 9-10; Polish Question and Russian war aims, 91-96; Polish project of March 3, 1915, 275-282
Mallet, Louis, 457-458
Marash, 366, 372
Marie, Queen of Rumania, 301

Maritza River, 70, 114, 319, 333
Marmora, Sea of, 84, 113-114, 131, 195, 210, 217
Marne, Battle of the, 13, 41-42, 76
Marosh River, 138
Mecca, 241, 357
Mecca, Sherif of, 356, 360
Mecklenburg-Schwerin, Duke of, 332
Mediterranean Sea, 64, 71, 110-116, 126, 172, 188, 235, 242, 262, 428, 449
Meiafarkin, 370
Mensheviks, 206; war aims controversy, 466-476, 483
Mersina, 138, 233-234, 238, 242-243, 428, 430, 456, 458
Mesopotamia, 65, 190, 241, 352, 355; Sykes-Picot Agreement, 358-362, 365, 368, 370
Messina, Straits of, 71
Milyukov, Paul N., Russian Minister of Foreign Affairs (1917), 203, 408; fall of Stürmer, 436-442; war aims controversy, 466-476
Minister of the Court, 403
Ministry of Foreign Affairs (Russian), proclamation to the Poles, 10, 14, 110; proclamation to the Czechs, 118-119, 132, 168-169, 183, 226, 232, 245, 289-290, 363, 366, 371, 373, 375, 390-391, 401-402, 411-413, 423-424, 431, 468-469
Mitava (Mitau), 303
Mogilev, 304, 339, 400, 402

· 541 ·

Index

Monastir, 35, 176, 297, 311, 348, 397
Montenegro, 136–137, 150; the Treaty of London, 243–272, 274, 295, 321, 325–326; occupied by Central Powers, 348–350; Allied war aims announcements (1916–17), 442–453, 484
Morava River, 158
Moscow, 7–8, 16, 410
Moslems, 173, 357, 381, 438
Mosul, 360–361
Murmansk-Petrograd Railroad, 442
Mush, 375

N

Nabokov, Konstantin, Russian Chargé in Great Britain (1917), London Conference on Anatolia, 453–459
Narenta River, 172, 248–249
Nationalists (Russian), 205–206
National Spanish Bank, 422
Navy, Ministry of the (Russian), 128–129, 262–263, 264, 366, 376, 378
Nazi-Soviet Pact (1939), 407
Near East, 80, 86, 365, 420
Nedjef, 85
Negev, 360
Nemits, A. V., Captain First Rank, 110–116, 129–131
Neratov, Anatolii A., Russian Deputy Minister of Foreign Affairs (1906–1917), 233–234; 289, 345, 402–403, 405, 422–423, 436; Acting Foreign Minister, 442, 445, 447, 453
Nestorians, 369
Netherlands, 55–56, 106
Neuilly, Treaty of (1919), 320
Nicholas I, Emperor of Russia (1825–1855), 84
Nicholas II, Emperor of Russia (1894–1917), 4–5; proclamation to the Poles, 9–10; Czech Question, 16–17, 19, 45, 77; declaration of war on Turkey, 81, 91; Polish Question, 96; announces Russian war aims to Paléologue, 99–108; Sazonov's report on Straits, 113–114; the Straits Agreement, 185–243, 251–252, 263, 265; Polish project of March 3, 1915, 275–282, 300–301; becomes Supreme High Commander, 304, 338, 340; threatened dismissal of Sazonov (1915), 344–347; Russian aims in Armenia and Anatolia, 386–387; the Polish Question (1916), 390–394, 395; the fall of Sazonov, 397–406, 409; deposition of Constantine of Greece, 431–436; fall of Stürmer, 436–442; Allied war aims announcements (1916–17), 442–453; Franco-Russian Agreement on Germany, 459–466; abdication, 466, 467, 486
Nicolson, Sir Arthur, 86–87, 226, 357
Niemen River, 47, 49, 72
Nikolai Nikolaevich, Grand Duke, Russian Supreme High Commander (1914–1915), Viceroy of Transcau-

· 542 ·

Index

casia (1915–1917), 5, 8, 10, 51–54, 62, 89–91, 133–134, 189–190, 193–194, 239, 263, 276–277, 289, 300; Viceroy of Transcaucasia, 304; Russian 1915–16 Armenian campaign, 352–354, 366, 380–381, 422–423
Nikolayev, 65, 128
Nish, 32, 39, 141, 152, 157, 160–161, 166, 170, 172–174, 177–178, 271, 322, 324, 326, 331, 348
Nivelle, General, 443
Nolde, Boris, Baron, 391–394, 397–398
North Sea, 187
Noulens, Joseph, French ambassador to Russia (1917–1919), 474
Novogeorgievsk, 304
Novorossisk, 79

O

Ober-Ost, Military Government of, 383
Octobrists, 201, 203
Oder River, 131
Odessa, 27, 112
Okhrida, 311
Okhrida, Lake, 32, 269
Oleg, 206
Orange Books (Russian), 212
Ordu, 374, 376
Orléans, House of, 177
Orthodoxy (Russian), 64, 89–90, 173–174, 183, 204, 365, 419
Ottoman Debt, 379
Ottoman Empire, See Turkey.
Ovtche Polje, 330

P

Painlevé, Paul, French Foreign Minister and Premier (1917), 443, 482
Palatinate, 47, 49
Paléologue, Maurice, French ambassador to Russia (1914–1917), 3–5, 10, 44–46; military objectives of Allied Powers, 50–54, 77–79, 81–82; learns Russian aims at Straits, 97–100, 121–124, 176; the Straits Agreement, 185–243; Allied Rumanian negotiations (May–Aug., 1915), 288–309; Russian aims in Armenia and Anatolia, 363–374; Franco-Russian Anatolian Agreement, 374–82; France and the Polish Question, 382–394, 395; fall of Sazonov, 397–406, 409–410, 412; fall of Stürmer, 436–442; Franco-Russian Agreement on Germany, 459–466; Russian war aims controversy, 466–476.
Palestine, 103–104, 190–191, 202; demanded by France, 234–238, 239, 242, 355–356; Sykes-Picot Agreement, 358–362, 366; Jewish national home, 418–419, 430
Panama, 485
Pančevo, 294, 301
Pan-Slavic, See Pan-Slavism
Pan-Slavism, Pan-Slavic federation, 15; "Pan-Slavic Mother," 16, 64, 129–130, 195
Papadzhanov, Mikhail I., 205
Paris, 14, 22, 26, 40, 43, 104,

Index

170, 172, 191, 212, 241, 254, 292, 300, 358–359, 362, 369–370, 385, 387, 410, 425–426, 439, 444, 455, 464, 481, 484–486

Paris Convention of 1856, 132

Paris Peace Conference (1919–1920), 460

Pashich, Nikola, Serbian Premier, 30–41; Serbian war aims, 138–142; second round of Balkan negotiations, 142–163; aftermath of Italian occupation of Valona, 169–175, 178, 271–272, 285, 294; final round of Allied negotiations with Bulgaria (May–July, 1915), 309–320; Bulgaria joins Central Powers, 320–335, 336

Peloponnesus, 435–436

Pera, 240

Perister, 330

Persia (Iran), 65–66; question of Russian intervention, 84–88; modification of Anglo-Russian Convention of 1907, 228–232, 238, 352–353, 360, 363, 365, 368, 371, 375, 380, 438, 485

Persian Gulf, 211

Petrograd (St. Petersburg before 1914; Leningrad after 1924), 3–6, 16, 23, 27–28, 61, 71, 108, 141, 145, 152, 172, 180, 183, 217, 221, 224, 226, 240, 247, 254, 259, 268, 271, 277, 284, 289–290, 293–294, 310, 347, 362–363, 385, 395, 400–402, 404, 410, 421, 425–426, 428, 431, 442, 444, 450, 455, 457, 460, 464, 480, 484, 486

Petrograd Conference of 1917, 410, 455, 459–466

Pichon, Ferdinand, French Foreign Minister (1917–1920), 443

Picot, Georges, Sykes-Picot Agreement, 358–362; Russian aims in Armenia and Anatolia, 363–374; Franco-Russian Anatolian Agreement, 374–382

Piedmont, 174

Pinsk, 304

Pirot, 348

Planca, Cape, 176, 225–256, 264, 268, 325

Plevna, 62

Pograditsa, 154

Poincaré, Raymond, President of the French Republic (1913–1920), 53, 237, 263, 265, 395

Pokrovskii, Nikolai N., Russian Foreign Minister (1916–1917), 408, 442; Allied war aims announcements (1916–1917), 442–453; London Conference on Anatolia, 453–459; Franco-Russian Agreement on Germany, 459–466, 482

Poklevskii, Russian ambassador to Rumania, 25; Allied Rumanian negotiations (May–Aug., 1915), 288–309

Pola, 141, 261

Poland, Russian proclamation to Poles, 9–11, 13–15, 20, 43, 45, 47–48, 50, 56, 62, 73, 82–83; Russian Council

Index

of Ministers discusses future of, 89–96, 102, 105, 107, 124–125, 127, 173, 203, 213, 239, 274; project of March 3, 1915, 275–282; conquered by Central Powers, 303–304, 343–344, 351; France and the Polish Question, 382–394; fall of Sazonov, 397–406; fall of Stürmer, 436–442; Allied war aims announcements (1916–1917), 442–453; Franco-Russian Agreement on Germany, 459–466; promised independence by Russian Provisional Government, 469–470, 471, 484
Polish Question, See Poland
Pontic Taurus, 376
Pope (Roman), 248
Posen, 47, 49, 92, 95, 102
Prague (Praha), 15
Prilep, 330
Pripet Marshes, 274
Progressive Bloc, 344
Protopopov, A. D., Minister of Internal Affairs (1916–17), 409–410, 442, 448–449
Provisional Council of the Russian Republic, 485–486
Provisional Government (Russian), 466–486
Prut River, 28–29, 169, 288, 290–293, 300, 302, 413
Przasnysz, 275
Przemysl, 13, 62, 117, 275, 278

Q

Quadruple Alliance, 270, 341–342

Quai d'Orsay (French Ministry of Foreign Affairs), 121, 188, 224, 343, 386, 388
Quarnero, 248

R

Racconigi Agreement, 20, 430–431, 445
Radical Socialists (French), 343
Radoslavov, Vassili, Bulgarian Premier, 30–41; second round of Allied Balkan negotiations, 142–163, 283–284, 285; final negotiations with Allies, 309–320; Bulgaria joins Central Powers 320–335
Rasputin, Grigorii, 89, 346; 402, 405–409, 411, 437, 460
Red Sea, 361
"Red Zone," 359–361
Revolution (Russian) of 1917, 408, 441, 466–486
Rhineland, 47, 49, 106; Franco-Russian Agreement on Germany, 459–466
Rhine River, 58, 62, 130, 368, 461–462
Rhodes, 172
Ribot, Alexandre, French Premier and Foreign Minister (1917), 443, 459; St. Jean de Maurienne Agreement, 470–471, 474; Kerenskii seeks revision of Allied war aims, 476–486
Riga, 304
Rijeka (Fiume), 140, 249, 261, 268, 314, 321, 330
Robeck, Admiral de, 282

Index

Rodd, Sir Rennell, British ambassador to Italy, 22, 26, 262–263
Rodosto, 131
Rodzyanko, V. I., President of the Fourth State Duma, 6, 199, 441
Roman, Prince, 12
Roman Catholicism, 93, 173–174, 277, 279, 364
Romanov Dynasty, 16
Rome, 22, 26, 141, 261, 288, 322, 345, 454
Rumania, Russian negotiations with (Aug.–Oct., 1914), 20–21, 23–30, 36–39, 42, 47, 50, 57, 74–76, 122, 132–133, 141–142; second round of Allied Balkan negotiations, 142–163; Italo-Rumanian bloc, 163–169, 170–171, 176; Russo-Rumanian coolness, 179–184, 207, 228–229, 254, 256, 259, 261, 271–272, 275, 283; negotiations with Allies (May–Aug., 1915), 288–309, 310–312, 314, 316, 325, 332; Allied effort to save Serbia, 335–340, 342, 351, 376, 388; Russo-Rumanian negotiations (Jan.–July, 1916), 394–397, 408; intervenes in war, 411–418, 432; defeated by Central Powers, 436–442; announcement of Allied war aims (1916–17), 442–453, 484
Rupel, Fort, 432
Russo-Rumanian Agreement of October, 1914, 27–29
Ruthenia (Trans-Carpathian Ukraine), 9, 42, 183; Allied Rumanian negotiations (May–Aug., 1915), 288–309

S

Saar Valley, 462
Samarra, 361
Samosh River, 413
Samothrace, 113–114
Samsat, 366, 372
Samsonov, General, 13
Samsun, 373–374, 376–378, 422
San Giovanni di Medua, 249, 265, 321
San Giuliano, Marquis, Italian Foreign Minister, 22; Italian war aims, 137–138; death of, 142
San River, 278
San Stefano, Treaty of (1878), 157
Santa Sophia, Cathedral of, 64, 114
Sarakamysh, 189–190
Saratov, 206
Sarrail, Jacques, General, 432–435
Saseno, 141–142, 248, 268
Save River, 139
Savenko, Anatolii I., 205–206
Savinskii, A. A., Russian ambassador to Bulgaria, 31–32, 144, 285; final round of Allied negotiations with Bulgaria (May–July, 1915), 309–320
Sazonov, Sergei Dmitrievich, Russian Foreign Minister (1910–1916), 5–8; proclamation to the Poles, 9–10, 14;

· 546 ·

Index

Czech Question, 15–20; Italian and Rumanian negotiations (Aug.–Oct., 1914), 20–30; first round of Macedonian negotiations 30–41; formation of Allied Powers, 42–44, 44–46; presentation of Twelve Points, 46–50; military objectives of Allied Powers, 50–54, 55; Straits Question (1912–14), 65–67; negotiations with Turkey, 70–76; breaks relations with Turkey, 80–82; Britain promises Constantinople and the Straits, 81–88; future of Poland, 89–96, 97–99, 108–109; Russian aims at Straits, 110–116; separate peace with Austria-Hungary, 120–124; Russian attack on Straits, 128–134; second round of Balkan negotiations, 142–163; Italo-Rumanian bloc, 163–169; aftermath of Valona incident, 169–175; fourth round of Macedonian negotiations, 175–178; Russo-Rumanian coolness, 179–184; the Straits Agreement, 185–243; the Treaty of London, 243–272, 274–275; Polish project of March 3, 1915, 275–282; Gallipoli campaign, Greece, and Bulgaria, 282–287; Rumanian negotiations (May–Aug., 1915), 288–309; final negotiations with Bulgaria (May–July, 1915), 309–320; Bulgaria joins the Central Powers, 320–335; Anglo-French occupation of Salonika, 335–340; dismissal threatened, 344–347; fall of Serbia and Montenegro, 349–350; Djemal Pasha intrigue, 354–358, 362; Russian aims in Anatolia and Armenia, 363–374; Franco-Russian Anatolian Agreement, 374–382; France and the Polish Question, 382–394; Russo-Rumanian negotiations (Jan.–July, 1916), 394–395; dismissed, 397–406, 407–409, 418, Anglo-Russian Anatolian Agreement, 420–422, 424, 429, 430, 437–438, 447; appointed Russian ambassador to Great Britain, 455

Scala Nuova, Gulf of, 453, 455, 457

Scheldt, River, 56

Schilling, Baron, 182–183, 235–236, 250–251, 293–294, 364, 405

Schleswig, 45, 106

Schleswig-Holstein, 47, 49, 55, 60

Scutari, 265, 348

Sedan, 390

Sejm, Polish, 92–93, 392–393

Sert, 375

Sembat, Marcel, 54, 222

Senate, Russian Imperial, 392

Serbia, 20, 22, 28–29; first round of Macedonian negotiations, 30–41, 42, 47, 50, 104–105; defeats Austrians, 116, 122; Serb vs. Italian ambitions, 135–142; second round of Balkan negotia-

· 547 ·

Index

tions, 142–163, 166; reaction to Italian occupation of Valona, 169–175; fourth round of Macedonian negotiations, 175–179, 186, 242; the Treaty of London, 243–275, 284–285; Allied Rumanian negotiations (May–Aug., 1915), 288–309; final Allied negotiations with Bulgaria (May–July, 1915), 309–320; Bulgaria joins Central Powers, 320–335; Allied efforts to save, 335–340, 343; occupied by Central Powers, 348–350, 385, 412, 414, 418, Allied war aims announcements (1916–17), 442–453, 484

Serbo-Bulgarian Treaty (1912), 161, 332

Serbo-Croatian Kingdom, 39, 11, 172, 250–251, 295–296, 326

Seres, 146, 283, 310, 314, 317, 432

Sereth River, 298, 300–301

Sevastopol, 79

Shcheglovitov, Russian Minister of Justice, Polish Question and Russian war aims, 91–96, 280–281

Shebeko, N. N., 347

Shiak, 154

Shidlovskii, Sergei I., 203–204

Shiite Moslems, 85

Shuvaev, General, Russian War Minister, 397

Šibenik (Sebenico), 137, 167, 172, 252

Silesia, 47, 102, 258

Sinope, 373–374, 376, 378

Sivas, 366, 370, 373, 376–378

Skobelev, 484–485

Skoplje (Uskub), 330, 348

Skumbi River, 154, 165

Slavic States, 58, 81, 94–95, 175, 179–180, 199, 201, 204; the Treaty of London, 243–272, 296, 469

Slavonia, 139, 270, 325–326

Slovaks, 19, 47, 49, 105

Slovenes, 49, 138–139, 141, 173–174, 258, 270–271, 295–296, 299, 304, 312, 328, 330

Smyrna (Izmir), 67; offered to Greece by Britain, 190–198, 201, 267, 286, 314, 316, 337, 427–428, 430–431; London Conference on Anatolia, 453–459; St. Jean de Maurienne Agreement, 470–471; promised to Italy, 481

Social Democrats (Russian), 7

Socialist Revolutionaries, war aims controversy with Kadets, 466–476, 483

Sofia, 31–32, 143, 145, 152, 155, 157, 170, 177, 178, 274, 284–285, 288, 310, 316, 322, 324, 328, 332

Somesh (Somesul) River, 291, 296

Somme River, 396

Sonnino, Sidney, Italian Foreign Minister, 142, 169; the Treaty of London, 243–272, 298, 306–307; final Allied negotiations with Bulgaria (May–July, 1915), 309–320; Bulgaria joins Central Powers, 320–335; fall of Serbia and Montenegro, 349–350;

Index

Italy's Anatolian demands, 424–431; Allied war aims announcements (1916–17), 442–453; London Conference on Anatolia, 453–459; St. Jean de Maurienne Agreement, 470–471; Kerenskii tries to revise war aims, 476–486
Sophia, Queen of Greece, 34
Sopot, 311
Souchon, Admiral, 79, 141
Souha Planina, 330
Soviet of Workers', Soldiers' and Peasants' Deputies (Petrograd), war aims controversy, 466–476, 484
Split (Spalato), 137, 150, 170, 254, 256, 268, 319, 321
State Bank (Russian), 64, 393
State Council, 279–280, 392
State Duma, See Duma.
Stavka (Headquarters of Russian Supreme High Commander), 13, 51–54, 96, 118, 128, 168–169, 183–184, 232–236, 239, 263, 276–277, 281, 288–289, 300, 302; moved from Baranovichi to Mogilev, 304, 305, 307, 339–340; Russo-Rumanian negotiations (Jan.–July, 1916), 394–399; the Polish Question and fall of Sazonov, 397–406, 412, 440
Stockholm, 409
Stockholm Conference, 482–483, 485
Stolitsa, 124–128
Stolypin, Peter A., Russian Premier (1906–1911), 201, 437

Straits, 57–58, 60; importance of to Russia (1908–1914), 63–67, 70, 73–74, 76–78; promised to Russia by Britain, 81–86, 94, 96; France informed of Russian desires, 97–110; definition of Russian aims, 110–116; proposed Russian attack, 128–134, 141, 149, 178, 180–184, 243, 246, 267, 274–275; British Gallipoli campaign, 282–287, 288, 300, 318, 341, 342, 355–356, 376, 382, 426, 429, 431, 438, 441, Allied war aims announcements, 442–453, 454, 456, 465, 471, 481
Straits Agreement, negotiated, 185–243, 255–256, 259, 267, 273, 339, 357, 363, 365, 372, 382, 388, 426–427; Italy adheres to, 428–429, 438, 440; publicly announced, 442–453; 464, 473–474
Struma Valley, 283
Strypa River, 397
Stürmer, Boris Vladimirovich, Russian Premier and Foreign Minister (1916), Russian aims in Armenia and Anatolia, 363–374, 383, 393; the Polish Question and the fall of Sazonov, 397–406, 407–408; performance as Foreign Minister, 409–411; intervention of Rumania, 411–418; Anglo-Russian Anatolian Agreement, 418–424; Italy's Anatolian demands, 424–431; deposition of Constantine of Greece, 431–436; fall

· 549 ·

Index

from power, 436–442, 444–445, 448, 470
Styria, 130, 328
Suchav (Suceava) River, 168, 289, 296
Suez Canal, 221, 241, 485
Sultan of Turkey, 231, 354, 365
Supilo, Frano, 140–141, 174, 178
Sunnite Moslems, 85
Suvla Bay, 323
Suwalki Triangle, 92, 383
Sykes-Picot Agreement, negotiated, 358–362, 364, 373, 379, 420, 426
Sykes, Sir Mark, Sykes-Picot Agreement, 358–362; Russian aims in Armenia and Anatolia, 363–374, 418
Syria, 103–104, 191, 211, 220; promised by Russia to France, 232–238, 239, 355–357; Sykes-Picot Agreement, 358–362, 363, 365, 419, 425–426, 456
Syrmia (Srem), 176, 305, 325
Szebeko, I. A., 280
Szegedin, 291, 414

T

Talaat Pasha, 77, 214
Tannenberg, Battle of, 13
Tarnopol, 13, 304
Tatishchev, B. A., 405
Taube, Baron, Russian Acting Minister of Education, Polish Question and Russian war aims, 91–96, 280
Taurus Mountains, 236
Tavricheskii Palace, 6, 448

Temesvar (Timisoara), See Banat of Temesvar
Tenedos, 113, 217
Tereshchenko, M. I., Russian Foreign Minister (1917), 473–474; succeeds Milyukov, 476; seeks revision of Allied war aims, 476–486
Theiss River, 138, 288, 290–291, 296, 302, 413–414
Thessaly, 435
Thomas, Albert, 393–394; Acting French ambassador to Russia (1917), 474, 478
Thrace, 35, 38, 40, 67, 74, 114, 132, 143–145, 150–151, 153, 155, 162, 167, 214, 217, 284, 287, 311, 315–318, 323, 338
Tibet, 232
Tigris River, 361, 375
Tirana, 154
Tiflis (Tbilisi), 124, 352–353, 423
Tittoni, 425–426
Townshend, General, 352
Trans-Carpathian Ukraine See Ruthenia
Trans-Jordan, 360
Transcaucasia, 65–67, 70, 74–75, 85, 94, 112, 116, 124–128, 189–190, 199–200, 205, 242, 304, 351; Russian campaign of 1915–16, 352–356; Russian aims in Armenia and Anatolia, 363–374; Franco-Russian Anatolian Agreement, 374–382, 422–423, 471
Transylvania, 23–30, 35, 42, 47, 56, 105, 120, 155, 180, 183; Allied Rumanian nego-

Index

tiations (May–Aug., 1915), 288–309, 368, 394–395, 439
Trebizond, captured by Russians, 353, 367, 371, 373–374, 376, 379, 422, 470
Trentino, 21, 42, 56, 137, 140; the Treaty of London 243–272, 396, 424
Trepov, Alexander F., Russian Premier (1916–1917), 442; Allied war aims announcements (1916–17), 442–453
Trieste, 21, 42, 137, 141; the Treaty of London 243–272
Triple Entente 20–23, 25–26, 32, 34, 36, 39, 66, 70, 72; 74–75
Troaid, 113
Trotskii (Bronstein), Lev D., 409, 459, 467–468, 484
Trubetskoi, G. N., Prince, proclamation to the Poles, 10–11; views on Constantinople and the Straits, 72–74, 75, 78; ambassador to Serbia, 158–163; Italo-Rumanian bloc, 163–169; aftermath of Italian occupation of Valona, 170–175, 240–241, 271–272, 296, 312
"Tsargrad" (Constantinople), 114, 200, 205–206
Tsarskoe Selo, 99, 226, 347, 366, 390
Tseretelli, Iraklii, 468
Tunisia, 244
Turco-German Treaty of Alliance (1914), 67–69
Turkey (Ottoman Empire), efforts to form pro-German block, 25, 28–29, 36; Allied Balkan negotiations (Aug.-Sept., 1914), 33–41, 42, 57–58, 62; Straits Question (1908–1914), 63–67; alliance with Germany, 67–69; proposes alliance to Allied Powers, 69–76; joins Central Powers, 76–82, 83, 113; early defeats in Transcaucasia, 116, 129–130, 133, 137–138, 143–144, 153, 172, 177–179; the Straits Agreement, 185–243, 244–245, 247, 250, 269, 278; Gallipoli Campaign, 282–287, 307–308; final round of Allied negotiations with Bulgaria, 309–320; Bulgaria joins, 320–335, 340, 342, 343, 51; Russian 1915–16 Armenian campaign, 352–354; Djemal Pasha intrigue, 254–258; Sykes-Picot Agreement, 358–362; Russian aims in Armenia and Anatolia, 363–374; Franco-Russian Anatolian Agreement, 374–382; Anglo-Russian Anatolian Agreement, 418–424; Italy's Anatolian demands, 424–431, 437; Allied war aims announcements (1916–1917), 442–453; London Conference on Anatolia, 453–457, 464; St. Jean de Maurienne Agreement, 470–471, 482
Turkish Army, 70
Turkish Navy, 65, 67–69, 110–116, 144
Turkish Straits, See Straits
Twelve Points, presented by

Index

Sazonov, 46–50, 53, 77, 82, 104, 408
Tyrol, 105; the Treaty of London, 243–272

U

Ukraine, Russian proclamation to Austro-Hungarian Ukrainians, 9, 11–12, 20, 27; Ukrainians of Bukovina, 28, 56, 64, 89–90; 94, 105, 169, 199–205, 335
Uniates, 89–90
United States of America, 46, 419; Allied war aims announcements (1916–17), 442–453; Russian war aims controversy (1917), 466–476; Kerenskii seeks revision of Allied war aims, 476–486
Unkiar Skelessi, Treaty of (1833), 113
Urmia, 365–366, 370
Urmia, Lake, 363
Urussov, Prince, 346

V

Valievo, 122
Valona, 21, 48, 104, 136–137, 140–141, 156, 165; occupied by Italy, 169–171, 248, 268
Van, 127, 241, 369, 374, 379
Vardar River, 127, 241, 369, 374, 379
Varna, 338
Vatican, the, 14, 173
Venizelos, Eleutherios, Greek Premier, 31–40; second round of Allied Balkan negotiations, 142, 163, 170; British offer of Smyrna, 190–198; first resignation, 197–198, 285; returns to power (Aug., 1915), 329; Anglo-French occupation of Salonika, 335–340; deposition of King Constantine, 341–436, 453, 470; returns to power (1917), 480, 481
Ventspils (Windau), 303
Verdun, Battle of, 367, 393, 396
Verdun, Treaty of (843), 461
Vienna, 19, 244, 347
Vilna, 274, 304
Vistula River, 13, 48–49, 73, 102
"Vistula Region" Poland, 92
Viviani, Rene, French Premier (1914–15), 341, 393–394
Vizo River, 413
Vladimir, Saint, 12
Voiussa River, 248–249, 268, 325
Voivodina, 139
Volga River, 204
Volosca, 248–249
Vranja, 348

W

Wallachia, 440
War Council (British), 438
War Ministry (Russian), 366, 377
Warsaw, 16, 62, 274, 276; evacuated by Russians, 303, 324, 392
Warsaw, Government-General of, 91–92, 276, 277–279, 383
Washington, D.C., 14, 471
Western Front, 186, 411

Index

Wielopolski, Wladislaw, 279–280
Wielospolski, Zygmunt, 279–280, 400–401
William II, Emperor of Germany (1888–1918), 34, 332
William of Wied, Prince of Albania (1914), 136
Wilson, Woodrow, President of the United States (1913–1921), 46; Allied war aims announcements (1916–17), 442–443; Russian war aims controversy, 466–476; Kerenskii seeks revision of Allied war aims, 476–486
Winter Palace, 3–5, 486
Witte, Sergei Yu., 82, 437

Y

Yanushkevich, General, Russian Chief of Staff (1914–15), 131–132
Yaroslav Osmomysl, 12
Yezd, 231
Young Turks, 63, 66–67, 74, 196
Yudenich, N. N., General, 190, 352–353
Yugo-Slavs (South Slavs), 123, 138, 141, 174–175; the Treaty of London, 243–272

Z

Zagreb, 174
Zagros Mountains, 352
Zaimis, Greek Premier, 338
Zara (Dalmatia), 252, 255, 261, 264
Zara (Armenia), 374, 379
Zavirev, 243; Djemal Pasha intrigue, 354–358
Zeitun, 370
Zemlin (Semlin, Zemun), 305, 325
Zionism, 419
Zographos, Greek Foreign Minister, 285–287
Zone "A", 360–361
Zone "B", 360–361
Zulfagor, 231